UNIVERSITY OF KNOWLEDGE

GLENN FRANK, B.A., M.A., LITT.D., L.H.D., LL.D., *Editor-in-Chief*

PRINTED AND BOUND IN THE UNITED STATES
OF AMERICA BY THE CUNEO PRESS, INC.

Every Branch of Knowledge
Man Possesses
May Be Applied To Some Good
Purpose

THE ANGEL MUSICIANS
From the painting by Van Eyck (1366-1441).
Altar piece in St. Bavon Cathedral, Ghent, Belgium.

UNIVERSITY OF KNOWLEDGE

GLENN FRANK, EDITOR-IN-CHIEF

MUSIC AND ITS MAKERS

THE STORY OF MUSICAL EXPRESSION

BY

WESLEY LA VIOLETTE, Mus. D.

Professor of Musical Theory and Composition
School of Music, DePaul University, Chicago

•

UNIVERSITY OF KNOWLEDGE, INCORPORATED

CHICAGO

The Editor wishes to express his indebtedness to the publishers who have permitted use of material which is in copyright or of which they have the rights of permission, as follows:

To J. Fischer and Bro., Music Publishers, Edna St. Vincent Millay and Deems Taylor, *The King's Henchman.*

To G. Ricordi and Co., Inc., Music Publishers, Puccini's *La Bohème* and *Madame Butterfly.*

INTRODUCTION

It may seem to some that to include a book on music in this series in the midst of the economic dislocation, political distraction, and social dishevelment that haunt the spirit of civilized men the world around is a little like fiddling while Rome burns. Would it not be better to declare a moratorium on the arts until we have made a better job of assuring food, clothing, and shelter to the millions? I feel profoundly the mood that makes such a question possible. And I should say "yes" to it if I did not believe that the arts—and music most of all—can help rather than hinder us in making conquest of the forces that today threaten the stability of our social order and the security of our lives.

Faced by a temptation extraordinary to surrender to materialism, Jesus of Nazareth rebuffed his tempter with the conviction that "Man shall not live by bread alone." And the great Mohammed once said, "If any man have two loaves of bread, let him trade one for a narcissus. The bread is nourishment for the body, but the narcissus is nourishment for the soul." We should be ready by now to admit the soundness of these ancient words of wisdom that have come down the centuries to us from Christ and Mohammed.

Under the pressure of the drop in public income during depression periods, we sometimes suspend from our schools much of the training in the arts we have introduced in recent years, on the short-sighted assumption that the arts are luxuries that must give way before necessities when the purse grows lean. I think a little more careful consideration will show us the folly of such judgment. For the arts are vital to the sort of education we need if, in the years ahead, we are to master instead of being mastered by this vast, complex, and swiftly moving technical civilization born of science and the machine.

The mastery of our machine civilization requires not only as good an education as our fathers had but a broader and better education, whether it be the formal education of the schools or that self-education which series of this sort seek to serve. Our fathers faced a simpler world. They could get along with an education that would be wholly inadequate for modern life.

Among other things, the education for the future must educate the whole man, not just his reasoning powers. It must educate his physical, emotional, and social reactions as well as his reasoning processes. We once thought our job was done when we had trained a man to think straight. This belief rested on the assumption that men *thought* their way into their *living*. We now know that men *live* their way into their *thinking* more than they think their way into their living. Because this is true, the education for the future must, in addition to the more obvious diets for the mind, include those stimulations and disciplines that sensitize and enrich men's capacity for worthy emotional and aesthetic response to some of the overlooked needs of modern life.

Here, I think, is one of the great and liberating ministries of music and the allied arts. Music, for instance, is not just a thing to relieve the tedium of tired hours, not just a thing to be bought and paid for in concert halls, not just a thing reserved for professional performers, not just a thing to tickle the tired business man and amuse his bored wife, but a thing that can develop in men the capacity for rich and creative emotional and aesthetic response to things that the starkly rational mind, however well trained, may wholly miss, and, in the missing, leave men's lives infinitely poorer.

Music is, of course, a science as well as an art. Just as the art of surgery rests upon the sciences of anatomy, physiology, and pathology, so music as an art sinks its roots deep in the soil of music as a science. Music, as a science, thus takes its place along with the other sciences in our education and makes a like contribution. But music, as an art, may, I think, make some distinctive contributions to the life of our time.

Let me suggest three such contributions that music may make to the future of American civilization.

First, *music can help men to cultivate the art of sensitiveness.* I do not mean merely a sensitiveness of response to delicacy of sound or loveliness of color. Training in the arts obviously cultivates that sort of response. I mean sensitiveness to the needs and conditions of man and his society.

Whether we shall be able to achieve complete control of the new powers arising out of science and the machine and bend them to better human use may well depend upon whether we can educate ourselves to a greater sensitiveness of spirit so that our political, social, and economic life shall be in the hands of men who actually feel a kinship with humanity, men who can *feel* the tug of famine in China as keenly as they might feel the cry of hunger from a brother's child, men who can *feel* the tragedy of starved minds in the hinterland of their own states as poignantly as they might feel the pathos of the idiot-chatter of an abnormal offspring, men who can be *stirred* by an annual report of industrial accidents, deaths from preventable disease, or the spiritual slavery of illiteracy as they might be stirred by a brutal murder by gangsters on the next street corner, men to whom evidence of stupidity, blundering, or malevolence in political, social, or economic leadership is as compelling a cry for help as the ravage of a plague. To such sensitiveness of spirit I am convinced the arts in general, and music in particular can contribute.

Second, *music, can help men to become participants instead of spectators in the leisure-life of the nation.* During office-hours, we Americans are a singularly self-sufficient people, but, after office-hours, we are pathetically dependent upon bought-and-paid-for diversion. There is a gap somewhere in the soul of a people that troops into the theater, but never produces a folk-drama, that crowds into concert halls, but never throws off a folk-song as a spark from a glowing iron. To the over-coming of this American disease of *spectatoritis* the arts can contribute.

Third, *music can bring to our all-too-materialistic civilization the priceless boon of beauty.*

A nation that forgets beauty will in time find even the foundations of its technical and economic achievements crumbling. A people dares not allow beauty to become the exclusive possession of antique dealers and millionaire collectors unless it wants to face a social reckoning sooner or later. Beauty is not a thing that can be bought by a rich nation; beauty, save as a museum piece, is something born in the soul of a sensitive people. And beauty—we must not forget—has a very intimate bearing upon the social content or social discontent of a nation. Social unrest finds its readiest recruits among men who have never been able to find beauty and joy in their jobs and in their environments. It is an old observation that hungry men turn radical, but what we are likely to forget is that men with full stomachs may still be hungry with a gnawing hunger for the things that make life free and adventurous and abundant. Maybe statesmen have overlooked beauty as a campaign issue, for men do not revolt against a government that is making their work, their lives, and their environment beautiful. Beautiful homes, beautiful factories, beautiful offices, beautiful cities, beautiful landscapes, beautiful relations in business and industry, a community, state, and national life that stimulate and satisfy men's hunger for beauty—these are the things that turn the ruin of revolt into the radiance of creative living. Beauty is better and cheaper than the big stick in assuring a contented and orderly life.

To these three supreme needs of our time the arts stand to make productive contribution. And music reigns as the queen of the arts!

GLENN FRANK, *Editor-in-Chief.*

WESLEY LA VIOLETTE, *Mus.D.*
Author

Wesley La Violette, distinguished American composer, was born in Minnesota in 1894.

He graduated from the School of Music at Northwestern University. From there he went to the Chicago Musical College, finally earning his Doctor of Music degree from that famous institution.

In 1933 Dr. La Violette was invited to join the faculty of the Theory Department in the School of Music at De Paul University in Chicago.

As a composer of distinction in his own field, La Violette has written in all the larger forms of music. An opera, "Shylock," to a text from Shakespeare's "Merchant of Venice," won the award of the David Bispham medal from the American Opera Society, given for distinctive contributions to that field. The composer recently finished a Symphony. Among his compositions should be named a Concert-piece for Piano and Orchestra, three String Quartets, a Piano Quintet, two Sonatas for Violin and Piano, numerous works for small and large orchestra, as well as many songs and piano pieces. In some seasons his works have reached the unusual total of more than thirty performances by major organizations.

PREFACE

Music is the language of the soul. Throughout the centuries, in all lands and among all peoples, man has found expression for his emotions—joy and sorrow, pleasure and pain, love and hate—through the medium of music. Music is an integral part of life itself. The barbarian beats upon his crude drums—and rhythm lives in the jungle. In our modern cities, the carefully groomed conductor raises his baton—and a sophisticated audience is carried away by the emotional intensity of a great symphony.

For primitive man, music was part of his life, like eating, drinking, making warfare, making love. Our music is rather more complex, and may seem harder to appreciate. Yet man is endowed with a natural capacity to enjoy and understand the rich storehouse of musical treasures which is our heritage. With the expenditure of a little effort, anyone may enjoy this inexhaustible wealth which lies all about us.

As never before, our modern civilization offers us countless opportunities to listen to great music. In earlier ages people had to make their own music—or to go to the concert hall in order to listen to the music played by great soloists and orchestras. The music lover had to spend many hours in tedious practice upon an instrument for which he may have had no particular talent. In church, in popular music halls, at choral societies, people could hear music, and they did; but the inventions of the phonograph and the radio have bestowed upon us riches which they would have considered fabulous. Recorded music approaches perfection and makes it possible not only to listen again and again to the best performances of the finest musicians, but to listen to the music one wants to hear at the moment one wants to hear it.

The radio has been the most potent factor of all in bringing good music to millions of listeners. Every hour of the day some kind of music is broadcast from concert halls, opera houses, hotels, and radio studios. Radio chains deluge the entire world with the concert performances of internationally famous orchestras. The finest operas, the most exciting symphonies—all flood into one's living room with the turn of a dial. Aladdin's lamp was not more miraculous.

Neither the phonograph nor the radio, of course, has supplanted the concert hall. The best way of all to appreciate music is still to attend actual concerts or operas. There is pleasure in seeing live musicians playing living music, in forming part of a listening group. The glistening instruments, the rhythmic movements of violin bows, the response of every member of the orchestra to the conductor's skill—all contribute to the fascination of the concert hall.

Nor is it true that it no longer is desirable to learn to play an instrument. The most effective means of discovering hidden beauties in music is to participate in it. All the subtle shadings in tone, all the nuances of individual interpretation, assume increased value for us when we have learned through actual experience the difficulty of producing them. In music, the sense response of the ear should come first; then the physical, technical, mechanical, and intellectual approaches can be added. The more we love music, the more we will want to know about it; and the more we know, the more we shall love it.

When Congreve said "Music has charms to soothe the savage breast, to soften rocks, and bend the knotted oak" he was expressing in emphatic form the emotional power which music undoubtedly has. Out of musical experience comes an emotional pleasure that makes life richer, more meaningful, and more endurable.

This book deals with generalities where principles seemed more important than technical data. Emphasis has been placed upon contemporary works and opinions, in order that we may know more of the music and attitudes of our own time. In this volume there has been an honest attempt to write of today's music in terms of music already known, so that there can be established some point of relationship between the past and the present.

To listen to music is to engage in one of the high and exciting adventures of life. Through experiencing and understanding the great musical works which are available to most of us, one may achieve intimate and uplifting fellowship with Bach or Beethoven, Stravinsky or Moussorgsky. Indescribable beauty and exaltation are the rewards for those who draw aside the curtains and enter the realm of music.

Chicago
January 24, 1938

Wesley La Violette

Dr. La Violette's associates in the writing and editing of this volume were Mrs. Wesley La Violette, Leon Stein, M.Mus., Boris Kremenliev, M.Mus., and Franklin J. Meine.

ACKNOWLEDGMENT

From the most primitive times until our own day man has responded to rhythm and has created music. What a story there is between the beat of a tom-tom and the playing of a great modern orchestra! Music now occupies a very important place in our lives. Our interest in chamber music, oratorios, symphonies, and operas is increasing. We have tried to illustrate this evolution of our musical tastes and to represent the creative spirit behind it which has found expression in a number of remarkable instruments and in the writing of modern music.

We were successful in securing pictures from some old and rare books for use in the section dealing with the history of music. We desire to thank the following persons, institutions, and corporations for their co-operation:

The Newberry Library, Chicago
C. G. Conn, Ltd., Elkhart, Indaina
Federal Art Project, Cambridge, Mass.
The Musical Leader, Chicago
Chicago City Opera Company
Chicago Symphony Orchestra
National Broadcasting Company, Inc.
Boston Symphony Orchestra, Inc.
The Art Institute of Chicago
German Railroads, New York, N. Y.
Columbia Broadcasting System, Inc.
Haensel and Jones, New York, N. Y.

J. BRADFORD PENGELLY
Picture Editor

TABLE OF CONTENTS

Introduction vii

Preface x

Acknowledgment xiv

Music Through the Centuries 17

The Romantic Movement 85

The Development of National Schools 101

Instruments of the Orchestra 121

Great Symphonic Works 135

Opera: Union of Music and Drama 175

Stories of the Great Operas 191

Chamber Music 284

The Ballet 301

The Piano—The Instrument of the Millions . . 313

The Men of Music 319

Men Who Are Making Music Today 341

Glossary of Musical Terms 380

Courtesy E. W. Forkert

INTERIOR OF THE SCALA THEATER, MILAN, ITALY

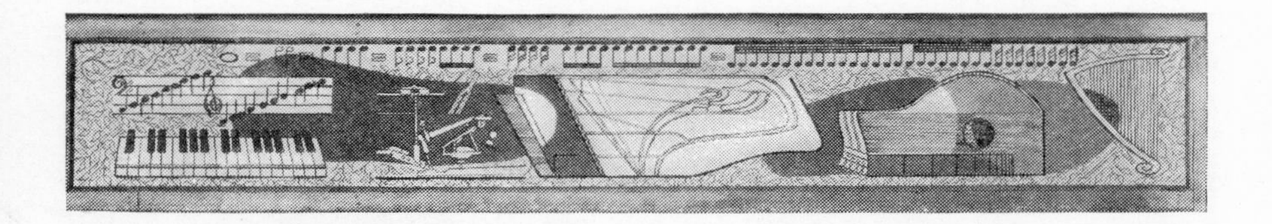

MUSIC THROUGH THE CENTURIES

THE ORIGIN OF MUSIC

"IN THE BEGINNING WAS RHYTHM," said an eminent musician of the last century. Everyone, no doubt, has observed how bodily work and movements are often co-ordinated in a general rhythmic pattern. Whether we watch a carpenter at work with his saw and hammer, or a mechanic operating a stamping machine in an automobile factory, —in every motion the element of rhythm is obvious. Note the rhythm involved in the running of a football player, or in the passing of a basketball between players, or in the movements displayed in a tennis match! If you watch accomplished athletes, you will see some of the most finished and complex of rhythmic motions.

MUSIC AMONG PRIMITIVE PEOPLE

Primitive people did not have football games, but they had many other ways of expressing rhythm. By studying primitive tribes, such as exist today in Africa and Australia, we can get some idea of the earliest musical expressions.

Being children of nature, these natives get their simple suggestions of rhythm by observing certain natural phenomena. The regular motions of the sun, the moon, and the stars, the swaying of the trees and grasses in the wind, and the antics of animals convey many rhythmic patterns. Primitive peoples probably imitated these with bodily movements which gradually developed into dances. Many common occupations, such as sowing, digging,

Courtesy the Atchison, Topeka and Santa Fe Railway Co.

INDIAN DANCERS AT SANTA CLARA PUEBLO, NEW MEXICO

or paddling, can be made more effective and more agreeable with the accompaniment of a song. It is conceivable, then, that the earliest musical endeavor began with rhythmic motions.

But these early dances could hardly have existed without some sort of accents in the form of sound. Probably simultaneous with bodily movements, the practice of accompanying them by clapping hands, or stamping the feet, was developed. The next step was the use of simple instruments. By merely pounding on a hollow stump, many intriguing and weird sounds could be produced. The hollow shell of a coconut, filled with pebbles, made an excellent rattle. Finally, the human voice could be used to emphasize rhythmic beats by shouting, grunting, and imitating the cries of animals and birds. These sounds gradually took on the nature of singing.

Music and dance are rarely separated among primitive people. Tribes now in existence perform their dances and songs for ceremonial purposes, such as rites of worship, curing of the sick, re-

Courtesy Mason Warner

NATIVE FIJIAN WAR-CLUB DANCE

joicing over births. When rain is scarce, they seek to move the gods by imitating the sounds of a storm; when they desire success in their hunting for game, they imitate in pantomime the search for prey.

In addition to drums and rattles, the primitives probably made whistles from reeds; or, possibly, a crude stringed instrument was devised when an inventive person heard the twanging of his bow string as he shot off an arrow. But all this we can only surmise and speculate about by means of comparison with the few remaining savage tribes.

EGYPTIAN MUSIC

Although we have no records of the musical activities of the pre-historic primitive people, we are far more fortunate in our inquiry into early Egyptian music. There are many hieroglyphic symbols and pictures on their monuments which have come down

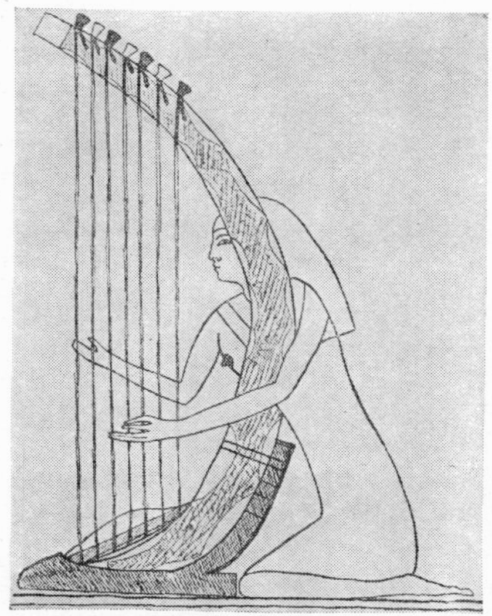

Courtesy The Newberry Library, Chicago

EGYPTIAN HARP OF THE MIDDLE EMPIRE

to us and which tell us something about the music and the musical instruments of the early Egyptians.

These people had several kinds of harps. There was a small bow-shaped harp which was carried on the shoulder, and also one of the same shape, but medium-sized and played in a seated position. Another type of harp was elaborately decorated and as tall as a man. Another important string instrument was the lyre. It was shaped like the letter U. The top ends were bridged by a cross bar from which were stretched five or more strings. By placing the lyre on a table or by holding it in a horizontal position under the arm, it was played by plucking the strings with the fingers or with a little ivory instrument, called a plectrum.

The pearshaped string instrument which we call a lute was already known in Egypt. It had from one to five strings which gave forth different tones when stopped in different positions against its fretted neck.

Two other stringed instruments should be mentioned, the Nefer which is akin to the guitar, and the Nanga which is a cross

EGYPTIAN TAMBOURINE OF THE TWELFTH DYNASTY

Courtesy The Newberry Library, Chicago

between a guitar and a harp. There were two kinds of flute: one which was played directly from one end, and another which was held transversely and played from the side.

For rhythm, in place of drums, the Egyptians used hand clapping. They did, however, have some percussion instruments, especially cymbals. They were from five to seven inches wide, usually made of brass, and they were played only by dancing girls. Tiny cymbals, called castanets, were small enough to be played by the thumb and one finger of the same hand.

In the worship of the goddess Isis, a species of rattle, called a sistrum, was used. It had a metal frame with a handle, and loose bars were fitted through the sides of the frame.

Egyptian pictures and picture writings also throw some light on the life of the musicians and their music. While the singers were of the highest caste—priests or even kings—the players belonged to the slave class, and their professions were handed down from father to son. Sometimes as many as six hundred players took part in a performance.

There has been some controversy as to the kind of musical scale the Egyptians used. Most of their instruments that have been found seem to indicate that their musical scale was made up of whole and half tones. There was at least one flute, however, that played a scale of half tones.

Courtesy The Newberry Library, Chicago

ANCIENT ASSYRIAN TRUMPETERS

ASSYRIAN MUSIC

It is very probable that when the Assyrians conquered Egypt, the conquerors took over some of the high artistic traditions of the conquered nation.

Like the Egyptians, the Assyrians had small harps that could be carried in their hands, and other types, varying in size. The dulcimer, which is still in use among Hungarian and gypsy orchestras, was already known to them. It consisted of a shallow box across which were stretched metal strings. Played by hitting the strings with little hammers, it is a primitive forerunner of the piano. Both single and double flutes were in use. The latter were really two flutes fastened together in a V shape and joined at the mouthpiece.

From pictures and inscriptions we gather that the Assyrians stamped their feet for rhythmic effects, instead of clapping their hands. We might conclude from this evidence that they made louder music than the Egyptians, and in view of their extreme militarism this conclusion is probably justified.

HEBREW MUSIC

The Bible makes many allusions to music, and, whether or not we can accept them as historical evidence, it is well known that the Israelites loved music. Probably they learned much from the Egyptians, and took with them what they knew when Moses led them out of their captivity to Palestine. In the new land music had an important part in their lives. King David arranged a musical service for the Temple, and the service of the contemporary Jewish Synagogue is founded on his arrangement. The psalms of David, recorded in the Bible, are excellent songs. In the early Hebrew temples all the singers and musicians were men; but women were allowed to take part in music for funerals, festivals, and other social affairs.

Hebrew musical instruments were, on the whole, similar to those of the Egyptians. The psaltery of which we hear so much in the Scriptures was a rectangular instrument with a flat wooden sounding board and thirteen strings. It is a relative of the dulcimer and the zither. A quaint horn which is used in the Synagogue service today, and which is capable of producing two tones, was

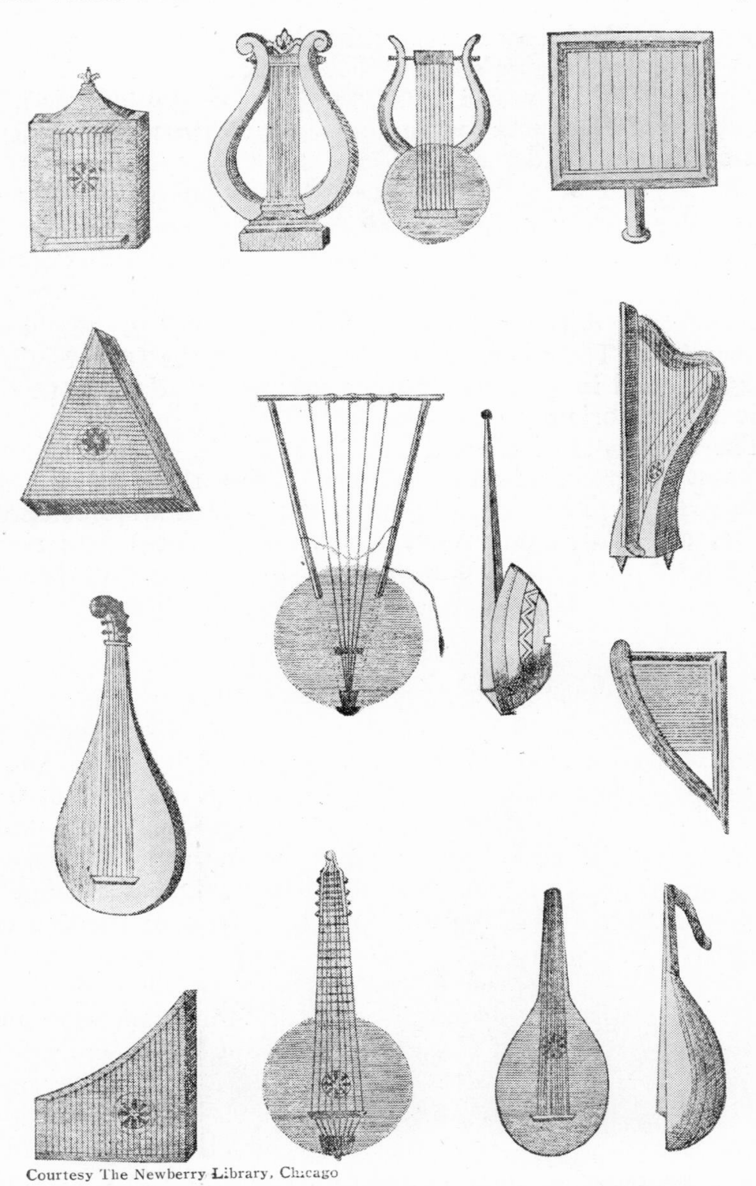

Courtesy The Newberry Library, Chicago

COLLECTION OF EARLY HEBREW MUSICAL INSTRUMENTS

known to the Hebrews already four thousand years ago. It was nothing else than a ram's horn. The timbrel, also familiar to us through the Bible, was a small tambourine. In addition, the Hebrews used trumpets for announcements, proclamations, religious ceremonies, and warfare.

THE MUSIC OF THE GREEKS

With the Greeks we get our first definite example of written music. There are about ten fragments of Greek composition extant, and they date from the fifth century B.C. to the second century A.D. These records, musical notes in the form of Greek letters, chiseled into stone tablets, reveal a good deal about their music and theories.

The two types of scale, the major and minor, in our present tonal system, are based on two of the seven scales that were used by the Greeks. The principle of what intervals were consonant (pure), and which ones were dissonant (impure) was rigidly followed up to the sixteenth century and is still a problem of theorists to this day.

PRIMITIVE PANDEAN PIPES

THE ANCIENT LYRE

Greek music was completely subordinate to poetry and its function was merely to emphasize and give life to some poetic text. Its chief element was rhythm, melody being relatively unimportant; and rhythmic beats were derived from the meter of the poetry. And since there was no music without poetry, it is natural that poetry and music were written by the same person.

VOCAL MUSIC

The poetry thus sung—for Greek music was mainly vocal—was generally also accompanied by instruments. These, too, served only to bring out the rhythm, by playing tones above the melody of the voice. We must not imagine the resulting combination sounded like anything our ear is accustomed to hear. The instrumental part was chosen according to very definite rules, but they are incomprehensible to us.

Of Greek instruments the lyre and the aulos were the most common. The lyre had a bellied sounding box, while its relative, the cithara, had a flat sounding box. In the fifth century both had about seven strings; but the number of strings increased up to eleven in later times. The musical effect of these string instruments must have been rather crude, for they were not equipped with a fingerboard. The aulos was a wind instrument with a reed in the mouthpiece, and consequently gave a sharp and penetrating sound, similar to that of the modern oboe.

Besides various trumpets, harps and pipes, one other important instrument should be mentioned. It was invented by Pythagoras and called a monochord. Consisting of a hollow wooden box with one string and a movable fret or piece of wood, it was able to give sounds of different pitches when the fret was moved up and down the string.

NORTH AFRICAN NEGRO WITH NATIVE DRUM

Courtesy The Art Institute of Chicago

It is well to realize the significance of ancient Greek music. Its theories and principles dominated Western Europe for centuries, and it is difficult to speculate what our music would be if Greek musical traditions had not come down to us.

MUSIC AMONG THE ROMANS

The music of the Romans was that of the Greeks. In fact, music was not held in such high esteem in Rome as it was in classical Greece. The Romans gradually separated music from poetry—at least, we no longer hear of poems being sung. Music in Rome, especially in later times, degenerated into an unwholesome art; it was employed to excite sensual pleasure, and gaudy performances; superficial virtuosity became the rule rather than the exception.

THE ARABS

We must at least briefly mention the music of the Arabs, for it is from them that some of our most important instruments were derived. The viols, the ancestors of our modern violins, and extremely popular from the thirteenth to the seventeenth centuries, were a modified and improved form of the Arabic viols. The kemangeh and the rebab or rebeck, as the Arabian viols were called, were played with or sometimes without a bow. The el-houd was a lute similar to our guitar. Although the Arabs had many kinds of drums, they seem to have definitely preferred the stringed instruments. All their music was played in *unison,* that is, all the instruments played the same melody at the same time, emphasized only by the beat of the drums.

ALGERIAN MUSICIANS WITH THEIR INSTRUMENTS

Courtesy The Art Institute of Chicago

CHURCH MUSIC IN THE EARLY MIDDLE AGES

It was through the Christian Church that our music experienced its earliest awakening. We learn from the Gospels, as well as from several church fathers, and from the Roman writer Pliny, that the early Christians sang in their assemblies. They took their psalms from the Jews, but very soon they created their own hymns. After 323, when Christianity triumphed as a religion over paganism, the happy Christians expressed their joy in a jubilant Alleluia, which means in Hebrew: "Praise ye the Lord." In the monasteries of Syria and Egypt the musical liturgy was first instituted, and from there it was enthusiastically taken up in the fourth century by St. Ambrose, the zealous Bishop of Milan.

In the sixth century, Pope Gregory the Great, motivated by a growing demand for reform of Church music, gathered all the existing melodies, purified and altered them, and created numerous new hymns. He specified which melodies were to be sung on a certain day, and thus arranged a varied liturgy for the entire church year.

We can hardly overestimate the significance of the Gregorian chants, as the new tunes were called. The chants soon became the foundation of the religious service and they retain their importance in that capacity up to this day.

Not only has it been retained by the Catholics as an imperishable vehicle for religious expression, but the whole structure of subsequent musical development rests upon the Gregorian chant. Bach, Mozart, Berlioz, and many others, even twentieth-century composers like Vincent d'Indy and Respighi have returned to Gregorian themes for material and inspiration.

GREGORIAN CHANTS

Gregorian chants have come down to us in manuscripts of the ninth century and later. They were recorded with queer signs called *neumes* which resemble modern shorthand characters. These neumes were certainly a definite improvement over the Greek system of notation which never could have sufficed for the complicated counterpoint of the fifteenth century.

A signal step toward progress was taken when some monk, now unknown to us, invented a red line which represented a fixed tone, and placed the neumes above and below it to indicate higher

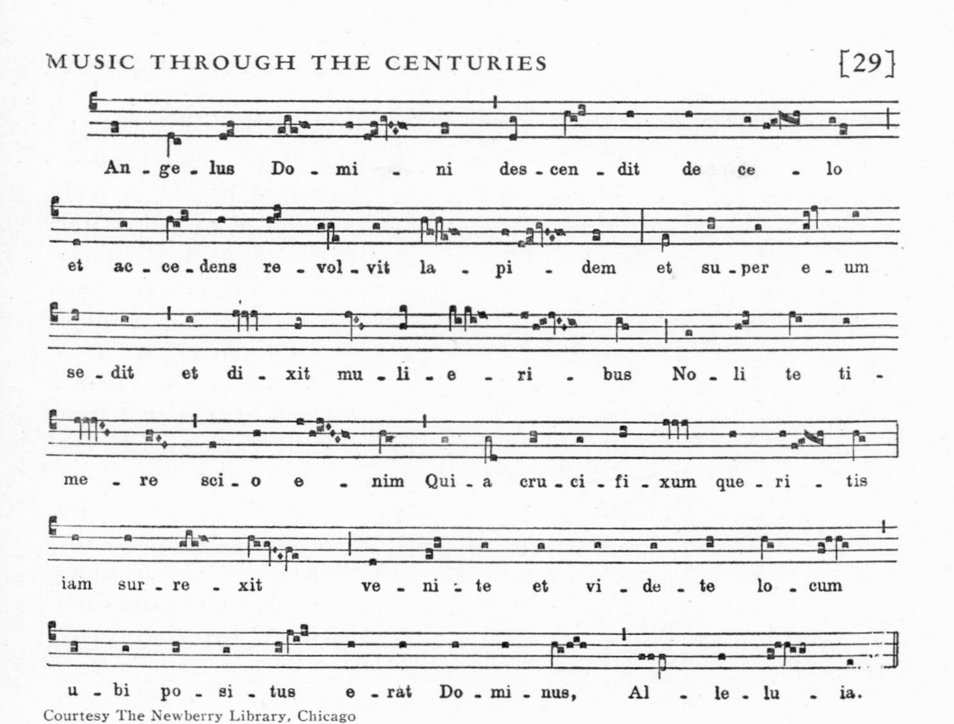

Courtesy The Newberry Library, Chicago

"ANGELUS DOMINI," A GREGORIAN CHANT

and lower pitch. Soon another yellow line was added to indicate the tone C, while the red line corresponded to F.

In the early part of the eleventh century, a famous theorist, Guido d'Arezzo, devised a four-line staff and used both the lines and the spaces between them to indicate the pitch. A fifth line was added by the thirteenth century, while the neumes were gradually disappearing. In their stead, lines and spaces were being filled with the black squares of different size which render medieval musical manuscript so picturesque.

The Gregorian chants were disseminated all over Europe with the spread of Christianity.

The Irish monks particularly fostered the chant and made valuable contributions. Famous schools sprang up in the monasteries of St. Gall, Nietz, Fulda, and Reichenau. Charlemagne was anxious to incorporate the chant in the Frankish realm, as a further unifying element among his diverse subjects.

MONUMENT TO HANS SACHS AT NUREMBERG

SECULAR MUSIC IN THE MIDDLE AGES

With the development of knighthood that was concurrent with the Crusades in the twelfth century, a new art evolved: a beautiful manifestation of the musical urge of the *troubadours* who flourished in that part of southern France called the Provence. The troubadours were inventors of songs which wandering minstrels sang for them. The minstrels carried with them a harp or, later, a viol, the ancestor of the violin. Among the troubadours were men of high rank, knights, counts and even kings, notably Richard the Lionhearted.

The melodies of the troubadours generally express themes of love and nature, as well as melancholy and lamentation. Their *chansons*, or songs, are of delightful freshness and originality with their exquisite melodies and fine rhythms, the latter being dependent upon the meter of the verses.

About a century after the troubadours appeared the German *minnesingers*. They were poets, singers, and actors at once, and, unlike the troubadours, they included men of lower rank, such as ordinary burghers. The songs of the minnesingers were art songs; they were not true folk songs.

With the further development of city life the art of the minnesingers deteriorated and gave way to that of the *meistersingers*. Consisting largely of members of the burgher class, and organized into guilds, the meistersingers made up an important class in the cities. Their members were rigidly classified according to ability; those who could invent new melodies were ranked as masters, while those who could not yet read music fluently were pupils. The meistersongs were made up of biblical as well as secular subjects. They were full of coloratures, and in view of the difficulties involved in their execution, we must have some respect for the men who sang them. Undoubtedly the melodies of the Protestant churches were influenced by the meistersongs.

FOLK SONGS

We come now to a musical form which can be regarded as the highest achievement in the music of the Middle Ages. This is the folk song, which came to perfection during the fourteenth century.

The earliest German folk songs which have come down to us date back to the twelfth century. They are all spiritual songs. We cannot trace secular songs farther back than the thirteenth century, although it is very possible that they existed along with the art of the minnesingers and meistersingers. It is certainly conceivable that these singers exerted a good deal of influence on the songs of the common people.

The spiritual folk song is said to have originated from the Kyrie Eleison ("Lord have mercy") in which the laity participated. Soon the Latin words were substituted for various versions in the vernacular. The farmer, the blacksmith, the cobbler, every-

Courtesy The Art Institute of Chicago

GERMAN MINNESINGERS OF NOBLE BIRTH
(From a medieval illuminated manuscript.)

body sang it at work. Other spiritual folk songs were made by translating Latin hymns, and new songs also arose through inspirations derived from the crusades.

The folk song was the common expression and property of all people, high and low, king and knight, plowman, monk, and student. They sang of love, of drinking, of heroes, of adventure, and of children; there were "humorous, satiric, and obscene songs; —narrative songs, ballads and romances, day songs, equestrian songs, watchmen's songs—" and songs dealing with all walks of life. Often spiritual texts used the same melodies as secular songs; especially during the Reformation, many old secular melodies were utilized for Protestant hymns.

Although the fourteenth century was the period of the classic German folk song, there was similar activity in other European countries. Russia had perhaps a greater wealth of folk songs than any other country in Europe, and its songs were based largely on epic themes of the twelfth century. In Spain, likewise, epic romances were popular, while England had a particular bent toward the ballad. But almost everywhere, in France, England, Scotland, or Denmark, the same familiar and homely subjects and emotions were characterized in folk song.

It is important to remember that up to this point we have dealt only with *monophonic* music in contrast to *polyphonic* music, which is a later development. All these folk songs were sung as a *single* melody, without the accompaniment of a different melody. Oriental countries still retained the monophonic style; it was the achievement of western Europe to contribute the polyphonic style. While the two styles existed side by side in the fourteenth century, the people had as yet no urge to hear or to express themselves in a many-voiced music. This was due to the fact that polyphony was still inferior to monophony. With the fifteenth century, however, the new style gained predominance.

POLYPHONIC MUSIC—PRIMITIVE TYPES

The greatest step in the advance of music was taken when the earliest attempts were made to sound two different voices simultaneously. Naturally, this momentous step was not the work or invention of one man. Such revolutionary innovations usually occur in various places simultaneously, when a certain stage of development has been reached.

Such a stage was reached about the ninth century. At least our earliest report of the first kind of polyphony comes from the pen of the eminent Irish scholar, John Scotus Erigena, who spent many years of his life at the court of Charlemagne. He describes in detail the art of the *organum* style, which was the earliest and most primitive attempt to sing another melody with the traditional chant. The very gradual and cumbersome development in the direction of the brilliant polyphonic contrapuntal style of the fifteenth century is of such interest as to justify a brief account of the earliest steps.

When the early medieval theoreticians searched for the most fitting sort of melody to run parallel to the given chant, they naturally followed the aesthetic laws concerning consonances, as laid down by the Greeks. The latter considered only those intervals consonant or pure, that is, agreeable to the ear, that approached as nearly as possible the effect of *unison* (one and the same sound). The octave, the fifth and the fourth were, therefore, the only permissible intervals. The first polyphonic style, the organum, consisted of improvising a second voice to the Gregorian chant, which ran parallel to it in fourths, like this:

Today some find the succession of fourths rather disagreeable. However, the severity of the fourths is somewhat tempered by the opening and closing where the two voices merge into unison. Even more austere was another type of organum which insisted on a progression of fourths from the very beginning to the end.

During the twelfth century a new style, called the *discantus*, appears which already prescribes the principle in counterpoint and in music in general. Parallel motion is discarded, and an improvised second voice running in alternating fifths and octaves to the *cantus firmus* is insisted upon. Here, too, only "Greek" consonances are permitted, but the contrary motion alleviates to a large extent the hardness of the music.

It seems that England claims the distinction for having first recognized thirds as consonances. The practice of singing in thirds to a chant had been in use during the thirteenth century. This was a remarkable step forward. Soon a new kind of style developed, which consisted of improvising thirds below the chant but actually singing these thirds an octave higher. Thus the pleasing effect of sixths was achieved:

This arrangement sounds much better. The style was called *fauxbourdon* (false bass) and was usually executed with thirds sung both above and below the cantus firmus. Here we have something that approaches modern music. The fauxbourdon persisted in the Church for many centuries, and can be heard even today in Rome.

FURTHER IMPROVEMENTS

Having already traced the origin of two-voiced music, we need merely to indicate some of the succeeding steps which the new art took. For from the fourteenth century onward music mainly elaborated and enlarged on the principles that were already established. We note how the second voice gradually assumed independent rhythm instead of stiffly following the cantus firmus, note for note. But the rhythmic complications that arose herewith had to be supplemented by improvements in the methods of notation. In the thirteenth century we encounter measured notes, that is, each black square note was assigned a definite time value. The supplementary voices which had been improvised were now actually worked out in detail and written down.

Several bold changes occurred in the cantus firmus. Traditionally this leading melody had been taken from the Gregorian chant, but in a new musical form, called the *conductus,* the cantus firmus was an invention. In another type known as *motet* the text of the Gregorian chant is paralleled and elaborated by a different text in the other voices. A really audacious step was taken when secular texts totally independent of that of the chant were assigned to the other voices. Thus there arose a curious combination of the secular and spiritual elements. One might find one or two love songs or any popular melodies set above the slow, long, sustained notes of a spiritual chant. The ecclesiastical melody soon came to be played by instruments, or in some cases the spiritual tradition was completely abandoned and a secular song was given to all voices, including the cantus firmus or tenor.

Very early an element entered into the motet which was to be of vital importance to music. This was the practice of having one voice imitate the motif or melody of the other. One of the earliest forms of imitation appeared in England in the *rondellus* which is in reality a *canon.* The latter is a song in which several voices sing the same melody but different intervals apart. A remarkably advanced rondellus dated about 1240 has been handed down to us. It is a delightful spring canon, called "Sumer is icumen in," and is written for four tenors and two basses. Thus the English played an important part in the early development of polyphony.

In France, the renowned organist and composer Philippe de Vitry (1290-1361) and his contemporaries devised rigid rules for the writing of good counterpoint. By counterpoint we mean the semi-independent voice or voices that accompany or run counter to a given melody. Thus in the organum style the Gregorian chant is the cantus firmus and the accompanying voice is the counterpoint. The writing of counterpoint is an extremely refined art and follows fixed rules which aim to achieve an aesthetically pure effect. In other words, these rules served no other purpose than to produce agreeable music, and for many centuries a good counterpoint was the essence of a musical composition.

During the time of Dante and Petrarch we find many celebrated musicians in Italy. Especially in Florence flourished a brilliant school of poets, composers, and organists. By this time musicians were recognized as worthy artists upon whom were conferred the highest honors by kings and nobles.

Courtesy The Newberry Library, Chicago

PART OF THE MANUSCRIPT OF AN ITALIAN MADRIGAL

THE NETHERLANDS SCHOOLS

By far the most outstanding in fifteenth-century music was the Netherlands school. The Low Countries (including Holland, Belgium, and a part of northern France) played an important role in the commerce and manufacturing of the early Renaissance. It is not surprising that the art of music should prosper there.

The music of the early Netherlands is generally divided into a first, second, and, by some authorities, even a third school. The main representative of the older, or first, school was William Dufay (1400-1474). He probably benefited from the works of the first great English composer, John Dunstable, who was particularly famous for the wealth of melodies in his works. Dufay was an excellent contrapuntist; each voice, even the bass, of his compositions has a melody and an independent function, despite the relative preference given to the upper voice.

The Netherlands musicians were equally capable in both secular and spiritual music. Of the first the *chanson* was the most important form, but little distinguishes it from spiritual music. The Mass was a new form of the latter. It consisted of the Kyrie, Gloria, Credo, Sanctus, and Agnus Dei, which were composed in the polyphonic style, in contrast to the monophonic Gregorian chant. Dufay even introduced the secular melodies into the Mass, and his innovation was eagerly imitated by his successors to such an extent that it aroused the opposition of the Church. At the Council of Trent in 1545 the Church, while considering Lutheran heresy, also proposed to condemn the polyphonic style in the Catholic services. It was only by the supreme style of Palestrina, who proved that religious devotion and art could be combined, that polyphonic music was saved for the Church.

Two men are outstanding in the second Netherlands school, which roughly falls between the years 1450 and 1550. Joannes Okeghem, the great master of the second half of the fifteenth century, and one of the world's greatest music teachers, lived most of his life in France where he served as court composer to Charles VII and Louis XI. Okeghem developed the practice of imitating melodies throughout the composition and abandoned the preference given to the upper voice. Four voices instead of three were now generally employed, and each voice was totally independent, although they all stood in a very definite relationship to each other.

Courtesy The Newberry Library, Chicago

JOSQUIN DES PRÉS

The greatest of all Flemish composers was Josquin des Prés, who was a pupil of Okeghem. He was a prolific composer and did much to transplant the music of his country into Italy. During his life Josquin enjoyed tremendous popularity, but his florid counterpoint later won for him the opposition of the Church. His contemporaries called him the "Prince of Music," but he remained in oblivion for centuries, until, recently, his works have been revived.

Through the Netherlands schools the art of counterpoint attained its highest perfection. Monster canons of thirty-six voices are known, as well as canons that can be read forward, backward, and upside down (mirror canons). But these extravagances only illustrate the facility with which these musicians composed a good counterpoint, and the exceptional extremes in which they indulged were largely an expression of joy at having mastered their material.

THE GERMAN SONG

While the musicians of the Netherlands brought counterpoint to an unheard-of complexity, German composers developed a distinctly characteristic musical form, the German *lied.* The French were writing their chansons with freely invented melodies, without employing spiritual or secular canti firmi. But in Germany, the lied was built up on the old folk song of the twelfth and thirteenth centuries. The old tune was used as a cantus firmus in the tenor voice and three other voices, soprano, alto, and bass, were constructed around it. These three voices usually were related to the tenor by varying the main theme.

The oldest collection of these polyphonic songs dates back to 1450. Humanists and scholars of that time were very fond of music and several of them eagerly collected these songs. That Luther was a great devotee of music and that he composed several chorals himself are well-known facts. More surprising it is that

Courtesy J. Bradford Pengelly

LUTHER INTRODUCED TO THE HOME OF FRAU COTTA
Luther composed several chorals and was a great lover of music.

the austere Calvin occupied his leisure hours playing the lute. It is characteristic that all the universities of this time had chairs of music. And it is a strange paradox that while these humanists and theoreticians were so ardently devoted to the Greeks and were earnestly trying to imitate them, they cultivated an art which was indeed very different from that of their models.

The earliest school of folk song composers was centered in the chapels of the dukes of Bavaria and Württemberg, and the Imperial Chapel of Maximilian at Innsbruck. The school was represented by Heinrich Isaak and Ludwig Senfl.

MUSIC NOTATION AND PRINTING

We have already seen how the earliest music was written in neumes, how the five-line staff originated, and that in the thirteenth century mensural notes were introduced. The men who were particularly instrumental in developing the latter were the two Francos, Franco of Cologne and Franco of Paris.

Today our notes are divisible into halves; the whole note is made up of two halves, the half of two quarters, the quarter of two-eighths, and so on down to the sixty-fourth notes. But the early mensural notes were divided into three parts, so that a measure of three beats was considered perfect. The perfect triple measure was to represent the Trinity. Later a small circle at the opening of the line indicated the "perfect" time, and when the "imperfect" two-beat measure began to be used, it was indicated by a half circle. The latter is still used to indicate our common four-four time.

Different shapes distinguished the individual notes from each other in their different time values. Some were square, others oblong or diamond-shaped. In the fourteenth century the notes of longer time value were colored red and shorter ones filled in with black. The red ones were soon left white, and so they have remained to this day.

The art of printing music employing movable type was invented in Venice in 1498. Venice became the leading center of music publishing, but other great centers soon rose in Paris, Nuremberg, and Amsterdam.

Let us bear in mind, however, that although musical notes had been assigned definite time value, it must have been somewhat difficult to sing a melody by sight. The lines were not as yet sub-

Servite . Euouae . Dñicis diebus.
Alle luia . Euouae Tempore pascali.
Eatus vir qui non
abiit in consilio impiorum:
et in via peccatorum non
stetit: et in cathedra pesti-
lentie non sedit, Sed
in lege domini voluntas
eius: et in lege eius meditabitur die ac no-

Courtesy Cuneo Press, Chicago

FIRST APPEARANCE OF MUSIC IN A PRINTED BOOK
Page of Psalter printed by Fust and Schoeffer in 1457.

divided by bars into measures, the notes were still awkward and cumbersome, and the rhythm, especially in the Netherlands schools, was extremely complicated. And yet this music, with its crafty syncopations, and its baffling symbols and directions, was usually sung at sight—a remarkable feat, even though executed largely by professional singers who were members of chapel choirs!

THE A CAPPELLA STYLE OF THE SIXTEENTH-CENTURY, PALESTRINA

We have seen how the chapels furnished the principal medium for the cultivation of music. The sixteenth century is characterized by a blossoming of the *a cappella* style *(cappella:* chapel) under the dominant figure of Palestrina, the greatest Italian composer of church music.

Courtesy The Newberry Library, Chicago

GIOVANNI PIERLUIGI DA PALESTRINA

Giovanni Pierluigi was born in the village of Palestrina, the name of which was later added to his name. True to tradition he was organist and leader of the chapel choir in his own village; later he became a papal singer in the Sistine Chapel. To his great dismay he was dismissed in the same year, but he soon obtained the post of chapel master at St. John Lateran in Rome. Finally, in 1571, he was elected chapel master of the Vatican, and he retained this high position until his death.

Palestrina lived at the same time and in the same city as Michelangelo, but the difference between their personalities was as great as the difference in their art. The dramatic, restless, passionately struggling human Titans on the ceiling of the Sistine Chapel exerted no influence on Palestrina, who sang in the very

Courtesy The Newberry Library, Chicago

EARLY ENGLISH TRANSLATION OF ONE OF PALESTRINA'S COMPOSITIONS

same chapel. Palestrina, like Michelangelo, devoted his entire life to the service of the Church, but his art was calm and impersonal, simple and clear. He was an industrious composer, having ninety-three masses, three hundred and fifty motets and a vast number of hymns, songs and madrigals to his credit. The music of Palestrina was pronounced by the ecclesiastical authorities to be in the only true *a cappella,* that is, church style. In the complex polyphony of the Netherlands the religious text had been so obscured that the words could not be understood. Palestrina underlined the text, so to speak, by having the voices move along independently, syllable for syllable, at the same time blending them with the intricate style of the Netherlands. His music represents the relationship of the Church to God; it has no consideration for the sufferings and passions of the individual. The Palestrina style is outward simplicity itself, for all display of technique and crafty artifice have been discarded.

Brilliant schools of music flourished in both Rome and Venice during the *a cappella* period. The Roman school was headed by Palestrina; the Venetian was founded by a master of the Netherlands school, Adrian Willaert. Born in Flanders, he received his musical education in Paris, made a tour through Italy, then became chapel master to the King of Hungary and Bohemia, and finally settled down in Venice. As chapel master at St. Mark's he thrilled the public by employing a double choir and two organs during the services. The double chorus was the original contribution and specialty of the Venetian school, and many eager German students like Schütz and Hassler flocked to Venice to receive instruction from its famous masters. Already Italy was beginning to assume leadership in music, and by the end of the sixteenth century it definitely emerged as the dominant musical country.

ORLANDO DI LASSO

Up until then, however, the Netherlands school held its own. It produced its last great master in the person of Orlandus Lassus, who was the most interesting figure in the musical world of his time. He was the first musician to represent the aristocratic artist typified by the painters Titian and Raphael. At home everywhere, admired, honored and enriched at great courts, he was a true international character. Despite his roaming existence he managed to compose some 2,400 works. He was a master in all fields of

ORLANDO DI LASSO
From an engraving by C. Deblois after an old German print.

Courtesy The Newberry Library, Chicago

music, spiritual and secular, vocal and instrumental, and several countries claim Orlando di Lasso (as he was known in Italy) as one of their great musicians.

PROTESTANT CHURCH MUSIC

In Germany the Reformation exercised a profound influence on the composers of the sixteenth century. Under the leadership of Luther the congregational hymn was made the core of the musical part of the religious service. The hymns were sung in unison by the congregation, but sometimes they were also rendered antiphonally by the choir. Consequently composers busied themselves with making four- and five-voice arrangements of hymns as well as folk songs which were adapted to a religious text. The most noted German Protestant composers were Michael Praetorius, Johann Walker, and Johann Eccard, a pupil of Orlando di Lasso. The foremost composer of this Protestant movement was the great

Nuremburg master, Hans Leo Hassler, whose polyphonic arrangements of spiritual and secular melodies are exquisite.

Only one composer of note during this period remained faithful to the Catholic church, namely Jacobus Gallus, known as Jakob Händl in Germany. He wrote numerous motets and madrigals, and he is sometimes referred to, with some exaggeration, as the German Palestrina.

In Switzerland, the Reformed church under Zwingli was definitely hostile toward music and prohibited it in the church service. But Calvin in France was more lenient; in fact, he even attempted to do what Luther had done for Germany, namely, to arrange melodies suitable for the Calvinistic congregations. While German composers were elaborating the chorales, the French developed the Psalms. Especially noteworthy are the four-voice arrangements by Claude Gaudimel set to the versification by Marot and Beza. Later these were translated into all languages and adapted by all the Reformed churches.

Much of the Protestant church music in America came originally from England. There the earliest Anglican chant was derived from the Catholic plain song in the sixteenth century. The English church anthem is derived from the Italian Palestrina. Development of English church music practically ceased during the domination of the Puritans.

MUSIC IN SPAIN

Spanish church music has been little known until very recently. During the fifteenth century, while the Netherlands schools flourished, there were also very notable masters in Spain, whose early ballads and romances, with their elements of vehemence and passion, were typically Spanish. The sixteenth century is dominated by two great names, Cristobal Morales and Ludovico da Victoria. Their polyphonic music is simpler and more choral in character, similar to the Palestrina style. It was written only for male voices and the minor mode prevails, thereby giving an impression of intense seriousness.

THE MADRIGAL

The flowering of the vocal style in secular music occurred in a new form called the madrigal. We have already met this form in the Florentine school of the fourteenth century, but it was

MVSICA TRANSALPINA.

CANTVS.

Madrigales tranſlated of foure, fiue and ſixe parts, choſen out of diuers excellent Authors, vvith the firſt and ſecond part of *La Verginella*, made by Maiſter *Byrd*, vpon two Stanz's of *Arioſto* and brought to ſpeake Engliſh with the reſt.

Publiſhed by N. Yonge, *in fauour of ſuch as take pleaſure in Muſick of voices.*

Imprinted at London by Thomas Eaſt, the aſsignè of William Byrd. 1588.

Cum Priuilegio Regiæ Maieſtatis.

Courtesy The Newberry Library, Chicago

TITLE PAGE OF BOOK OF MADRIGALS PUBLISHED IN 1588

Courtesy The Newberry Library, Chicago

A MADRIGAL BY WILLIAM BYRD, OF THE ELIZABETHAN PERIOD

then still in its embryonic stage. In the beginning of the sixteenth century two new types of songs appeared in Italy, the *frottola* and the *villanella*. Both are popular dance songs, both are rhythmically lively and well marked, and both have trivial and commonplace words for a text.

These two rustic forms were the precursors of the sixteenth century madrigal. Originally a pastoral or love song, the madrigal soon took almost any religious, moral, pastoral, or domestic subject for its text, never long and serious, but of a spontaneous and trifling nature. It is usually written for four or five voices which take up a theme independently and are divided into definite sections. Madrigals were all in the *a cappella* style, which designation no longer applies only to church music of the Palestrina style, but includes all vocal music without instrumental accompaniment.

Again it was the Netherlanders who were the pioneers in the field. Under Adrian Willaert the Venetian school composed a great number of madrigals which became exceedingly popular. The new form was at once imitated by musicians in all countries, and a vast amount of vocal music grew up around it.

ELIZABETHAN MUSIC

Elizabethan England was not only a period of national glory and a golden age of literature, but it was the heyday of English music as well. There was unparalleled musical activity among both professional and lay musicians. The madrigal achieved perfection and an individual form; church music also found expression, in such great masters as Byrd and Gibbons. And of especial interest is the universal zeal displayed in playing such instruments as the virginal, the lute, the recorders, and the viols.

Secular music in Elizabethan England centered about the madrigal. It took most of its melodies from the street, the farm, and the people; from the Netherlands it took its counterpoint, and from Italy both counterpoint and popular songs. Thus it is a successful fusion of various foreign and indigenous elements.

Madrigals were enthusiastically cultivated by the laity. In almost every home one might find the family seated around a table singing madrigals. Even the maids and servants might be asked to come in and help out. In fact, some families would not hire a maid if she was not able to sing or read a musical part.

Foremost of the English madrigal composers was John Wilbye, who ranks among the greatest of English composers, Thomas

Courtesy The Newberry Library, Chicago

AN ANGEL PLAYING A MEDIEVAL VIOLA

A detail from "La Verge de la Llet," fourteenth century. (Museum Diocesa, Valencia.)

Weelkes, John Bennet, and especially Thomas Morely, who wrote the melody for Shakespeare's well-known song, "It Was a Lover and His Lass" in *As You Like it.* Most of the madrigalists were also accomplished lutanists.

INSTRUMENTS IN ELIZABETHAN MUSIC

Often madrigals were also played by instruments only. A chest of viols or a set of recorders, or both, belonged to every well-to-do home; and the lute was practically universal. The viols were the precursors of the modern bowed instruments, and had been in use since the twelfth century. They are probably derived from the Arabians, by whom they were transmitted to the Moors in Spain. The troubadours had already used them in the eleventh century. In the fifteenth century viols began to be made in different sizes to correspond to the various pitches. The treble (the highest) viol was called violino (little viola), the viola da gamba (leg viola) had a tenor pitch and resembled our modern cello. Others were the viola da braccio (arm viola) and the bass violone (big viola). A set of such viols constituted a "chest" or "consort" of viols, which in its function was comparable to the modern string quartet.

Recorders can be regarded as the precursors of the flute. They were played directly from the end, not from the side as is the present-day transverse flute. A rich but soft and mellow tone was characteristic of the recorders, which were, like the viols, built in various sizes from the bass to the soprano pitch.

The lute was of ancient descent and had been popular among the Arabians. Throughout the Middle Ages it was used as accompaniment to a single voice, especially in Italy. Closely resembling the guitar, it differs from the latter in its superior tone and in the shape of its back, which is pear-shaped, while the guitar has a flat back. Queen Elizabeth and Mary Queen of Scots were accomplished lute players. It became fashionable for the gallant gentleman to present his sweetheart with a bouquet of lute strings. The tuning of the lute was rather difficult, for the strings were extremely sensitive to influences of temperature, moisture, and the like. A real virtuosity was developed on the lute, and consequently composers felt inspired to write solo pieces expressly for it. This was the first step to the instrumental style, which was to gain undisputed dominance from the seventeenth century onward.

Courtesy The Art Institute of Chicago

EUROPEAN INSTRUMENTS OF THE TWELFTH TO SIXTEENTH CENTURIES

The virginal found particular appeal among young ladies. It was usually slender and triangular in shape, but smaller and earlier virginals were oblong and rectangular, and when played were placed on a table. Belonging to the family of key instruments, and the species called harpsichord, it is an important predecessor of the piano. Soft but precise tones were produced by the plucking of the strings with small metal or leather plectra which were operated by the keyboard.

As a composer for the virginal, William Byrd was important. He belonged to a family of talented musicians, and has been called the English Palestrina. During a time when Protestant England was persecuting Catholics, Byrd stood in such high favor with the Queen that he remained unmolested. Byrd's virginal pieces are significant in the development of instrumental music and especially of a new form, the variation, which makes use of a well-known popular or church melody by artistically embellishing and transforming it. Apart from Byrd, Orlando Gibbons and John Bull are the principal figures in Elizabethan virginal music. Their compositions are mainly built up on plain-songs or popular tunes, especially of folk dances. There is an extraordinary abundance of ornament in the forms of delicate trills, and also a considerable amount of meaningless fast scale-playing. The novelty of instruments which could produce tones faster and easier than could human voices impressed these early instrumental composers. It is a natural, childish joy in a new toy, quite different from anything that the *a capella* style had permitted. We must also bear in mind that the virginal music was written for an instrument that was far more delicate than the piano of today. Such ornamentation would be intolerable on a modern instrument.

GENERAL MUSICAL DEVELOPMENTS

In all European countries, there was a noticeable development of instrumental and vocal music. Germany eagerly accepted the Italian madrigal and in general fell under the sway of Italian influence. Orlando di Lasso of Munich composed German madrigals in the Italian style, and the famous Hassler even wrote madrigals to Italian words.

The lute was universally popular in all of Europe. In France a refined lute music grew up under J. B. Besard, Charles Mouton, and Denis Gaultier. Poland, where music flourished in the royal court, contributed precious lute songs and dances which bear the typically Polish elements of melancholy and rhythmic vigor.

THE ORGAN—COMPLEX AND VERSATILE

Up to the fourteenth century, the organ was extremely unwieldy, for it took from eight to ten men to operate the bellows, while the keys could be depressed only by pounding with the fists and elbows. Pedals were invented during the fourteenth century, and a century later the first reed pipes were used. But the organ did not achieve mechanical pliancy and majestic beauty until the seventeenth century.

One of the earliest and most famous of organ composers was Paul Hofhaimer (1459-1537), who was organist at the court of Emperor Maximilian I in Vienna. Under his influence a notable school of organists grew up in Switzerland, Austria, and Germany. The compositions for organ were confined in the beginning to transcriptions of ecclesiastical and secular songs and dances, and, as in the case of the early virginal pieces, they were embellished considerably. In Italy, the real creators of organ music were Andrea and Giovanni Gabrieli, both organists at St. Mark's in Venice. The Venetian masters distinguished themselves by inventing various new, purely instrumental forms, such as the *fantasia,* the *toccata,* and the *ricercare.* The latter employs the principle of imitation and is important as a precursor of the great artistic form of the eighteenth century, the fugue.

LE MVSICHE
DI IACOPO PERI
NOBIL FIORENTINO
Sopra L'Euridice
DEL SIG. OTTAVIO RINVCCINI
Rappreſentate Nello Sponſalizio
della Criſtianiſsima
MARIA MEDICI
REGINA DI FRANCIA
E DI NAVARRA

IN FIORENZA
APPRESSO GIORGIO MARESCOTTI.
M D C.

Courtesy The Newberry Library, Chicago

TITLE PAGE OF THE OPERA "EURIDICE"

THE SEVENTEENTH CENTURY—THE OPERA

At the opening of the seventeenth century the opera came into being. The spirit of classical antiquity which permeated all of Italy during the Renaissance also inspired composers with the ambition to revive the music of the Greeks. But there were no records of the works of classical composers to speak of, save three Greek hymns which could not be deciphered. Disregarding the lack of information, Vincenzo Galilei, father of the great astronomer, boldly set to music a number of poetic works with the accompaniment of an instrument. The innovation was greeted with enthusiasm, and gave rise to a movement which swept over Italy like a wave and soon spread to all the European countries.

The real history of the opera begins with the performance in the year 1600 of the opera *Euridice* by the Italian Jacopo Peri. It was generally believed that with this work, the Greek tragedy had been revived, but in reality it was a totally new creation. Peri and his colleagues declared that music should be the servant of poetry, and felt that counterpoint had destroyed this natural relationship by assuming too much independence. They wished to exterminate the art of counterpoint altogether, and a dry, declamatory style, the *stile recitativo*, was to take its place. The recitativo or *rappresentativo* consisted of an accompanied melody and was therefore in sharp contrast to the independence of all the voices as characteristic in contrapuntal polyphony.

In accordance with the prominence of the melody in the recitativo, the accompaniment was merely noted in a kind of musical shorthand. Only the bass was written out, and little numbers placed above the bass notes indicated the chords to be played. This system of a figured bass was called the *basso continuo* or thorough bass. A certain freedom of execution was given the player by this generalized notation, and the thorough bass became very popular and was extensively used until the end of the eighteenth century.

Euridice was soon followed by Gagliano's *Dafne*, which was staged with all sorts of dazzling scenic effects. Among others, a mechanized dragon amazed the unsophisticated audience, and already we notice tendencies which later led to the spectacular operas of Wagner.

Courtesy The Newberry Library, Chicago

FIRST PAGE OF SCENE FROM PERI'S "EURIDICE"

THE COLOR OF MODERN OPERA

Claudio Monteverdi is a dramatic figure in the rise of the opera. Even twentieth century realism has not produced an audacious genius of the caliber of Monteverdi. He expressed the spirit of his time admirably; it was a realistic age, and like his contemporary, Shakespeare, Monteverdi dauntlessly made use of his elaborate inventory of realistic expressions. He deliberately violated the rules of counterpoint by his revolutionary, unprepared dissonances and made his music express precisely the desired effects. After Monteverdi, the new harmonic style became preeminent throughout Europe.

A few years before the death of Monteverdi, the first popular opera house was opened in Venice. The earlier opera performances had taken place under the auspices of wealthy princes in their palaces, but now a veritable democratic institution arose which admitted anyone for a small admission price. The whole machinery of operatic routine, the virtuoso singers, the impresarios, the stirring scenic splendors, the applauding audience, and all the glamour connected with evening performances—all this had its beginning in Venice. The fame of this city rang throughout Europe, and even German princes maintained boxes in the Venetian opera house for their families.

Monteverdi used an elaborate orchestra, which contained a large number of chordal instruments like the harpsichord, organ, and lute. These did not play continuously with the rest of the orchestra; on the contrary, various sections of instruments were used to fit different effects and scenes. The orchestra frequently alternated with the singers and played short movements, called sinfonias, describing some aspect of nature, like the sea, a forest, or a storm.

Later composers were markedly influenced by this early opera, which was regarded with wonder throughout Europe.

THE OPERA IN FRANCE

During the seventeenth century when French literature drifted toward its great classical period, the French genius was little inclined merely to imitate the *nuove musiche*, as the new harmonic style of the Italians was called. But under the protection of the influential minister Mazarin, an Italian by birth,

JEAN BAPTISTE LULLY

Italian singers were invited to Paris to perform in operas. In 1647 the *Orfeo* of Luigi Rossi and other operas were produced, and despite protests for religious and financial reasons, the operas were a success.

But these operas were all Italian operas by Italian composers. The first French opera was *Pastorale* by the composer Robert Cambert, who a few years later produced another more important opera, *Pomone*. This opera, repeated 146 times, was the first to be performed in the newly opened Académie Royale de Musique, 1671, created under Louis XIV and subsidized by the government for the cultivation of operas.

It was of utmost importance for the future of the French opera that the great French musician Jean Baptiste Lully took over the leadership of the Académie Royale. He was born in Florence, but had been taken to France in his early boyhood to work as a kitchen boy in a private household. Since he was an excellent violinist, Louis XIV took him into his court orchestra. Lully soon acquired fame as a composer of church music and dances, but his talent lay particularly in the field of ballet. Given the directorship of the opera, he composed some twenty operas to texts furnished by the great tragic poet Quinault. It was natural for Lully to give an important place to ballet in his operas, and thus he established a tradition which has persisted down to this day. In fact, the French have always had a special talent for dancing, and it would be no exaggeration to say that the French opera was based on the ballet. A host of dances, the rustic *bourrée,* the graceful minuet, and the lively gavotte are all French dance forms. These dances abounded in Lully's operas, and European instrumental music drew nourishment from them for more than a century.

In Italian opera the chorus had been reduced to insignificance. Lully, however, made frequent use of choruses to support mass scenes and add to the magnificence of the French opera under the Grand Monarch.

THE OPERA IN ENGLAND

Music in seventeenth-century England rises and falls with the frequent and disturbing political events. The troublesome times during the reign of the unfortunate Charles I gave little opportunity for music to flourish. During the Puritan regime, while the art was not completely suppressed by Cromwell, nevertheless the cultivation of church music was certainly checked. But with the restoration in 1660 of Charles II, the Merry Monarch, English music again flourished.

The development of the English opera began with two or three performances at court of operas by the French composer Cambert, who had come to England as the master of music to the king. The real founder of opera in England was Henry Purcell, who was especially interested in developing a musical drama and composed altogether fifty-four dramatic pieces and a great deal of incidental music. Purcell's most famous opera is *Dido and*

Aeneas, written to the libretto by Nahum Tate. Italian influence is very evident, especially in his use of the *basso ostinato*, frequently employed by Monteverdi. This "ground" bass, as it is called in English, consists of an ever recurring theme which lends a characteristic charm to the composition.

THE OPERA IN GERMANY

The Italian opera gained a strong foothold in Germany under the patronage of the music-loving Emperors Ferdinand III and Leopold I. In fact, both of these monarchs and some of their successors were accomplished composers. In Vienna, Leopold founded an Italian opera house which produced almost ten new works every year. Munich, too, could soon boast a permanent Italian opera. Johann Kasper Kerl, who was conductor of the Munich opera, was the first German composer to write Italian operas to Italian texts. Kerl was succeeded in his post by Italian musicians. Of these Agostina Steffani was the most eminent; indeed, his operas as well as his chamber duets (written for two voices and harpischord accompaniment) possess a remarkably finished form as attained by the classical composers of the eighteenth century.

Another Italian opera was established in Dresden in 1662 which became famous under the direction of another Italian composer, Carlo Pallavicino.

The opera had been introduced into Germany by Heinrich Schütz, better known as a composer of church music. His opera, *Daphne*, written to the words by the eminent poet Martin Opitz, and produced in 1627, represents the first opera in German. Further development was temporarily halted by the disturbances and horrors of the Thirty Years' War, but at last in 1678 the German opera was established.

The Hamburg opera would have been able to maintain itself had there been worthy poets to furnish libretti for the composers. But librettists exhibited too much the characteristics of their time, a vulgar realism and crude humor recalling the vaudeville stage. Not infrequently a whole menagerie of animals was led onto the stage. Murders were displayed right before the audience, and red-stained water added color to the scene. A striking contrast is furnished by the French opera of this time, which recruited such poetic talents as Molière and Quinault.

Despite the degraded character of the libretti, a host of very able musicians offered their energy to the Hamburg opera. Such celebrities as G. Philip Telemann and Handel wrote operas for it. However, the typical personality of the Hamburg school was Reinhard Keiser. A charming, flattering nature, somewhat shallow, very talented and extremely productive both in operatic and sacred music, Keiser could have been an outstanding composer had he been more profound. He wrote no less than 116 operas, but they are stereotyped pieces owing, perhaps, partly to the formal nature of the *thorough bass* system, so widely in use at this time. Yet his compositions do possess some structural and aesthetic features which are characteristic of later seventeenth- and early eighteenth-century music.

THE ORATORIO

When in the early part of the seventeenth century the admirers of classical antiquity began to experiment with the harmonic style which soon led to the first opera, other musicians in Rome cultivated dramatic pieces with spiritual texts which developed into the oratorio. In 1600 Peri's *Euridice* was enacted in the "oratory" or chapel of St. Philip of Neri in Rome. In this oratory from which the new composition takes its name, there had been numerous performances of sacred music, the so-called *Laudi Spirituali*.

These were sacred dialogues in madrigal form, composed by the best composers of the day, and they enjoyed wide popularity. Musically, the *Laudi Spirituali* are the precursors of the oratorio, but textually the latter is an outgrowth of the medieval mystery play. Thus the opera and the oratorio are of independent origin, although the recitative style was common to both of them. The spiritual operas were performed with costumes, scenery, and dances, but soon a narrator took over the function of the theatrical paraphernalia. With this step the real oratorio began.

The first oratorio appeared in Rome in 1619. There developed two types, the *oratorio Latino*, based on a biblical text, and the *oratorio volgare*, which was written to a free text, containing religious, moral, and worldly elements.

Giacomo Carissimi composed mainly biblical oratorios. His achievement lies in the fact that he attained a successful blending of the old choral and the new harmonic style. There had been a strong tendency among reformers like Monteverdi to neglect contrapuntal polyphony altogether, but it was soon realized that it was not so easily dispensible. Carissimi freely utilized the principles of the old art and applied them to the choruses of his oratorios.

The biblical oratorio was soon superseded by the *oratorio volgare*. But this, too, never reached the height of the oratorio of Protestant Germany, for the Bible was inaccessible to the ordinary layman in Catholic Italy and thus prevented individual exaltation and personal contact with the Scriptures. The Italian oratorio soon became a purely dramatic entertainment edifying the audience with the legendary adventures of the saints and teaching a moral amid a good deal of earthly realism.

HEINRICH SCHÜTZ (1585-1672)

In Germany, the development of the oratorio rested largely on the works of Heinrich Schütz. His long sojourn in Italy and

HEINRICH SCHÜTZ

Courtesy The Newberry Library, Chicago

years of study in Venice made Schütz fully acquainted not only with the art of the many-voiced chorus but with the revolutionary monodic style as well. He was able to assimilate all of these contrasting principles, and introduced upon his return to Germany an art which contained both the time-honored polyphony and the modern harmonic style of the Florentine school.

It has been mentioned already that Schütz brought the opera into Germany by the performance of *Daphne* in 1627. But his main activity lay in the field of church music. Here he pursued the path of the Italian oratorio composers. He wrote a number of "dialogues" and so-called "histories," for solo voices and orchestra. A delightful realism is evident in these sacred works, for the characters in them are lively and folk-like.

RELIGIOUS WORKS

Schütz was an extremely versatile composer. In the secular field he wrote an opera and a ballet, *Orpheus and Eurydice,* madrigals and arias. His religious works include four church passions, over a hundred spiritual concerts, and a great number of motets, spiritual concerts, "histories," Psalms, and sacred choruses. His *History of the Joyful and Blessed Birth of Jesus Christ,* a Christmas oratorio, charming in its unadorned homeliness, may be regarded as the first real German oratorio.

Thus Schütz had cultivated the Italian dialogues into the form of the oratorio, and from there it was taken up by a long list of talented German church composers, until it was later developed by Bach to an unparalleled perfection.

THE ORCHESTRAL SUITE

Composers of the first half of the seventeenth century manifested a special predilection for incorporating popular dance tunes into instrumental compositions. The most important dances at this time were the *pavan* or *paduan*, and the *galliard*. The pavan was a slow, stately dance, used for wedding marches, aristocratic processions, and the like. It was written in four-part time and consisted primarily of walking. But the galliard, in three-part time, was fast and lively. In Germany the pavan and galliard were regularly combined into one dance. The customary dance, even in the sixteenth century, was composed of a slow part in the first half, and ended with a wild and gay dance in the second.

These dance forms were eagerly adapted for the clavier instruments; English virginal composers like William Byrd reveled in them. Soon it became customary to include not only two, but five or six dances in one composition, and usually the folk tunes were varied and embellished. The resultant artistic piece was called a *suite*. One of the earliest and best composers of orchestral suites was Hermann Schein. He applied the polyphonic principle to popular dance tunes, but bold modern dissonances resembling those of Monteverdi were not lacking.

The orchestral suite was a specialty of German composers. In the latter part of the seventeenth century, however, the French musician Lully, director of the Parisian opera, exerted a deep influence on the suite. The result was the refined, versatile suite as we know it. Frequently the various dance forms of the suite were based on the same tune, varied rhythmically and thematically. Orchestral suites were supplied with overtures, an innovation the Germans took over from Lully. These later became important as an introduction to oratorios. The overture to Handel's *Messiah* is a familiar example.

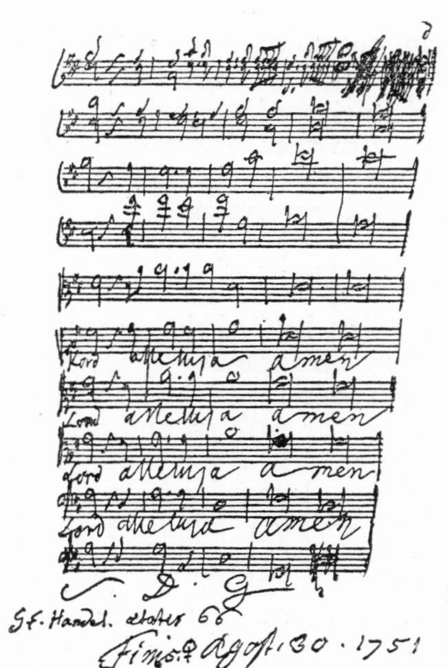

MANUSCRIPT OF THE "AMEN CHORUS" FROM HANDEL'S "MESSIAH"

THE SONATA AND THE CONCERTO

The revolution in music which ushered in the harmonic style during the latter part of the seventeenth century manifested itself in the beginning mostly in vocal music. The development of instrumental music followed almost a century later.

The first instrumental forms were modest and free, providing for four or five instruments. A very early form was the *trio*, consisting of two violins and a *basso continuo* executed by a keyboard instrument and some string bass like the viola da gamba. This so-called trio was the standard ensemble throughout the seventeenth century, until it was superseded by the string quartet of Haydn.

The Italians again were the first to devise satisfactory forms for the instrumental ensemble. Arcangelo Corelli (1653-1713), a brilliant violinist in Rome, established the sonata form. It was based on the law of contrast. The first movement was of a restrained, *adagio* (slow) nature, relieved by an *allegro* (fast) second movement. The third and fourth likewise progressed from a slow to a fast tempo, so that the scheme of the entire sonata was an alternation between slow and fast. In the latter half of the eighteenth century the sonata generally followed a three-part plan, beginning and ending with a fast tempo. Corelli himself wrote highly perfected and significant solo sonatas and trio sonatas which serve as models up to this day.

A favorite form which originated about the time of Corelli was the *concerto*. This rests on the contrasting effects between soloists and full orchestra. The concerto might be written for a solo instrument or for a combination of several (*concerti grossi*) which alternated with the orchestra. Concertos were based on the sonata form, usually consisting of three movements. In this field Corelli, Stradella and Alessandro Scarlatti were the most outstanding composers.

MUSIC FOR KEYBOARD INSTRUMENTS

In the field of organ music one can already detect the line which was to lead to Bach. The most worthy Italian precursor of the great Leipzig organist was Girolamo Frescobaldi, who seems to have been an extraordinary virtuoso. But he also wrote

GIROLAMO FRESCOBALDI

Courtesy The Newberry Library, Chicago

very excellent counterpoint in his fantasias, toccatas, and caprices for the organ.

Jan Pieters Sweelinck was the outstanding Dutch musician of his time. A great number of German organists flocked to Amsterdam to learn from him. He was perhaps the greatest composer in the fugal style up to the time of Bach. A very famous pupil of Sweelinck was Samuel Scheidt, who created many lofty Protestant chorals from secular folk songs.

Germany had three great organists at this time; the celebrated J. J. Froberger, a happy, international traveler; Dietrich Buxtehude, organist at Lübeck; and Johann Pachelbel of Nuremberg. All of these were composers as well as organists. They were very proficient in the art of fugal composition and thus prepared the soil for the greatest of all, Johann Sebastian Bach.

THE CLAVIER

While Lully directed the opera in Paris, French composers developed the suite for the clavier (a general term for any stringed keyboard instrument). The four-part suite, consisting of an *allemande, courante, sarabande,* and *gigue,* was created by Jacques Champion de Chambonnières, the first harpsichordist of Louis XIV. The new form was developed into a brilliant and extremely colorful composition by the Couperins, a family of numerous talented musicians, like the families of Byrd and Bach. François Couperin (1668-1733), known as the "Great Couperin," com-

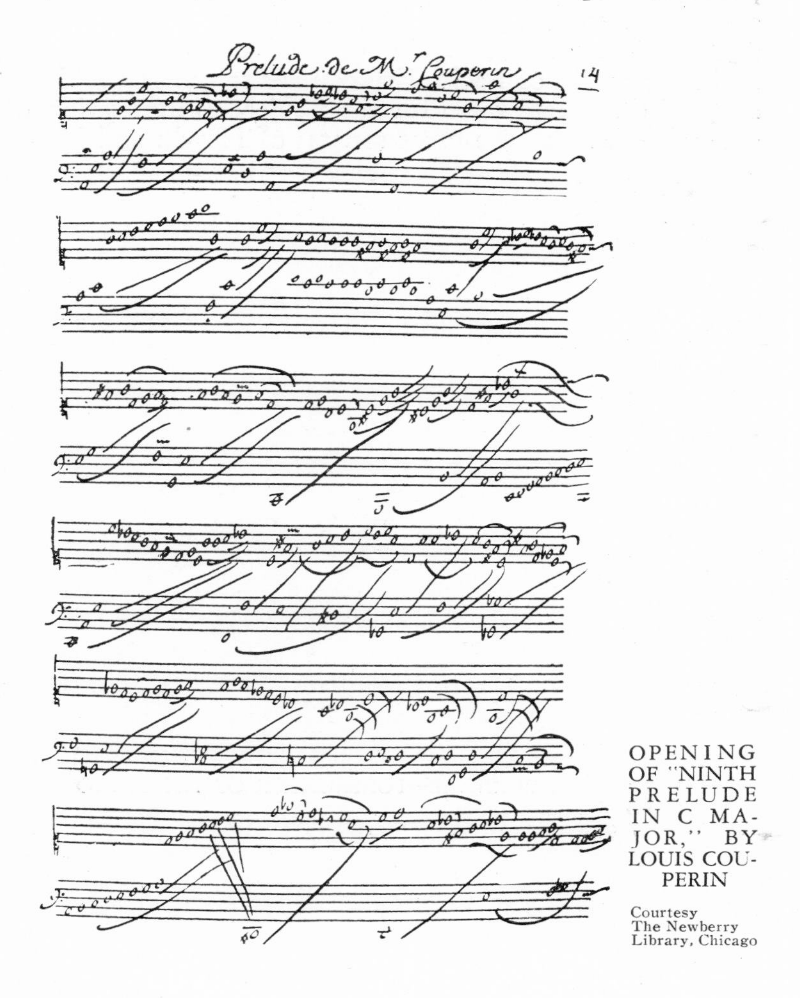

OPENING OF "NINTH PRELUDE IN C MAJOR," BY LOUIS COUPERIN

Courtesy The Newberry Library, Chicago

posed numerous suites for the harpsichord and exerted a profound influence on Bach.

Froberger also achieved fame as a composer of French suites, which in their gracefulness and delicacy present a sharp contrast to his exuberant organ toccatas and fantasias.

The predecessor of Bach as cantor of St. Thomas in Leipzig, Johann Kuhnau, should be mentioned for his interesting *Biblical Sonatas* for the harpsichord. They are significant for their pictorial wealth. The art of portraying scenes and actions of life in musical compositions had been attempted by several earlier composers, notably Carissimi. Kuhnau in his *Biblical Sonatas* pictures anger, melancholy, joy, and exciting events. This sort of descriptive music appears later in some of Keiser's works and above all in the works of Bach. Kuhnau is also remembered for having adapted the sonata form for the clavier, an innovation which led somewhat later to the great sonatas of Haydn and Mozart.

THE VIRGINAL—FORERUNNER OF THE PIANO

THE OPERA AND ORATORIO DURING THE EIGHTEENTH CENTURY

The music of the first half of the eighteenth century was, at least externally, completely under the sway of Italy. The harmonic style, the thorough bass system, the opera and oratorio, and various instrumental forms like the sonata and concerto—all of these had their origin in Italy. These musical innovations and developments came to a climax in the eighteenth century. It was a period of magnificent flowering, unparalleled in the history of music, and epitomized by such great figures as Bach, Handel, Rameau, and Scarlatti. Each country could boast a glorious musical school of its own, but all of them were permeated with Italian conventions and traditions. European princes cultivated the Italian opera with an extravagance hitherto unknown, and Italian musicians and composers were invited to direct the musical activities of foreign courts. Finally, the Italian musical terms which are in use today were universally adopted as standard in the eighteenth century.

SCARLATTI AND THE NEAPOLITAN SCHOOL

The traditional supremacy of Venice in the field of the opera was taken over by Naples around the turn of the seventeenth century. This city was acquiring world fame through the works of Alessandro Scarlatti (1659-1725), director of three conservatories in Naples.

A striking characteristic of the century was the sense for form. The aim of artists was to produce an aesthetic, harmonious whole, and not merely to reproduce life realistically. The various musical forms of the day, the sonata, the suite, the aria, the choral, and finally the fugue, all satisfied the refined taste for proportion and harmony. Feeling was artistically controlled but not suppressed by the form; the latter rather enhanced and elevated the meaning of feeling, and therefore the artistic form was not of less importance than the content.

In Scarlatti's operas and those of the Neapolitan school in general, the *aria* was the formal expression for the human voice. The aria consisted of three definite, rigid parts, the third of which was a repetition of the first; therefore this aria was known generally as the *da capo aria* (the "repeat" aria). In this form the Neapolitan

ALESSANDRO
SCARLATTI

Courtesy The Newberry
Library, Chicago

school achieved perfection. The singers were expected to improvise embellishments to these arias, and although they were granted a certain freedom of expression, there was also a danger of empty virtuosity.

The Neapolitan operas have often been viewed as a mere series of arias, connected by occasional recitatives. While the aria was designed to express lyrical feeling, the recitative was to express the dramatic action. The *recitativo secco* was accompanied with a thorough bass, executed by a harpsichord, while the later *recitativo accompagnato* was furnished with orchestral accompaniment, which was worked out in detail. Scarlatti's operas are by no means meaningless; his recitatives still contain action and life, and it was not till half a century later, when the opera composers almost disregarded the meaning of the poetry and action altogether, that a reformer like Gluck was needed to restore the proper relationship between poetry and music.

Scarlatti is also important for having furnished the form of the symphony which later became popular under Haydn and Mozart. The Italians called the overture to an opera a *sinfonia.* It consisted of three movements, *allegro* (fast), *andante* (slow), and a dance-like *allegro.* The succession of contrasts proved exceedingly satisfying, and was therefore adopted for the sonata and the concerto, as well as the symphony.

Besides Scarlatti, we must mention Giovanni Battista Pergolesi (1710-1736) and Leonardo da Vinci (1690-1730) for their importance among the Neapolitan masters. In addition to ten operas, Pergolesi managed to compose thirty-six violin sonatas, twelve cantatas, three masses, a symphony, and a number of motets, psalms, and lessons for the harpsichord—truly a remarkable productivity for a brief life of twenty-six years.

Leonardo da Vinci was a descendant of the great Renaissance painter. He was primarily an opera composer, and his significance lay mainly in his development of the orchestral accompaniment for the recitative.

The Neapolitan school exercised a profound influence on composers in other countries, especially Germany. Johann Adolf Hasse, originally an operatic tenor in Hamburg, not only composed in the Italian manner, but was looked upon as the head of the Neapolitan school when he moved to Italy. Most of Handel's operas are in that style, as are the early operas of Gluck. Even the operas of Mozart and Haydn show markedly the influence of the Neapolitan school.

RAMEAU AND THE FRENCH OPERA

The French opera was continued in the spirit of Lully by successive composers, most of whom had been under his tutelage, but in the first half of the eighteenth century the Lully opera was definitely superseded by the operas of Jean Philippe Rameau (1683-1764).

This somewhat eccentric composer did not have an opera produced until his fifty-first year. He had battled for many years against theoreticians and musicians, but finally he established an unshakable reputation both as a composer and theoretician. Louis XV appointed him chamber composer, and raised him to the

Courtesy The Newberry Library, Chicago

JEAN PHILIPPE RAMEAU
From a lithograph at the Paris Opera Library, after a drawing by E. Nesle.

nobility. Rameau's greatest achievement was his establishment of modern harmony by his *Traité de l'harmonie.* In his operas he continued the cultivation of the ballet and chorus, and while he closely followed the accepted forms of the day he enriched his music with a bold, modern harmony. His harpsichord music, his theoretical works, and some twenty operas easily place him as the greatest French composer between Lully and Gluck.

GEORG FRIEDRICH HANDEL (1685-1759)

The greatest of English composers was a German by birth. The son of a barber-surgeon in Halle, Handel was matriculated as a law student at the Halle university. His superior musical abilities, however, soon gained him a place in the musical world in Berlin, Halle, and Hamburg. In the latter city he worked for the opera under Keiser. At this time Handel fought a duel with the composer Mattheson, and he would have lost his life if it had not been for a brass button on his coat which bent the point of his opponent's sword.

After four years of labor and troubles at the Hamburg opera, he sojourned for four years more in Italy where he fully acquainted himself with the Italian opera, met Corelli and the two Scarlattis, and was himself enthusiastically received.

Upon his return to Germany he became chapel master to the Elector of Hanover, but soon left for a visit to England. Here the success of his opera *Rinaldo*, composed within two weeks before its performance, was so great that he decided to overstay his leave of absence and remain in England permanently. In 1719 Handel opened the Academy for Opera, for which he wrote a large number of Italian operas. Most of them—he wrote forty altogether—are now in oblivion, but they deserve a revival purely for their musical richness, their exquisite arias and splendid choruses. Owing to rival interprises and to the ridicule heaped upon the Italian opera in the successful *Beggar's Opera* by Gay and Pepusch, Handel's opera house failed and he himself was financially ruined. He tried his luck once more with another undertaking, but his health broke down under the strain of many difficulties, and he was compelled to seek a cure at the springs of Aachen. His vigorous constitution and an insurmountable willpower soon overcame the illness, and returning to England he now abandoned the opera and concentrated on the oratorio.

GEORG FRIEDRICH HANDEL

HANDEL'S ORATORIOS

In the oratorio Handel produced his best work and expressed the fullness and depth of his spirit. His oratorios are really religious operas; in fact, he at first intended them to be staged, but the opposition of the Bishop of London caused him to present them in concert form. In his oratorios, *Belshazzar, Israel in Egypt, Judas Maccabaeus, Samson, Messiah,* and others, Handel used for his text the dramatic stories of the Old Testament. There is no narrator in these oratorios, the text and music being sufficiently endowed with dramatic action. The struggles and sentiments of large masses are sublimely expressed by the chorus. Handel's unique talent was his ability to combine artistic quality with popular demand, as evidenced by the overwhelming effect of the magnificent "Hallelujah Chorus" in the *Messiah.* The well-known "Largo" from *Xerxes,* and the exquisite *Messiah* aria, "He Shall Feed His Flock" bear further testimony to this characteristic gift.

THE CHURCH MUSIC OF BACH

The works of Johann Sebastian Bach (1685-1750) represent the peak of the musical development of two preceding centuries. His *Passions* and his organ works have surpassed everything else in their field; he brought the art of the fugue to the point of perfection, and he is the last great, if not the greatest, master of the contrapuntal style.

To understand Bach properly one must always bear in mind that he was a devout and humble Protestant, and as such he expressed himself in almost all of his religious music. Thus we must view the *Passions* as the artistic participation of a firm and enthusiastic believer in the passion of Christ. Practically all of his religious music is spontaneous expression of an overflowing, grateful soul.

The Protestant chorale forms the center of Bach's creations. The polyphonic settings of his 371 chorales are masterpieces of perfection and simplicity. In his *Passions,* the chorale is the pediment supporting the entire colossal architectural structure. In these monumental compositions the chorale establishes an intimate relation between the congregation and the composer. The *Passions* were created for services during Holy week; and they can never rise to their full meaning as concert performances, judged by purely aesthetic standards.

The cantata of Bach's day was like a little oratorio, making use of all the instrumental and vocal devices available. The content of a church cantata corresponded to the liturgical significance of each individual Sunday. Bach himself wrote five sets of cantatas for the entire church year, and of these some two hundred survive. These cantatas are little worlds in themselves, containing everything that music can express.

Besides his cantatas, his chorales, and the *Passions* according to St. Matthew, St. John and St. Luke, Bach wrote a number of motets of awe-inspiring grandeur; also five masses, a Christmas and an Easter oratorio, and numerous preludes and variations on choral themes.

JOHANN SEBASTIAN BACH

Courtesy The Newberry Library, Chicago

BACH'S BIRTHPLACE AT EISENACH

Bach never went to Italy, and consequently his art is predominantly Germanic. The musical world of his day, imbued with Neapolitan strains, had little understanding for the vigorous style of a Bach. Of the tremendous bulk of compositions from his pen, only some four or five were published, and they were immediately forgotten after his death. Not until 1829 was his *St. Matthew Passion* resurrected by Mendelssohn.

Only as an organist was Bach esteemed by his contemporaries. An organ style is evident in all his compositions, instrumental and vocal. As a composer of organ music he is unequaled.

THE OPERA BUFFA AND OPERA COMIQUE

In the early part of the eighteenth century a reaction against the prevailing formalism showed itself in the shape of the comic opera.

In England, the *Beggar's Opera,* a gay musical comedy, satirized the Neapolitan Opera. Dr. John Pepusch furnished the melodies, with a thorough bass that was beyond all criticism, to

Courtesy The Newberry Library, Chicago

REPRODUCTION OF TITLE PAGE AND PART OF THE MANUSCRIPT OF PERGOLESI'S "SALVE REGINA"

Original now in The British Museum.

verse written by the poet Gay. The performances were a huge success.

The *théâtre de la foire* in Paris specialized in parodies on the grand opera and the serious drama. These performances gradually acquired the high-sounding name of *opéra comique*, in reality the modern operetta (light opera). In the operetta the dialogue is spoken.

In Naples, the very home of the opera, an independent comic opera was beginning to take form. After 1720 we frequently find light intermezzos between the acts of an opera performance. We have already mentioned Pergolesi as a composer of intermezzos and as a pioneer in comic opera. His intermezzo, *The Servant as Mistress,* consisting of a very simple but lively plot played by three characters, met with an enthusiastic reception in Naples. The little play contained delightful humor and such vivid characterization and animating music that it has survived in the operatic repertoire up to the present time.

The outstanding representatives of the French school of comic opera were F. J. Gossec and André Grétry. The latter's opera, *Richard the Lionhearted,* his best work, already foreshadows Wagner's "leitmotiv," in the steady recurrence and variation of its basic theme.

The Neapolitan school meanwhile developed the *opera buffa,* which was similar to the French comic opera, except that it contributed several new musical forms. The aria lost its pre-eminent position. An especially characteristic feature was the brilliant *finale,* in which the entire personnel joined. Many of the popular songs, which were thrown in with the opera buffa, were later developed by the Vienna classicists in their instrumental works.

GLUCK, THE REFORMER OF THE OPERA

The abuses of the Neapolitan opera during the eighteenth century have been mentioned. The grand opera had fallen into overindulgence of virtuosity, and the plots had become almost insipid with their excessive love element. The reforms which Gluck was to effect were necessary.

Christoph Willibald Ritter von Gluck (1714-1787) was a German by birth, but he spent most of his life in Austria, Italy, and France. During the early years of his career he composed a number of operas in the Italian style. Not until 1762, almost in

Courtesy The Newberry Library, Chicago

FRESCO IN VIENNA OPERA HOUSE REPRESENTING GLUCK'S "ARMIDE"

his fiftieth year, did he embark on his great reform with the performance of *Orpheus and Eurydice*.

In this new work, Gluck strove to bring out the dramatic action of the plot. Accordingly he placed music in a secondary position to the poetry. He did not allow the continuity of the action to be disturbed by sheer virtuosity and senseless ornamentation. The ballet and the chorus function as an essential part of the organic whole.

Gluck had once and for all reformed the opera along principles which were later followed by almost all the great opera composers, such as Berlioz, Weber, Wagner, and others.

MOZART AND THE GERMAN OPERA

The first German operetta, a version of the *Beggar's Opera*, was performed in the year 1752 in Leipzig under the title *The Devil to Pay*. It was taken up enthusiastically by the German poets, and represented the beginning of a movement which led to the *Singspiel* of Mozart. The composer Johann Adam Hiller (1728-1804) was especially popular with his operettas, *The Chase, Love in the Country,* and *The Village Barber*. His pieces contained captivating, folklike songs, which greatly stimulated the movement for popular melodies.

In 1778 a National Opera was established in Vienna by the progressive and art-loving Emperor Joseph II. The performance in 1782 of the *Abduction from the Seraglio* by Mozart set up an example for all German opera composers. The greatest of Mozart's *singspiele* is *The Magic Flute*, composed in the last year of his life. It has the virtue of combining the elements of popularity and depth. Love, the dominating subject, magic, and mysticism are charmingly interwoven and admirably expressed by the delightful music.

WOLFGANG AMADEUS MOZART

His greatest works were in the field of *opera buffa,* which he reshaped to suit his own talent. *The Marriage of Figaro* and *Don Giovanni* are charming and delightful. The characters are represented in a masterful manner. Mozart did not and could not quite follow the frivolous and farcical buffoonery of the Italians; he put more meaning and characterization into his texts, furnished mostly by the poet and adventurer Lorenzo da Ponte. A thoroughly playful opera is Mozart's *Cosi fan tutte* which has often been referred to as his *Midsummer Night's Dream.*

Mozart was a master in all fields of music, and later we shall have more to say about his instrumental works.

INSTRUMENTAL MUSIC IN THE EIGHTEENTH CENTURY

All instrumental forms of the seventeenth century came to a climax in the first half of the eighteenth. This period can be regarded as the flowering of music in Europe.

In all forms, Johann Sebastian Bach was the greatest master of his time. His organ works are unparalleled to this day. The preludes and fugues, toccatas and fantasias, and above all, his choral preludes, represent the sublime in musical expression. For

Courtesy The Newberry Library, Chicago

FACSIMILE OF MANUSCRIPT OF THE FIRST PAGE OF FIRST PRELUDE FROM BACH'S "WELL-TEMPERED CLAVICHORD"

the harpsichord and clavichord he wrote quantities of suites, concertos, and fugues. The *Well-Tempered Clavier* consists of a series of preludes and fugues, one for each key, to illustrate the feasibility of composing in any key, instead of the limited number of simpler keys which were used before his time. He showed that the tones of the piano could be tuned so as to fit the chromatic scale of twelve equal semitones on all keys, thus establishing the system of *equal temperament*. In this connection it should also be pointed out that he revolutionized the manner of playing keyboard instruments by assigning equal function to the thumb and little finger as well as the rest of the fingers.

In the field of orchestral music, Bach composed the six so-called *Brandenburg Concertos*, which rank among the best *concerti grossi* of the time. In addition he wrote four orchestral suites and a wealth of exquisite chamber music.

The other great figure in the field of instrumental music of this time is Handel. His suites for the harpsichord rank equally with those of Bach. Although the German masters borrowed the form of the suite from France, their works differ considerably from those of Couperin and Rameau, for example. Handel, like Bach, composed in all musical forms known to his time, and all of his works, whether *concerti grossi*, organ concertos, or chamber music, are products of an inexhaustibly inventive and vigorous genius.

François Couperin, who specialized in clavier music, and Rameau were the main representatives of French music. In Italy we must mention Antonio Vivaldi, many of whose violin concertos were transcribed for piano by Bach, and Giuseppe Tartini, who was the greatest violinist of his time. Benedetto Marcello, Pergolesi, Domenico Scarlatti, and P. Locatelli were all distinguished Italian composers of the period.

THE SYMPHONY

The symphony was an entirely new form and was a product of the same forces that created the comic opera.

The symphony cast off almost all of the traditions that clung to the musical forms up to the eighteenth century. The thorough bass system was abandoned; the contrapuntal setting definitely gave way to the *homophonic* or one-voiced setting, the upper voice became prominent, and by eliminating the frequent pauses, the individual units of the form became much longer.

The Italian operatic sinfonia, or overture, as used by Alessandro Scarlatti, furnished the form for the concert symphony. The three-movement composition was merely taken from the theater to the concert hall. As a result the symphony became the rage of the day and literally excluded all other forms. The *concerto grosso,* the suite, and the fugue disappeared; only the concerto for soloists maintained itself, for in it virtuosos were able to exhibit their technical accomplishments.

The new form was more natural, it is true, but also a little empty. It gave freer reign to the expression of the imagination and emotions, and thus satisfied the needs of the Age of Sentimentality and the later Age of Storm and Stress.

The new forces in music were best manifested by the Mannheim school. Here, in the orchestra of the Elector of the Palatinate, the violin virtuoso and composer, Johann Stamitz (1717-1757), put into practice his new ideas. The orchestra under Stamitz played very much like a modern orchestra, expressing not only *forte* (loud) and *piano* (soft), but also all the shadings in between, which are known in music as *diminuendo* (decreasing loudness) and *crescendo* (increasing loudness). In this way modern music is characterized by an infinite variety of shadings, in contrast to the more static quality of seventeenth and eighteenth century music, the dynamic force of which is brought out by the symmetry of the whole.

Stamitz may be viewed as influential in the development of the symphony, and with him a new musical period begins. The movements of his symphonies already have the structure of the later classical form, that is, each movement contains a main theme and a second theme, a development and a reprise of the first theme. He introduced the minuet, as we find it in the symphonies of Haydn, as an intermediary movement.

Characteristic of the Age of Sentimentality is the music of Carl Philipp Emanuel Bach (1714-1788), a son of the great Bach. In the sonatas of C. P. E. Bach a personal element is injected, and the composer sought to express something which was more fully expressed later by Beethoven. C. P. E. Bach is at his best in his clavichord sonatas, with their sudden changes, their tender expression, and graceful rococo figures. The clavichord was the favorite instrument of the day. The tone of the instrument is so tender and soft that it can hardly be heard in an adjoining room. Sentimental enthusiasts of the day would sit alone at the clavi-

ENGLISH HARPSICHORD OF THE EIGHTEENTH CENTURY

Courtesy The Art Institute of Chicago

chord and gently give expression to their emotions on the keyboard of their beloved companion.

Wilhelm-Friedmann Bach, a brother of C. P. E. Bach, was extremely gifted and achieved distinction as an organist and composer. His symphonies were especially noteworthy, but his brilliant career was obscured by the dissolute living to which he succumbed. One more member of the great Bach family should be mentioned, the so-called London Bach, Johann Christian, who represented the "gallant" style, and greatly influenced the young Mozart.

JOSEPH HAYDN AND THE SYMPHONY

Joseph Haydn (1732-1809) is called the "Father of the Symphony." Indeed, under Haydn the symphony reached such classical perfection that it stands as an eloquent symbol of the age of classicism.

Haydn was the son of a very humble family and passed his early boyhood in the little Croatian village of his birth. His father, a wheelwright, was an amateur on the harp, and his mother sang to his playing. From such unpretentious heritage and environment, the genius of Haydn rose to Olympian heights, but throughout his life he remained the modest, cheerful, and simple "Papa Haydn." Not only did Haydn develop the symphony, but he perfected the form of the string quartet, composed a great

JOSEPH HAYDN

number of piano sonatas, fourteen Italian operas, and hundreds of minuets, allemandes, Scotch romances, and divertissements. Above all he wrote five oratorios, including the *Creation* and the *Seasons*, for which he is perhaps best known.

The most delightful element in Haydn's symphonies is the ingenious thematic development of popular airs. He utilized many folk tunes which he remembered from his rustic childhood days, and incorporated them into his works, varying them to express every possible mood. Through this method, Haydn gave the symphony, which had been Italian in form and spirit, a distinctly German touch. Furthermore, Haydn always began his symphonies with a short, slow, and dignified introduction. In his middle slow movement he frequently used the variation form, which he took over from chamber music. Haydn wrote many of his earlier symphonies and chamber music in the thorough bass system, but later this method of writing disappeared permanently. The harpsichord, which up to his time had been an indispensable part of the orchestra—in fact, the orchestra was directed by the conductor who played the harpsichord himself—vanished in Haydn's day. Thus the modern orchestra was evolved and subsequently enlarged to the full scope it has today.

Although Haydn was many years older than Mozart, he did not fail to learn from his symphonies. Mozart is to be credited for weaving a *cantabile* melody into the rapid theme of a symphony. This merit Haydn readily recognized and adopted it in his symphonies, thus introducing a charming element of contrast, and preparing the path for Beethoven.

LUDWIG VAN BEETHOVEN (1770-1827)

WITH BEETHOVEN a new period of music begins. Although he is considered the greatest of classical composers, many of his works embody the tendencies of a great new movement, Romanticism.

Beauties of nature, the great object of reverence for the Romanticists, are most sublimely expressed in Beethoven's *Sixth,* or *Pastoral Symphony.* The Romanticist's idealistic conception of humanity as a universal brotherhood is nowhere more nobly expressed than in the Chorus of the Ninth Symphony. The French Revolution, which Romanticists thought would realize their utopian ideals, found an enthusiastic sympathizer in Beethoven. He wrote his Third Symphony, the *Eroica,* in honor of Napoleon Bonaparte, but when the latter declared himself emperor, the composer tore up the dedication in a rage.

His significance as a classical composer lies in the fact that he brought to perfection the forms of the symphony and sonata, and through them brought the harmonic style to a climax. He did not invent new forms, but he freed himself of formal conventions whenever he felt them to be burdensome to his genius. Thus in his *Ninth Symphony* he broke all previous traditions by introducing a chorus in the fourth movement. The traditional minuet which constituted the third movement of the classical symphony and sonata, he changed into a *scherzo* by imbuing it with a new element, humor.

LUDWIG VAN BEETHOVEN

The symphonies of Beethoven differ markedly from those of his predecessors. Their most striking characteristic is their individuality, each symphony being distinctly different from the others. Thus the *Sixth Symphony* depicts scenes of rural life; the *Ninth,* after indulging in demoniacal pondering during the first three movements, finally bursts out in an exalted hymn to joy; and almost everyone knows the hammering theme of the first movement in the *Fifth Symphony* in C Minor, in which one recognizes "Fate knocking at the door."

It has been mentioned that Beethoven brought the harmonic style to unprecedented heights. In his work, melody has become predominant, and all other voices merely serve to support and emphasize it. In this connection it is well to point out the song-like character of the melodies of Beethoven's slow movements, especially in his piano works. He drew inspiration from the simple quality and deep spirit of German song which is well illustrated by the fact that some of his *adagio* (slow) movements are frequently sung by choral societies.

Beethoven had an extremely original and dramatic personality. Despite his slovenly appearance, poor manners, and eccentricity, he was greatly admired by the aristocracy.

His personal life was a tragedy. A severe illness in his youth rendered him even more irritable than he was by nature. A far more fatal consequence of the same illness was his gradually increasing deafness. In his thirties, he was already distressed by his difficulties of hearing. He was completely deaf for the last ten years of his life, a fate which for a musician is a catastrophe. Although he could carry on his conversations only by means of notebooks, although he could not hear his own violin playing, which naturally sounded unbearably out of tune, Beethoven nevertheless composed some of his greatest works during this period. The *Eighth* and *Ninth Symphonies,* the *Missa Solemnis,* and his last quartets and sonatas were written when he could not hear a note of what he composed.

Before the time of Beethoven, the status of the musician was more that of a servant than an artist. Masters like Haydn, Mozart, and Bach were forced to earn their living by playing in orchestras and working like court servants for kings and petty princes. Beethoven never held a permanent position. He was an independent artist who was patronized by nobles and who maintained himself with the returns from his art. With Beethoven the modern musician makes his appearance.

Courtesy The Newberry Library, Chicago

ROSSINI BESET BY MULTITUDINOUS MUSICAL INSPIRATIONS
(From an anonymous caricature of 1850.)

ITALIAN OPERA IN THE NINETEENTH CENTURY

During the nineteenth century Italy, the land of the opera, produced again several outstanding operatic composers. The earliest of these, Gioacchino Rossini (1792-1868) became the favorite with all opera lovers during the first half of the century. A Europe which had suffered from the Napoleonic wars and was weary beyond words, found relaxation in the sweet and entertaining operas of Rossini. He was an extraordinarily inventive genius, who could jot down the most appealing melodies with the greatest ease and rapidity. His most popular work in the domain of the opera buffa, *The Barber of Seville,* is supposed to have been written within thirteen days. He composed thirty-five operas in all, most of which are comic operas, but he also achieved distinction in his serious opera, *Semiramide,* and in the field of French grand opera with his *William Tell.*

Vincenzo Bellini (1801-1835) is remembered for his operas *La Sonnambula* and *Norma,* both of which had wide appeal. His melodies reveal a strong romantic tendency in their somewhat

GIUSEPPE VERDI

Courtesy Italian Tourist Bureau

sentimental quality. More successful than Bellini was Gaetano Donizetti (1797-1848) whose *Daughter of the Regiment* was the favorite of Europe for three generations. Of his sixty-six operas, several still manage to hold their own among European audiences; of them, his comic opera, *Don Pasquale,* and *Lucia di Lammermoor* should be mentioned.

With Giuseppe Verdi (1813-1901) Italian opera rose to new heights. In his earlier works he revealed his intense patriotism, and the peoples of Naples shouted "Viva Verdi," a circumstance which brought him into frequent difficulty with the Austrian authorities. His celebrated *Rigoletto* was originally entitled *The King Amuses Himself;* the story was taken from Hugo's *Le Roi s'amuse,* but he was forced to change the title and make his king into a duke, because the authorities thought his story reflected upon the Austrian emperor, Francis I. He acquired international fame with *Rigoletto, La Traviata,* and *Il Trovatore.* As a mature composer, Verdi strove after a higher ideal in his operas, attempting to unite harmoniously text and music, and the final outcome

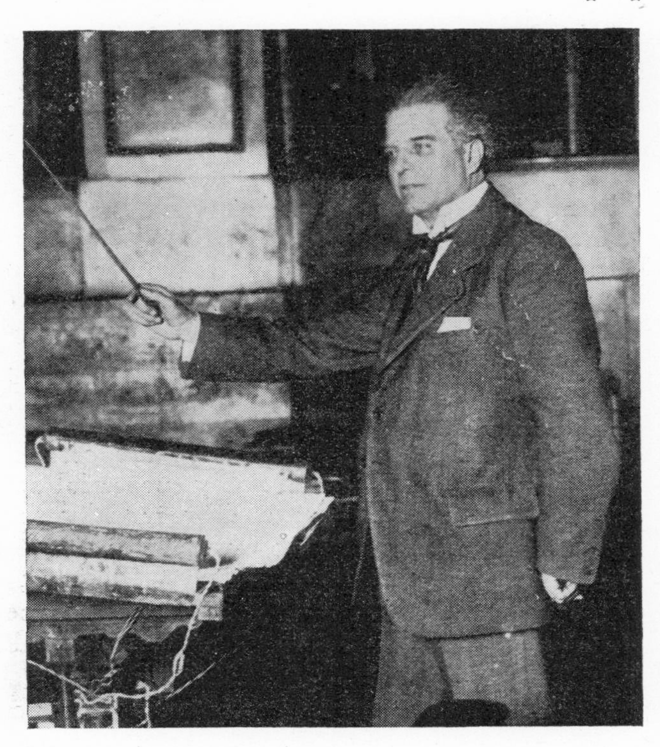

PIETRO MASCAGNI

Paul's Photos, Chicago

was the opera *Aïda*, in many respects his greatest work. It was especially composed for the festive occasion of the opening of the Suez Canal and was performed with great pomp in Cairo in 1871. Even in his old age he produced a masterpiece, *Othello*, and the delightful comic opera *Falstaff*. Verdi was one of the world's greatest composers and exerted a profound influence on the composers of the "Young Italian" school.

With the opera *Cavalleria Rusticana* by Pietro Mascagni, the element of realism entered the field of the Italian opera. This one-act opera with its freshness and passion was an instantaneous success. It was followed two years later, in 1892, by the equally passionate piece *I Pagliacci*, by Leoncavallo. The two short temperamental operas were presented together in subsequent performances, in which form they still constitute a favorite among opera-goers.

The most popular composer of the "Young Italian" school was Giacomo Puccini (1858-1924). His best opera is *La Bohème*, but his exotic *Madame Butterfly* and the somewhat sentimental opera *La Tosca* still possess popular appeal.

FRENCH OPERA IN THE NINETEENTH CENTURY

In France, opera composers broke completely with the classical traditions of Rameau and Gluck. The spirit of romanticism, as manifested in the literary works of Victor Hugo and Scribe, soon seized and dominated French opera. The first important example of this change was *The Mute Maid of Portici* by Daniel F. E. Auber (1782-1871). It is said that the performance of this vivacious romantic opera helped to precipitate the revolution in Belgium in 1830.

The French romantic opera, however, soon deteriorated into mere "spectacle operas," in which the creation of sensational effects was the chief aim. Highly successful among these sensational works were the operas of Giacomo Meyerbeer (1791-1864), whose most important work was done in the field of the French Grand Opera. In his opera, *Robert the Devil,* statues of nuns, brought to life by a demon, strip off their garments, and dance a ballet. But despite his occasional poor taste, Meyerbeer's operas reveal melodic beauty and dramatic power.

CHARLES GOUNOD

To this period of French opera also belong the operas, *Faust,* by Charles Gounod, and *Manon,* by Jules Massenet, both of which still enjoy a wide popularity. But the most popular opera of the day was *Carmen,* by Georges Bizet. With this work a realism based on national influence and environment entered French opera. Except for Wagner's operas, *Carmen* is played more frequently than any other opera on the modern stage. Among the more recent French composers of opera are Edouard Lalo, Charpentier, Vincent d'Indy, and Debussy. The French operetta is represented during this period by Jacques Offenbach and Charles Lecocq.

GERMAN OPERA IN THE NINETEENTH CENTURY

Beethoven's *Fidelio* may be regarded as definitely establishing German Opera. This, his only opera, is so markedly German in spirit that it has only with difficulty received attention in foreign countries. There is a strong moral element in *Fidelio,* for Beethoven needed the inspiration of some moral principle in order to compose exalting music.

The appearance of the romantic opera *Der Freischütz* in 1821 marked the rise of German national opera. Its charming music by Carl Maria von Weber (1786-1826), and the romanticism of the subject, met the enthusiastic approval of the German people. It is interesting to note how romanticism in all countries encouraged the development of a national art. Folk tales, popular tunes, and old traditions all entered into art and removed it from the universal, international conventions of the eighteenth century. Unfortunately for Weber, the libretti of most of his operas are very poor, and although his other operas, *Oberon* and *Euryanthe,* contain very fine music, they have for this reason not been very successful. Weber was a precursor of Wagner in his search for a higher dramatic ideal and in his aim of merging all the allied arts into one artistic expression in the form of opera.

In Vienna the operettas by the famous "Waltz King," Johann Strauss (1825-1899), created a sensation. His father had already developed the waltz into a finished musical form, and as a dance form the waltzes of Strauss were as significant as the minuets of the eighteenth century. In his operetta, *Die Fledermaus,* (The Bat), the younger Johann Strauss virtually reveled in the waltz. The waltz became the rage in Vienna in the nineteenth century. Today the waltzes of Johann Strauss, such as *The Blue Danube, Tales from the Venna Woods, Vienna Blood,* and *Artist's Life* are played, sung, or whistled by the man on the street, the world over.

German opera was brought to unprecedented heights by Richard Wagner (1813-1883). The history of the opera is embodied in the endless struggle between music and poetry. Wagner put new emphasis on the poetic side of opera: he wrote the li-

Courtesy The Newberry Library, Chicago

JOHANN STRAUSS, JR., LEADING HIS ORCHESTRA IN 1853
(From a contemporary lithograph.)

bretti himself, taking his material from medieval sagas. The conceptions of sacrificial love and redemption are his main themes. By uniting four of his operas into *Der Ring des Nibelung* he built a great coherent drama of gigantic proportions, such as had never been seen before on the operatic stage.

In order to enhance the action of the drama, Wagner discarded all those operatic accessories which arrested the dramatic development. He therefore eliminated the aria which was the showpiece of Italian opera, and placed a new emphasis on musical declamation, or recitative, which now came to the foreground for the first time.

LEITMOTIV

The *leitmotiv* (leading melody) is the foundation upon which rests the entire structure of Wagner's operas. He did not invent this device; it had been employed in opera by Weber and in symphonies by Berlioz. The use of the leitmotiv by Wagner is akin to the thematic development in the symphony, and thus, in a way, he enlisted the symphony in the service of opera. The leitmotivs are the themes which occur again and again in varying form, reminding the listener of the dominant ideas, and are, therefore, well characterized by calling them *reminiscent* melodies. Finally, the leitmotiv lends unity to the entire work.

RICHARD WAGNER

The unraveling of the dramatic action in Wagner's operas is, however, somewhat interrupted by his strong use of the orchestra. In playing its role of describing situations and expressing the emotions of the characters, the orchestra often indulges in lengthy digressions which are inimical to continuous action.

Wagner himself wished to be remembered as a dramatist rather than as a composer. In his youth he wavered somewhat between the two professions, and his development into a composer was the natural result of his search for an art that would harmoniously contain all the sister arts.

The four music dramas which make up *Der Ring des Nibelung* are *Das Rheingold, Die Walküre* (The Valkyries,) *Siegfried,* and *Die Götterdämmerung* (The Twilight of the Gods). Wagner's early operas, *The Flying Dutchman, Tannhäuser,* and *Lohengrin,* still show traces of the influence of Italian opera. The *Ring, Tristan und Isolde, Die Meistersinger von Nürnberg,* and *Parsifal,* represent the highest expressions of his genius. The sacred festival play *Parsifal* is built on the legend of the Holy Grail, and Wagner decreed in his will that it should never be performed anywhere except in the festival theatre of Bayreuth. Because of the efforts of King Ludwig II of Bavaria, this little city had already become the center of the Wagnerian cult during Wagner's lifetime. Wagner societies had sprung up in many foreign countries, and the operas had soon invaded every stage of Europe and America. To-

Courtesy German Railroads Information Office, N. Y.

NEUSCHWANSTEIN

Dream castle of King Ludwig II, patron of the arts and protector of Richard Wagner.

day they are among the most frequently produced works in the operatic repertoire.

Wagner had many followers, none of whom equaled him. The leitmotiv is freely employed by Richard Strauss in his operas, *Salome, Rosenkavalier, Electra,* and many others. The fairy-tale opera, *Hänsel and Gretel,* by Humperdinck, also follows in the footsteps of Wagner. A very successful composer of operas during the first two decades of the twentieth century was Eugen d'Albert, whose operas *Tiefland* (Lowland) and *Tote Augen* (Dead Eyes) achieved wide popularity.

THE GERMAN SONG

In Germany the *lied* or song was revised and underwent a new development during the eighteenth and nineteenth centuries. The movement for composing songs received great impetus from the poems of Goethe, Schiller, Heine, Novalis, and Uhland. Already Haydn, Mozart, and Beethoven had cultivated the song, while Karl Friedrich Zelter and Johann Friedrich Reichardt had set many of Goethe's songs to music. Reichardt had in fact declared that all he had to do was to recite the poems aloud, and melodies would suggest themselves to him spontaneously. But the finest and most beautiful songs were written by the Viennese composer, Franz Schubert.

FRANZ SCHUBERT

The life of Schubert (1797-1828) was short, uneventful, and incomplete. He was the son of a village schoolmaster, spent several painful years teaching in a country school, and struggled throughout his life for bread and recognition. He never married, never obtained a permanent position, and suffered all his life from loneliness and longing. Never during his lifetime did he achieve distinction as a composer or musician, and his publishers shamelessly took advantage of his indigence and kindheartedness. Yet Schubert possessed an ever-cheerful disposition and a productivity seldom equaled. In the short span of his eighteen years' activity, he composed over a thousand works, extending into every branch of music.

Great as is Franz Schubert's fame as a universal and prolific composer, his principal distinction lies in the fact that he was the

FRANZ SCHUBERT

ROBERT SCHUMANN

world's greatest composer of songs. Schubert had an extraordinary talent for inventing melodies which vividly expressed the meaning of poetry. And what melodies they are! They are so appealing, so singable, and so easy-flowing, that it is difficult for us to understand how Schubert's audiences could be indifferent to them.

Unique, also, was his use of the piano. The harpsichord, which had been the dominant keyboard instrument in the home and the concert hall up to Mozart's time, was gradually being displaced by the newly perfected pianoforte. The latter was capable of reproducing all shades of tones from *pianissimo* (very soft) to *fortissimo* (very loud). Beethoven had already occupied himself seriously with the piano and his piano sonatas were magnificent and epoch-making. In his piano accompaniments Schubert achieved wonders. In his songs, piano and voice are organically united and they blend perfectly. It is amazing to reflect that Schubert was able to compose eight songs, including the priceless *Erl King*, in one day. In addition to more than six hundred songs, Schubert left eight symphonies, of which the *Unfinished* is familiar to everyone, a great number of operas, masses, overtures, string quartets, and a vast bulk of vocal and piano works.

JOHANNES BRAHMS

In many of the songs of Robert Schumann (1810-1856) the piano predominates over the vocal part. Though sometimes Schumann's melodies appear somewhat dull, in them one will find an entirely original richness in the piano accompaniment. He particularly delighted in expressing ecstatic and supernatural impressions, as well as the ardor and passion of youth.

The same fate befell the highly gifted but long neglected Hugo Wolf (1860-1903) who was really an outstanding composer of the modern lied. He ardently studied and absorbed his poetic texts, and took infinite pains to reproduce precisely the intentions and feelings of the poet.

Johannes Brahms, on the other hand, merely reproduced the general mood of the poetry and created a rich but almost independent and original musical accompaniment. He went back to the German folk songs for inspiration. There is an indescribable elegiac charm in his songs, which are characterized by rich harmonies and rhythmic vitality. Finally, the songs of Richard Strauss have had wide appeal because of their dazzling tonal qualities.

PROGRAM MUSIC IN THE NINETEENTH CENTURY

Hector Berlioz (1803-1869) was a successor of Beethoven in more than one way. Taking as his point of departure Beethoven's *Pastoral Symphony*, in which country life and scenes are depicted, he further developed the practice of attempting to describe ideas, images, or moods with tonal effects, creating a species of music generally referred to as program music. Because he greatly enlarged the range of expression of the orchestra, he may be given the title, "Father of modern orchestration." Finally, it was he who introduced the *leitmotiv* into the symphony, and thus gave that form an added unity.

FRANZ LISZT

The music of Berlioz, like much of Beethoven's, is subjective, that is to say, it reflects the composer's personal experiences and feelings, and thus strongly reflects his personality. Berlioz wove his autobiography into his work in a manner far more obvious than Beethoven. In his *Roméo et Juliette* symphony, he further imitates his predecessor by introducing song into the symphony, but this attempt, followed by many other similar ones, has never been quite successful.

Berlioz is one of the great French composers, but during his lifetime he won far more appreciation in Germany and Russia than in his own country.

Program music was further developed by the brilliant piano virtuoso, Franz Liszt (1811-1886). He was an ardent admirer of Beethoven and Berlioz, many of whose orchestral works he transcribed, and he generously supported and encouraged Chopin, Wagner, and Schumann as well as almost every other young striving composer in Europe. He was no doubt the greatest piano virtuoso the world had ever seen, and his concert tours through Europe resembled the triumphal processions of a magnificent ruler.

His compositions strongly bear the stamp of virtuosity and are poetic. Many of his works, in fact, are piano transcriptions from famous orchestral compositions. But with his *symphonic poems* Liszt made an original contribution to orchestral forms. Symphonic poems lack the thematic development and, in fact, the whole structure of the symphony, being irregular and descriptive in character, but they require an orchestra of symphonic magnitude. With these short, one-movement, orchestral pieces Liszt laid down new principles which were followed by many later composers, notably Saint-Saëns and Richard Strauss. Liszt's compositions, owing to their virtuoso-like character, never produce their effect unless they are rendered in a virtuoso manner, a feat which is attained only with utmost difficulty. Beethoven can be appreciated even in mediocre performance, but under such conditions Liszt's works appear quite meaningless. This applies most of all to his piano works, which, because of their descriptive character, are also program music.

PIANO MUSIC OF THE ROMANTICISTS

During the nineteenth century the piano became an important and original vehicle of expression, just as did the clavichord in the time of Couperin. And just as various dance forms, in the seventeenth and eighteenth centuries, stimulated composers, so in the nineteenth century the dance influenced piano music.

Among the piano compositions of Schubert, his sonatas are far less important than his *Impromptus, Moments musicaux,* and *Ländler.* The latter form is a slow German dance in three-four time from which the waltz probably developed. Emphasis was from now on placed on short forms which, owing to their descriptive element, were called "character pieces."

Felix Mendelssohn-Bartholdy (1809-1847) is significant both as a symphonic composer and as a composer for the piano. Romanticism found expression in the brilliant music of this composer. To this fact the Overture to *A Midsummer Night's Dream* and the *Fingal's Cave* Overture, as well as the *Scottish Symphony* in A minor, bear eloquent witness. They beautifully reflect the happy life and disposition of a carefree artist. The son of a wealthy Jewish banker, Mendelssohn was a member of a refined and friendly family circle, and his life was extremely happy, although extremely short. In his short piano pieces called *Songs without Words,* he expressed his affection for his family, revealing at the same time a marked tendency toward sentiment which was his chief characteristic.

FELIX MENDELSSOHN-BARTHOLDY

FRÉDÉRIC CHOPIN

After the death of Haydn and Mozart, the formal, classical style suffered rapid deterioration. The works of those composers who still followed that tradition were sterile and insignificant. This is partly due to, or at least connected with, the predominance of the virtuoso style. Brilliant as the performances of Liszt and Paganini were, they represented, nevertheless, wholly superficial display and contained little creativeness.

These tendencies toward decadence were vigorously opposed by Schumann. He conceived of an organization, the *League of David*, the existence of which he only imagined, and with it he meant to carry on a war against the "Philistines," the decadent manufacturers of empty variations, rondos, and fantasias. In his piano works Schumann followed in the footsteps of Schubert. The *Ländler* forms the foundations in many compositions, such as *Papillons* (Butterflies), *Carnival*, and the *David's League Dances*. In a way they resemble the old suite, but they are less formal in structure.

Frédéric Chopin (1810-1849) was a composer Polish by birth who spent most of his life in Paris. He was instrumental in introducing Polish music to European musical circles. Like Couperin a century and a half earlier, Chopin centered his attention upon piano music. He drew from the rich sources of Polish folk music and adapted them for the piano, endowing them with delicately harmonic qualities. His mazurkas and polonaises are full of rhythmic vigor and piquant subtleties. His nocturnes and preludes are jewel-like in their elegance, grace, and high poetic quality.

THE DEVELOPMENT OF NATIONAL SCHOOLS

UNTIL THE MIDDLE OF THE NINETEENTH CENTURY music had been cultivated mainly in Italy, Germany, France and England. But with the rise of romanticism, another movement developed parallel to it. The awakening of national consciousness, characterized by a revival of medieval legends, also manifested itself in the field of music. Not only did this new nationalism give rise to romantic operas and songs, but it also led to the formation of music schools of a distinctly national character. France, Germany, England, and Italy all produced national composers, but also hitherto inactive countries now gave musical expression to their national culture. The Scandinavian countries, Bohemia, Russia, and the United States all exhibited musical activity that demanded recognition.

SCANDINAVIA

In Denmark the composer Niels Gade (1817-1890) aroused public attention with his *Reminiscences from Ossian.* His *Symphony in C Minor,* introduced to the German public by Mendelssohn in 1834, reveals a marked Nordic element. Gade became a leader of a host of Scandinavian composers, among whom A. Hamerik in Denmark, and Svendson, Sinding, and Grieg in Norway were the most important.

Courtesy The Newberry Library, Chicago

NIELS WILLIAM GADE
From the reproduction of a photograph from life by Hansen & Weller, Copenhagen.

Edvard Grieg (1843-1907) was the most outstanding of the Scandinavian composers. His orchestral suite to Ibsen's drama, *Peer Gynt,* invaded all concert stages in Europe and America. The music of Grieg is often based on old Norwegian folk songs and dances and on an old tonal system which is hardly fitted for the European harmonic system. An air of mel-

ANTON DVORAK

ancholy hovers over this old Norwegian folk music which achieves brilliant expression in Grieg's orchestral and piano works.

BOHEMIA

Frederic Smetana (1824-1884) is celebrated by the Bohemians as the father of Bohemian national music. As is well known, the Bohemians possess a marked musical talent manifested by their rich treasure of folk music. They have furnished European music centers with many distinguished musicians and composers during the eighteenth century. In his symphonic poem *My Fatherland,* Smetana depicted scenes of the history of his country, and through this work has won the appreciation and enthusiasm of the Bohemians. His operas, *The Bartered Bride* and *The Kiss,* contain the same popular elements that characterize Smetana's art.

Bohemia produced another talented composer, Anton Dvořák (1841-1904) whose symphony, *From the New World,* is particularly well known in America. He composed this work during his four-year residence in New York as director of the National Conservatory. In this symphony he made free use of themes suggestive of American Negro folk songs, a factor which probably accounts for its American popularity. He also composed several national operas, oratorios, chamber music works, and slavic dances.

Schwanda, by Jaromir Weinberg, is a popular contemporary opera making much use of Bohemian folk material.

FRANCE

César Franck (1822-1890) is generally regarded as the founder of the modern French school. His main work is the famous *Symphony in D Minor,* serious music with a structural unity,

CLAUDE DEBUSSY

which is emphasized by frequently repeated themes. There is an element of mysticism in many of Franck's works. He was not only the greatest modern French teacher, but his music also reflects the greatest religious influence since the time of Bach. Franck has written only one symphony, but a great many works for organ and piano; also chamber music. In the latter category he was instrumental in giving rise to an entire school of composers.

Vincent D'Indy (1851-1931), a pupil of Franck's, even surpassed his teacher in emphasizing the national element, which is evident by merely glancing at the titles of some of his compositions, such as his *Symphony on a French Mountain Song.*

The composers Edouard Lalo and Camile Saint-Saëns are noted for their contributions to the modern French symphonic style. Saint-Saëns composed numerous operas of which *Samson and Delilah* is best known. All of his works are typically French in character, with their perfect form, elegance, and uniformity.

With Claude Debussy (1862-1918) a whole revolutionary movement in music was inaugurated. He may well be regarded as the most daring innovator of the early century. He not only freely indulged in unheard-of dissonances to secure color effects, but he attacked the very tonal system which had been in existence for many centuries. This was a feat which only a barbarian or a maniac would have dared to do at a time when the infallibility of the diatonic system was still unshaken. Debussy employed in many of his works a whole-tone scale. His melodies and harmonies thereby produce exotic and grotesque effects. He strove to use harmony merely to achieve color effects and thus became the founder of impressionism in music. This is exemplified in his orchestral works, *Afternoon of a Faun, Nocturnes,* and *The Sea,* and in the opera, *Pelléas et Mélisande.*

ENGLAND

After the time of Handel, English music was by no means insignificant, but it remained in the background since it did not produce any great composers of international fame. There were many English composers of real talent, whose works were, however, eclipsed by the brilliant creations of the great international composers.

It would be tedious to enumerate the long list of important musicians from Handel's day to the Victorian period. But at least two names merit attention even in a short survey of this kind. John Field (1782-1837) is chiefly famous for his invention of the *nocturne*, a form which was subsequently taken up by Chopin. The leading English organist and church composer at the beginning of the nineteenth century was Samuel Wesley (1766-1837), a nephew of John Wesley, the famous founder of Methodism. He composed numerous motets which are considered the finest works of their kind during the period. His son, Samuel Sebastian Wesley, the outstanding musician during the early Victorian period, composed several Anglican anthems which are notable for their beautiful melodies and good counterpoint.

Courtesy The Newberry Library, Chicago

ARTHUR SEYMOUR SULLIVAN
From the reproduction of a photograph from life, by Walery, of London.

GILBERT AND SULLIVAN

Sir Arthur Sullivan (1842-1900) belongs to the later Victorian period. He was beyond doubt the most popular English composer. His numerous operas and oratorios are completely eclipsed by the enormous success of *H.M.S. Pinafore, The Mikado,* and *Trial by Jury. Pinafore* was produced seven hundred times in the same house in London, and was performed in the United States simultaneously by several companies. This success was partially due to the brilliance of the libretti written by W. S. Gilbert. These libretti are the most sparkling in the

English language and hardly have been surpassed in other countries. The music of Sullivan's light operas is of a light, sometimes trivial, character, and in its charm and gaiety has made an almost universal appeal. Gilbert and Sullivan operas were the rage of the time and their popularity has persisted down to our day.

MODERN ENGLISH MUSIC

The leading figures in modern English music are Charles V. Stanford (1852-1924), Charles H. Parry (1848-1918), and Edward Elgar (1857-1934). Stanford was an Irishman by birth and many of his melodies are equivalent to Irish folk music. This is especially evident in his opera, *Shamus O'Brien,* a charming dramatic work with spoken dialogues. Parry, a prolific composer and writer, has been often regarded as the founder of modern English music. Elgar's compositions, consisting of oratorios, overtures, symphonies and numerous orchestral and choral works, are notable for their sensuous colors and clever orchestration.

Among the very recent composers, England has produced numerous original figures. The most outstanding are Frederick Delius (1863-1934), Vaughan Williams, Granville Bantock, Cyril Scott, Gustave Holst, and Arnold Bax.

RECENT TRENDS IN MUSIC

Present music is in a state of transition. Old forms and traditions are being undermined and new ones are being tried. The situation has been aggravated by the confusions of the World War, which have disillusioned many creative artists. Realism became the dominant element in music. At the same time composers strove to emphasize again the most elemental forces of music, tone, rhythm, and dynamics.

The attack on the traditional tonal system by Debussy and his use of the whole-tone scale has already been referred to. He was followed in his search for a new system by Arnold Schönberg (1874-) who established atonality. In his system all the half tones of the old system are used, but the dominance of any one key is abolished. The old relationship of tonic and dominant keys does not exist in atonal music, and the progression of chords is un-

IGOR STRAVINSKY

hindered by any key relationships. Several composers have followed him in his atonality, such as the two German composers, Heinrich Kaminski and Paul Hindemith. The works of the latter are particularly significant for the revival of polyphony.

A further step has been made by certain innovators in searching for other tones outside those of the present diatonic system. Ferrucio Busoni has devised a third-tone system, that is, he divided each whole tone (now divided into half-tones) into thirds. A quarter-tone system has been even set up by the Czechoslovakian, Alois Haba. It must be borne in mind, however, that third and quarter tones have always been in use among Orientals, but their music is only homophonic (one voiced). Whether a polyphonic system can be constructed on such intervals as third and quarter tones, still remains a problem of the future.

The attempt to bring back the elements of music, rhythm and sound, to their real importance can be observed in the works of Igor Stravinsky. No sounds, whether drum beats, kettle strokes, or metal hammers, are beyond the consideration of this talented Russian composer. In the works of Hindemith new vigorous rhythmic qualities are evident.

FOLK MUSIC

Modern composers also make great use of the treasures of folk music. In England, the English and Irish songs gave great impetus to the new national school. The Hungarian composer, Béla Bartók, not only utilizes the old Hungarian tunes, but also writes them in severe counterpoint comparable to that of the late Middle Ages. Manuel de Falla freely draws on the Spanish folk songs and folklore.

JEAN SIBELIUS

The works of the Finnish composer, Jean Sibelius, strongly reflect the heroic sagas and the national background of Finland. His symphonies and symphonic poems, which are written in a strongly individual style, resembling Finnish folk music, have become favorite numbers on the concert programs of all nations. The Frenchman, Darius Milhaud, has utilized not only the folklore of Brazil in his work, *The Ox on the Roof,* but has also drawn on Negro jazz in his *Creation of the World,* as well as on Jewish popular elements in his *Popular Hebrew Melodies,* and *Jewish Poems.* Finally, we need only remind ourselves of the extensive influence of Negro songs and jazz on American composers, to estimate the importance of folk elements in modern music.

It is characteristic of the present time that composers express themselves in short musical forms. Whereas a century ago every self-respecting composer wrote several symphonies to assure his reputation, very few modern composers today produce such lengthy works. Chamber music, solo-concertos, concerti grossi, and small ensembles are as in style today as they were in the seventeenth century. Hindemith, Prokofiev, Stravinsky, and Kaminski have all produced numerous works of this kind.

BRAHMS AND RECENT GERMAN COMPOSERS

Johannes Brahms (1833-1897), was a successor of Beethoven and the last great master of the classical symphony. His music is ponderous and massive throughout, definitely reflecting his North German origin. In contrast to Schumann, whose works are sufficiently international to win the admiration of much of the world, the music of Brahms is quite national in character, a factor which stood in the way of immediate recognition.

Brahms spent his first years as a piano virtuoso, but he possessed very little of the virtuoso tendency for display, and was consequently ignored by many musicians. But Schumann enthusiastically supported Brahms and declared him Beethoven's successor. Liszt and his friends invited him to participate in the movement for the music of the future and both classicists and romanticists made a bid for his partnership. But Brahms remained aloof from all controversies and maintained an unconcerned, neutral attitude. He admired Bach and Beethoven, and he strove to imitate them. He took over the thematic development and periodic structure from Beethoven, while he followed Bach in his contrapuntal technique. The tradition of Haydn and Mozart, which demanded that a symphony must end with a light, cheerful movement, was definitely abandoned by Brahms. In his *Fourth Symphony,* for instance, the last movement, the *finale,* embodies the climax of the whole symphony. Thus he succeeded in what Beethoven had already attempted, the maintenance of dynamic tension to the very conclusion of the symphony.

Brahms was also a master of the variation form, which is best illustrated by the above mentioned finale of the *Fourth Symphony,* where he constructed a gigantic work out of a short theme in the bass. His orchestration is uniquely rich and full of contrasts, not between individual instruments but entire groups of them.

Brahms's external life was exceptionally uneventful. Bearing this in mind, it is sometimes incomprehensible how he could have created works of such fulness and originality. The answer lies in the richness of his inner life, his imagination, his natural bent toward seriousness and reflection. Quietly and unpretentiously, he lived his methodical, orderly life in Vienna, undisturbed by the aesthetic controversies of his contemporaries, but expressing himself in his creations.

The musical center of Germany during the first half of the nineteenth century was Leipzig. In the latter half of the century musical life again shifted toward Vienna. Even Brahms, the typical North German (he was born in Hamburg), spent most of his life in Vienna. This city became the home of four other famous recent composers; Max Reger, Anton Bruckner, Gustav Mahler, and Richard Strauss.

Reger's music contains the contrasting elements of a gloomy melancholy and a rustic and bold gaiety. His striking rhythms

MAX REGER

RICHARD STRAUSS

and transitions reveal a Bavarian temperament. His style is characterized by frequent chromaticisms and artistic counterpoint, which achieve their highest expression in his organ works.

In the works of Bruckner, the composer's Austrian personality is clearly visible. In his symphonies he freely gives expression to his piety and love of nature. The symphonic forms he frequently changes to suit his needs which sometimes renders them somewhat diffuse. But he possessed a typical Viennese talent for inventing song melodies and he clothed them in magnificent orchestrations.

Mahler was a pupil and a follower of Bruckner. He employs the same brilliant orchestral expressions, but his music differs decidedly from that of his teacher in its element of realism. Mahler's symphonies (he wrote nine of them) possess marked dramatic qualities, and all sorts of means are employed, whether trivial, comic or quaint, to paint the particular atmosphere realistically. His symphonies are characterized also by a colossal grandeur, and he boldly employed vocal solos and choruses to achieve the utmost in musical expression. In his Eighth Symphony, the *Symphony of a Thousand,* a thousand performers are actually required.

Richard Strauss has already been mentioned in connection with his operas and songs. The chief characteristic of his music is his ability to paint images and situations by means of tonal effects that sometimes are bizarre and startling. He is ever striving for novel effects, which abound in his symphonic poems, *The Merry Pranks of Tyll Eulenspiegel, Thus Spake Zarathustra* (after Nietzsche), and *The Life of a Hero.* As a conductor he was very successful and his works have become as popular in America as in Europe.

RUSSIAN MUSIC

The principal contributions that Russia has made to art have been in the branches of literature, drama, and music. It has been pointed out that Germanic music was not only emotional, but also highly intellectual. Another outstanding quality in Germanic music is its form, or organization of material. The ability to take a few notes and build them into a symphony, to take a small pattern of rhythm or fragments of a melody, and to mold it into a larger unit, these are traits and powers which many of the Germanic composers have inherited and developed over generations of musical endeavor.

But the music of the Slavic countries, to which Russia belongs, differs markedly from western music. In Russian music the emotional element and the love of the fantastic and imaginary dominate. In briefly characterizing Russian music, what are some of its most conspicuous qualities? Most obvious is its range of color, its love of sheer sound. Color in music usually signifies those qualities which result from the combinations of dissonance and consonance, or the unique tone qualities of any instrument or groups of instruments in combination. Color ranges from the somber hues in the *Pathetic Symphony* of Tschaikowsky, to the brilliance in the ballet of the *Rite of Spring* by Stravinsky. There is splendor in the imposing Coronation Scene in the opera *Boris Godounov* by Moussorgsky; there is tragedy and realistic hallucination in the closing death scene from the same opera, and all these images are faithfully mirrored in the sound color of the orchestra.

INFLUENCES ON TONE COLOR

A contributing factor in the Russian love of color has been the influence of the peasant life, the intermingling of the Byzantine, Slavic, and Asiatic elements. This is particularly evident in the music of the Russian Greek Orthodox Church with its elaborate liturgy. At the lower end of the color scale we find the tragic realism of an oppressed people, the pitiful poverty of a migratory peasantry. Russian music often appears more national than personal, and it is easy to respond to its exotic and powerful rhythms as well as to its harmonic or orchestral color.

In the music of Scriabin there is a racial vitality that drives him into ecstatic voodoo dances. The latter show a deep kinship with some of the Russian religious sects whose services develop into orgies of dervish dances. Some uninformed American essayists like to eulogize about the arbitrary or synthetic rhythms of a passage by George Gershwin. They write of it as highly advanced, even as international. Yet it is easy to see from the chorus in the opera *Sadko* by the Russian, Rimsky-Korsakov, that what for Gershwin had become an arbitrary meter was for Rimsky-Korsakov a natural meter of eleven quarter notes to the measure. This is a rhythm that is native to the Russians, springing from an art

PETER TSCHAIKOWSKY

Paul's Photos, Chicago

NICHOLAS RIMSKY-KORSAKOV

that is racial. Other examples could be cited from the savage songs of the Houri tribe in the Transcaucasus. Contemporary masters of mixed or crossed rhythms and meters could still learn much from this ancient music.

FOLK SONG

Folk song also has played a vitalizing role in the evolution of Russian music. Although there has been made much use of the actual folk melodies, their influence has been more pronounced in stimulating rhythm, scales, melodies, and color. An example of the so-called Russian minor scale is the opening theme of the *String Quartet in G Minor* by the French composer, Claude Debussy. There he makes excellent use of this minor scale, with its second step lowered a half tone. The scales established by the Gregorian chants have also found their way into the Slavic countries and into the music of the Greek Orthodox Church, and thus into the musical language of many of Russia's composers.

Moussorgsky made much use of folk elements, in actual songs and melodies, in folk lore, and in ideas from peasant life. This love of mythology and fairy tales has provided material for many Russian composers. An early example is the opera *The Great Stone Face*, by Dargomijsky, and a later one is Rimsky-Korsakov's suite for orchestra called *Scheherazade*.

HUMAN INTEREST

In considering either Russian music, literature, or drama, it is evident that part of its power is derived from its human interest. We are often sympathetic to it because it deals with humanity, humanity often unclothed, unfed, and unwept. This atmosphere is in the music of Moussorgsky, as it is in the plays of Maxim Gorky, in the novels of Dostoyevsky, and in Tolstoy's novel *War and Peace*.

Besides being interested in humanity at large, the Russian has been deeply fascinated by his own personality. This tendency toward introspection is found in Dostoyevsky, and comes to powerful expression in the last three symphonies of Tschaikowsky.

MODEST PETROVICH MOUSSORGSKY

Courtesy The Newberry Library, Chicago

MIKHAIL IVANOVITCH GLINKA

FORM

In contrast to the technical command of form possessed by many German composers, the form, or organization of material, in the Russian school is loose and disjointed. The works of Tschaikowsky hang together more by the force of his emotion than by intellectual skill in the development of musical ideas. Many of the Russian dramas and novels are a series of characterizations of individuals or episodes; and similarly, much of the Russian music also seems more like a series of moving, gripping episodes, than a coherent, well developed plot. Tschaikowsky and Moussorgsky may have suffered from various physiological or psychological disorders, but they also possessed a racial inheritance which made them as true to their race as they were to themselves.

THE RUSSIAN SCHOOL

The real founder of the Russian school was Mikhail I. Glinka (1804-1857). He was followed by a large group of famous composers, of which M. Moussorgsky (1839-1881), Nikolai A. Rimsky-Korsakov (1844-1908), and Alexander Borodin (1834-1887) were the most outstanding. Peter I. Tschaikowsky (1840-

1893) stands out as one of the greatest geniuses Russia has produced in music. He painted blocks of rich color on his orchestral canvas. His work varies in quality; sometimes it is trivial and sensational and sometimes it has grandeur and dramatic intensity. His musical descendant is the contemporary Miaskowsky.

Igor Stravinsky (1882-) and Serge Prokofiev (1891-) are two contemporaries who have made important contributions to music. Stravinsky's most important work has been done in the ballet, while Prokofiev has made contributions in the fields of chamber music and symphony, as well as ballet and opera.

Russia is being observed today for the outcome of its social changes which also embody great potentialities for influencing the development of music. Western music became stalemated before the advent of the Frenchmen Debussy and Ravel, who were influenced by Russian composers, especially Stravinsky. Prior to these three, there had developed a mid-European pretense to a universality in the tonal art, which was really only of and for the Western world. The Far East, which includes part of Russia, was forgotten. The music of the mountains, villages, and temples, which is so much a part of the East, had been lost in the city canyons of the Western world. It may be that the East and West shall meet in the tonal art of music. There are some who believe that the fusion begun in the land that gave birth to Soviet Russia will find its fulfillment in the United States.

MUSIC IN AMERICA

If one is to reach an understanding of current trends in American music, it is important to take a brief look backward. Much of our background is European rather than American.

From about 1730 until well into the nineteenth century the music of the United States was dominated by influences from England. Francis Hopkinson (1737-91) is known as the first secular composer, while the Reverend James Lyon was the first American composer of sacred music. Francis Hopkinson's song, "My Days Have Been so Wondrous Free," written in 1759, is the earliest piece of music written by an American composer.

THE NINETEENTH CENTURY

During the nineteenth century the spread of musical activities throughout the United States was rapid and general. Choral and operatic enterprises were launched. Symphony orchestras and chamber music groups were established, and music schools were founded. Meanwhile, the movement for musical education went on apace, resulting in the introduction of music in the public schools before the end of the third decade, and finally, in the organization of the National Federation of Music Clubs just before the close of the century. Explanatory symphony concert series for children and adults were started, and music criticisms appeared in the newspapers. A movement for Opera-in-English began in the nineteenth century, and soon a clamor for real American composers was heard.

Simultaneously, enthusiastic American music lovers began to search for native American folk music. It should be indicated here that our greatest art forms have come not from primitive societies but from highly developed cultures. Precultural societies can, and frequently do, influence the art of a nation, but the art of music is essentially an expression of culture and civilization. The Czechoslovakian composer, Anton Dvořák, who lived for a few years in New York, was of the opinion that the only basis for a distinctly American music was the Negro melody. Composers following in this tradition were Rubin Goldmark and the contemporary John Powell. Another group voiced the opinion that the hope of American music lay in the inspiration from Indian music. In this group are Charles Cadman, Arthur Nevin, Arthur Farwell, and others.

Courtesy The Foster Hall Collection, University of Pittsburgh

STEPHEN FOSTER AT 33
(From a contemporary daguerreotype.)

The slave songs of the South were said to have inspired Stephen Foster, whose songs, such as "Old Folks at Home," "My Old Kentucky Home," and "Old Black Joe," were so widely known that writers sometimes called them "folk songs." These songs have but few of the characteristics of Negro melodies which have appealed most forcibly to the later composers. These Foster songs lean toward the Negro "spirituals" in their facile sentiment. The rhythmic snap which subsequently laid the foundations of ragtime is absent from them, but it is found in the compositions of Powell and Goldmark, whose compositions show some Negro influence.

EDWARD Mac DOWELL

The first American composer in the nineteenth century who achieved a reputation at home and abroad was Edward MacDowell. There are many who rate him as the first American composer of distinction. Although the music of MacDowell shows a decided Germanic influence, it is indisputable that his rise to fame greatly stimulated the hope that eventually America was to produce great composers. MacDowell labored under the misconception of a forced nationalism. Some of his compositions as well as some of the titles show the tendency to make Indian music the basis of American music. On the other hand, he also made a conscious effort to free himself from these influences when he wrote some of his larger works for the piano or orchestra.

INFLUENCE OF FRANCE

The nineteenth-century influence of Germany on American composers was followed in the twentieth century by influence from France. This influence came first from César Franck, and then from Claude Debussy. It was natural that Franck should come first for he was as much Germanic as he was French in his inheritance. The influence of Debussy, with his love of chromatics, of colors, and of sensuous impressionism, struck America as effectively as it did every other western country. By 1915 it had infected both young and old composers. But its very limitations of style and technique made French impressionism incapable of expressing the largeness and the vastness that is typically American.

Debussy worked under a very pronounced influence from the Far East. When the Russian Stravinsky became famous in the second decade of this century, there came a clash between the Debussyites and the Stravinskyites. One was almost forced into one allegiance or the other. Many composers in America, as well as in Europe, made the mistake of unduly emphasizing color and manner. The desire to create was thought to be an adequate sub-

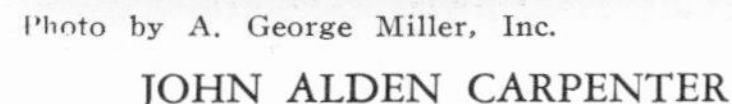

Photo by A. George Miller, Inc.

JOHN ALDEN CARPENTER

Courtesy Columbia Broadcasting System

DEEMS TAYLOR

stitute for the desire to learn how to create. This phase of American music lasted pretty well through the first twenty years of our century.

Probably the most distinguished music of this period has come from the pen of the Chicago composer, John Alden Carpenter. His piano pieces and songs first brought him into prominence. But these were followed by many larger orchestral and chamber works, and his music has been played in all the major musical centers in the world.

AMERICAN SONGS

Another misapprehension that many composers labor under is that if they are given a good poem it is not too difficult to write a song. A glance at any publisher's catalogue would make it appear that Americans write only songs. Songs are like books; of their making there is no end. Fortunately, the present decade has seen an important turn in the writing of American songs. Adequate technique is becoming increasingly evident. Songs by Carpenter, Charles, Ernest Bloch, Russell Bennett, Jacobi, as well as a long list of other important composers, show both craftsmanship and inspiration.

In the 1920's, American composers were indulging in volatile fancy and whimsical humor, along with an attempt to make ragtime and jazz into classical forms. But it did not take long to learn that music which appeals to the feet does not always appeal to the mind, not to speak of the higher emotions. The artistic and literary circles of Paris discovered the great American composer in George Antheil. His well-advertised *Ballet Méchanique* was a musical skyscraper made out of steel girders and rivets from Stravinsky's warehouses. Factories and the streets of New York can make their contribution to the house in which art and music dwell, but they cannot create human beings to inhabit it.

In the field of opera, Walter Damrosch, Horatio Parker, Deems Taylor, Louis Gruenberg, Charles Wakefield Cadman, and Howard Hanson have been honored by performances at the Metropolitan Opera House in recent years. In the field of orchestral and chamber music the works of Leo Sowerby, Arthur Shepherd, Randall Thompson, Virgil Thomson, Frederic Jacobi, Ernest Schelling, Loeffler, Roy Harris, and Gershwin have received particular attention.

CONTEMPORARY AMERICAN COMPOSERS

American music has suffered as much from too much publicity as it has from lack of it. Fortunately, though glamour and fame may present or refuse opportunities for the hearing of new works, they cannot stop the production and creation of new music. There are a number of high-minded, serious composers working in the United States whose names are known to only a few, and their works known to even fewer. They are not interested in writing music for the future, nor are they over-concerned with a false sense of nationalism. They know that whether or not a work bears the stamp of nationalism has little to do with its quality as music or art. A piano piece by Chopin is not better than one by Schumann because it is Polish, or one by Schumann better than Chopin's because it is German—not even for the Poles or Germans. All music must bear the stamp of the composer, and of the country and epoch that gave him birth. These are his inheritance. But they are a gift and cannot be acquired.

In surveying the contemporary scene in American music one sees a few tendencies that are even more important than the individuals who may represent them. These tendencies can be summarized in one sentence: they comprise a change of attitude toward the purposes and ideals of music, accompanied by a search for a technique that will most satisfactorily express the purposes and ideals of the composer. The serious American composer is coming to realize that his hope of musical salvation does not lie in anything but himself. With this awakening sense of responsibility, he is laying aside a false romanticism that would make music more literary than musical, that tries to force music definitely to speak a language that is not its own. Our conservatories and university schools of music also are slowly changing their attitudes. Their ideal is no longer to produce an individual who merely plays an instrument well; they rather seek to train a cultured musician first and a performer second; or better still, the performance is to be the expression of a cultured artist.

In attempting to create music that is American, our composers have turned to the life of the cities, and to the background of the American Negro and the American Indian. But America is more than this.

It will take a new Ninth Symphony to symbolize and express the noble simplicity and sublimity to be found in our distant horizons, or in the still canyons of our Far West. The earth that gave birth to Bach, to Beethoven, to César Franck, and to Brahms, is still a living, pregnant earth. Music and art that express only the elbowing excitement of Times Square, the brown-stone front of Fifth Avenue, the noise of Wabash Avenue, or the momentary quiet of Central Park will be timely art, but it may pass with the age that gave it birth.

If you have watched the purpling sun flame over the walls of the Grand Canyon after a mist of rain; if you have seen the symphonies in the sun-drenched chasms and snow-capped peaks of the Rockies, then you will know that these are silently waiting for their symbolical expression through music that shall be as universal as it is American.

Union Pacific Railroad photo

THE GRAND CANYON OF THE COLORADO

Courtesy C. G. Conn, Ltd.

MEMBERS OF THE VIOLIN FAMILY

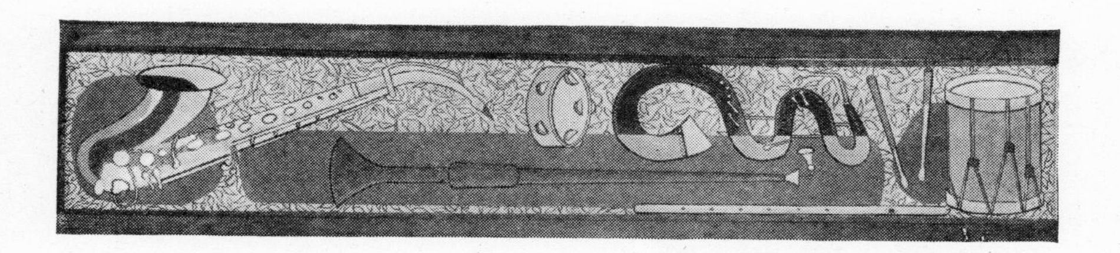

INSTRUMENTS OF THE ORCHESTRA

THE VARIOUS INSTRUMENTS in an orchestra are like the voices in a chorus. Just as it takes many voices of different qualities to make up a chorus, so it takes many kinds of instruments to produce the music which the symphony orchestra expresses. The voice, however, is far more limited in its possibilities than are those instruments which man has learned to manufacture after centuries of experiment. As a result, the music of a symphony is far more complex than the most elaborate music sung by a chorus. It is only by understanding something of the way in which the different instruments of the orchestra produce their music that we can learn to distinguish them. By knowing the characteristic qualities of the instruments, one can learn to appreciate the rich, complex combination of musical sounds heard when an orchestra is playing.

The members of the orchestral ensemble are divided into four groups, which are known as the string, woodwind, brass, and percussion sections. These names are derived either from the manner in which the sound is produced, or from the material of which the instruments are made.

THE STRINGS

In this group are included those instruments (four in number) which are normally played by drawing a bow across taut strings. Most strings are made of gut, although some are made of metal, and still others have gut cores which are wrapped with wire. They can produce several varieties of sound, depending upon the way in which the strings are caused to vibrate. They may be made to "speak" by plucking with the fingers, by drawing the horsehair surface of a bow across the strings, or by striking them with the wooden back of the bow.

The violin, the viola, the violoncello, and the double-bass, are all violins of various sizes. Just as the harp is famous for the delicate unearthliness of its music, so the violin is characterized by a sweet, rich tone which seems to reflect human emotion. Its ancestors go far back to the rebeck of pre-Christian Arabia. This was an instrument which had one string. In the sixteenth and seventeenth centuries the famous Italian instrument-makers perfected the violin as we have it now—a box made of many kinds and pieces of wood, shaped gracefully and skilfully to produce beautiful sound. On either side of the box are "S" shaped holes which permit the music to escape. Tones are created by air vibrations which are set up in the box when the strings are agitated. The latter are held away from the body of the violin by a bridge; this is arched so that the performer may play upon one string at a time. The length of the strings and, consequently, their pitch are regulated by pegs. The player further varies pitch while playing by pressing upon the strings with the fingers of his left hand while his right hand guides the bow across the strings.

The Violin

The violin is the smallest unit of the string section. It is a valuable solo instrument as well as the most important member of the orchestra. The violin is held between the chin and the shoulder while it is being played. Its tone, flexible and extremely expressive, has a very extensive range.

The Viola

From the time of its invention until comparatively recently, the viola seldom was played solo. Recently, as artists have become more proficient, it has grown in favor as a solo instrument. The viola is held in the same manner as the violin, but it is larger and possesses a lower range. Its penetrating voice adds dark, melancholy shadows to the color of the orchestra.

The Violoncello

The violoncello player sits with the instrument leaning against him. The 'cello rests on a spike which projects from the lower edge of the violin-box. He uses a much shorter and heavier bow than the violinist. The range of the violoncello is an octave lower than that of the viola, but it also extends well up into the register of the latter instrument. The 'cello is often heard as a solo instrument, its beautiful tone, wide range, and great technical possibilities making it increasingly popular.

The Double-Bass

The double-bass is the largest violin made. The player usually stands at the rear of the orchestra, holding against his body the instrument, which is often taller than himself. The performer must have strong fingers in order to press down the strings, which, almost as long as the instrument, are proportionately heavy. The tones produced by these heavy strings in this great box are too deep for much solo use, but they are as important in the orchestra as the bass voice is in a chorus. The double-bass greatly adds to the sonority and depth of the orchestral tone.

THE WOODWINDS

At the present time, membership in the woodwind section is not limited to those instruments which are made of wood, although many of them are. A woodwind is a tubular instrument

PRIMITIVE SHEPHERD'S PIPE

played by blowing air either into an opening in the side of the tube, or into a mouthpiece which is fitted with a single or double reed. A reed is a thin, flat strip of wood. Upon it partially depends the quality of the sound that issues from the instrument.

The Flute

The flute was played by the early Greeks, and the Egyptians also had a variety of flute which consisted of a very long tube closed at one end. The Greek and Egyptian flutes were played by blowing a stream of air across the open end of the tube. The modern flute is held sideways. The player blows air across a hole in the side at the upper end of the instrument, regulating the pitch by means of holes and keys which he manipulates with his fingers. Breath control is also of great importance in adjusting the pitch.

The Piccolo

The piccolo looks just like the flute, and is played in the same manner. It is, however, only half as big, and its range is an octave higher. It has a high, piercing tone.

The Oboe

The oboe is made with a double reed. The player blows air between the two reeds into the length of the instrument, instead of into the side, as with the flute. He controls the pitch by a system of keys and holes. The instrument is about two feet long, and is usually made of wood. Pastoral in character, the voice of the oboe is sweet and rich, and it is often used to add a plaintive quality to orchestral melodies.

Courtesy C. G. Conn, Ltd

THE OBOE

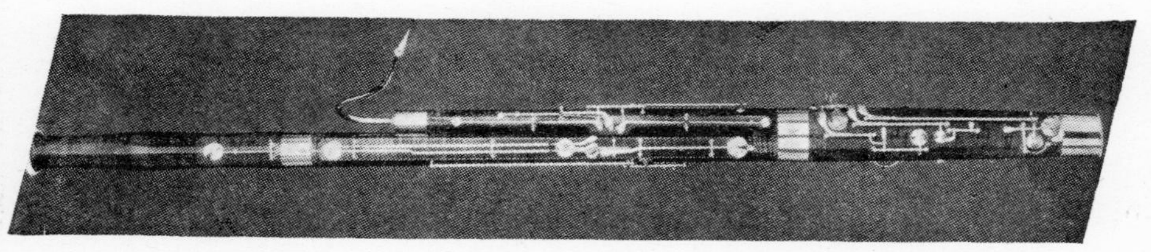

Courtesy C. G. Conn, Ltd.

THE BASSOON

The English Horn

This instrument is really not a horn at all, nor is it English. The name is probably a corruption of the French appellation *cor anglais,* which means "English horn"; the usage of the word "horn" in this connection is obscure. The English horn is actually an alto oboe, with a rich, mournful tone. Many famous melodies have been written for this beautiful instrument.

The Bassoon

The bassoon is the bass voice of the woodwind section, as the double-bass is the bass of the strings. Like the English horn and the oboe, it is played with a double reed. The bassoon is, however, so much longer than these instruments that it bends back upon itself and is fitted with a long, curved mouthpiece. It is sometimes the clown of the orchestra, but its rich baritone voice is frequently used to lend distinction to a melody.

The Double-Bassoon

The double-bassoon is longer, deeper, and gives a more solemn tone. Its low tones are often used to support and double the bass, or for special grotesque effects.

The Clarinet

The clarinet differs slightly in shape from the oboe, for its funnel-shaped end flares out into a bell. Instead of a double reed, the clarinet is fitted with a single reed which is fastened to a mouthpiece on the upper end of the tube. The instrument has an extensive range and is extremely adaptable within an orchestra. It has three voices: one is high, bright, and shrill; the second is tender and warm; and the third is low, dark, and gloomy.

The Alto Clarinet

Like the English horn, the alto clarinet (sometimes called the basset-horn) is also a woodwind. Its pitch is lower than that of the ordinary clarinet, and it also is played with a single reed. To facilitate the handling of its greater length, both the mouthpiece and the funnel-like lower end are bent into a shape resembling that of the saxophone.

The Bass Clarinet

The bass clarinet is pitched an octave lower than the ordinary clarinet and, like the other clarinets, it is played with a single reed. Characterized by a curved mouthpiece and a turned-up, funnel-shaped lower end, the bass clarinet closely resembles the saxophone in shape. It has a deep, heavy, melancholy voice of extreme richness in the lower register.

The Saxophone

The saxophone existed as an orchestral instrument long before jazz was introduced. It was invented by Adolph Sax in 1840 and was used at first only in brass bands. Composers later wrote parts for it into their orchestral scores. Shaped like the bass clarinet, but made in several sizes, the saxophone is made of brass instead of wood. For this reason, among others, some writers classify the instrument with the brass group, even though it is played with a single reed. It is coming into use more and more in serious works of contemporary composers. It is found in the scores of Debussy, Ravel, Sowerby, and others.

THE BRASS SECTION

The members of the brass section are also wind instruments. The players blow air directly into the cup- or funnel-shaped mouthpieces which are essential characteristics of this group of instruments. The vibrating medium consists of the player's own breath and lips, and a series of notes can be played by altering the lip tension. With the addition of three or four valves (which cut the tube into various lengths), a complete, chromatic scale which covers several octaves can be obtained. In the trombone, a slide is used instead of valves, but the result is the same.

The first horns used, to call together the members of a tribe, were made from tusks of animals. Methods were later discovered whereby instruments could be made of metal. The Romans found that volume and pitch varied with the length of the horn. Since a long, straight horn was unwieldy, instrument-makers bent and twisted the tubes into various shapes.

The French Horn

The player blows into this instrument through a funnel-shaped mouthpiece, controlling the pitch by means of his lips, supplemented by three valves. This type of instrument was originally a hunting-horn without valves. Today it is spoken of simply as "horn," not as "French horn." This is a most useful instrument in the orchestra. It blends with many other instruments in harmony, and it has an expressive quality well suited to long, sustained melodies. The rich, sweet tone of the horn can be impressive in its beauty.

The Slide Trombone

Instead of valves or keys, the slide trombone has an arrangement of overlapping slides which allows the player to regulate pitch by sliding part of the instrument back and forth. Its voice has a penetrating, thrilling quality which is often dramatic and noble in its sonority.

The Trumpet

This instrument is an oblong coil of narrow tubing which is fitted with a hemispherical mouthpiece and three valves. Its brilliant tones are associated with war, glory, and marching men.

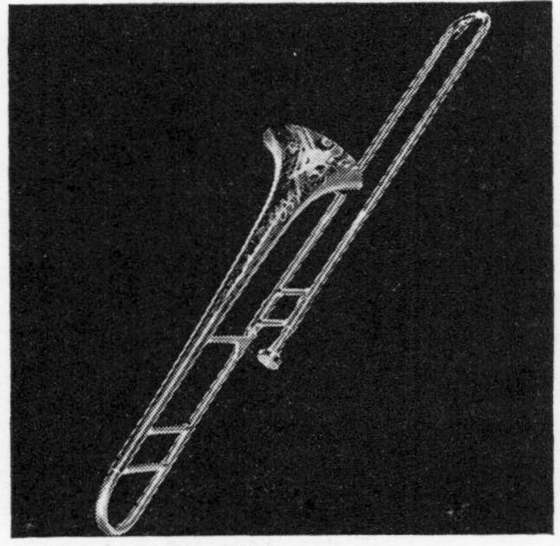

Courtesy C. G. Conn, Ltd.
THE SLIDE TROMBONE

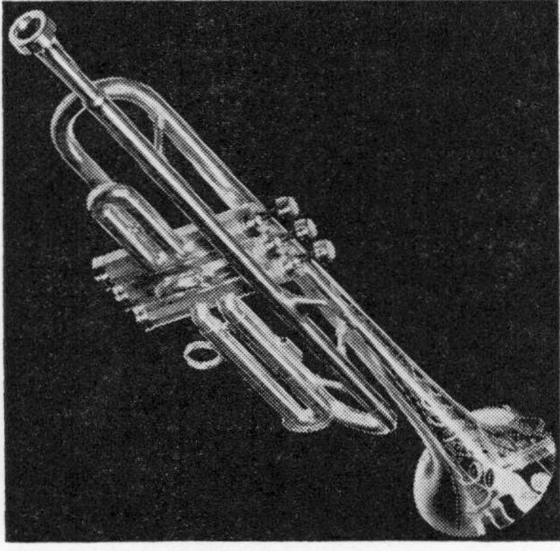

Courtesy C. G. Conn, Ltd.
THE TRUMPET

The Cornet

The cornet is a development of the post-horn, and is not a small trumpet, as many people believe. Its bore is larger and more conical than that of the trumpet, and a cup-shaped mouthpiece is used. The cornet lacks the brilliancy and incisiveness of the trumpet, but it is somewhat easier to play.

The Tuba

This is the largest of the brass instruments, and it is therefore the bass of the brass section. Its great tube twists upon itself many times in order to make it convenient to handle. The tuba has a rich, deep tone which Wagner used in many of his operatic works. The instrument is made in several sizes, but all are equipped with a cup-shaped mouthpiece and either three or four valves.

THE PERCUSSION INSTRUMENTS

The percussion section of the orchestra gets its name from the manner in which the instruments are sounded. Included in this group are the piano, the harp and other plucked instruments, the drums, the xylophones and their relatives, and the triangle, gong, cymbals, and castanets. The members of the violin family also belong in this category when the strings are plucked or struck with the back of a bow.

The history of the percussion instruments, like that of the horn and the flute, goes far back. The former were used by primitive tribes on occasions associated with war, religion, celebration, and woe. The beating of a drum is still exciting to most of us, whether we hear it in an orchestra, with a brass band, or by itself.

The percussion instruments are further classified in two large groups, viz., those which have a definite musical pitch and those which do not. Included in the second group are the gong, the castanets, the triangle, the cymbals, and all of the drums except the kettle-drums, or timpani.

The Harp

The harp is played by an individual who sits behind it and plucks the strings with his fingers. It is one of the oldest and largest instruments we have. The beautiful tone of the harp is associated with ethereal thoughts. The instrument consists of a wooden frame in which are set forty-six strings of different lengths. These strings produce different tones, since the shorter the string, the higher its pitch. Sébastien Érard, a French instrument-maker who lived in the latter part of the eighteenth century and the first part of the nineteenth, made it possible to play a harp in any key by inventing an ingenious arrangement of foot pedals whereby the length of the strings could be changed. The first harps of which we have pictures were played in Egypt, fifteen hundred years before the Christian Era. Harps were also favorite instruments in ancient Ireland, and we still associate them with the characteristic music of that country.

AN ANCIENT HARP

The Piano

The piano is, with the possible exception of the organ, the most important and widely used of our modern instruments. It was invented about 1709 by Bartolomeo Cristofori, a Florentine harpsichord-maker. The piano consists essentially of a series of strings which are stretched across a frame attached to a sounding board. The strings are struck by hammers which are activated by a keyboard. A set of pedals is used to increase or reduce the resonance of the instrument. Cristofori called his invention a "Gravecembalo col piano e forte" (harpsichord with soft and loud), and it is from this name that our words "pianoforte" and "piano" are derived. The instrument is chiefly used in a solo role, but it has been introduced into the orchestral ensemble in recent years to provide special effects and to supplement such instruments as the harp and the celesta.

The Kettledrums

The kettledrum gets its name from a resemblance in appearance to a primitive pot with an animal skin stretched over the top. There are three or more in most orchestras. Their range in pitch is very limited. Tuning is accomplished by manipulating a set of clamps and screws which tighten or loosen the membrane, thus raising or lowering the pitch. The drummer uses sticks to strike this membrane. The kettledrums are used for rhythmic patterns and special effects.

The Glockenspiel

The name of this instrument means "the playing of bells," and its tones sound like ringing bells. They are produced by striking metal bars of different lengths with a small hammer.

The Celesta

The celesta looks like a small upright piano, and like a piano it has a keyboard and pedals. The celesta has no strings, however; when the keys are struck, little hammers beat upon a series of steel bars or plates. Each of the latter is provided with a resonator or sounding box; these are partly responsible for the difference in quality between the tone of the celesta and that of the glockenspiel. By using the pedal, it is possible to play passages on the

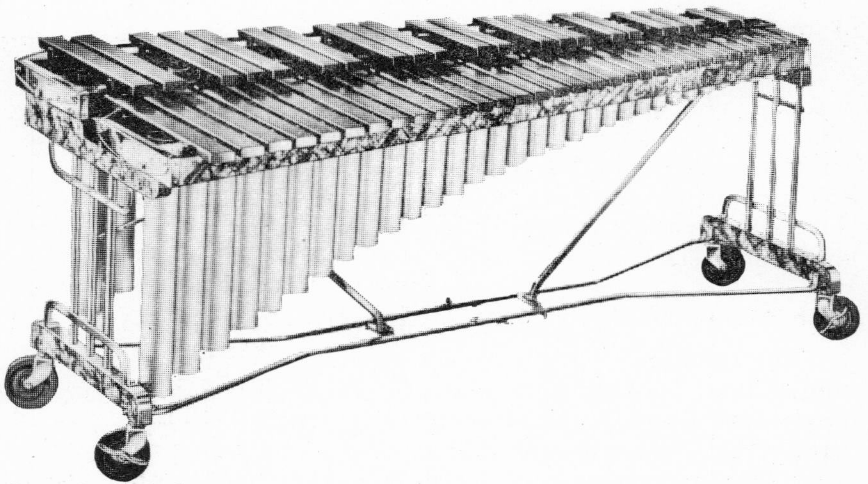

Courtesy Leedy Mfg. Co.

THE MARIMBA-XYLOPHONE

celesta which are quite clear and distinct, whereas the same passage played on the glockenspiel would sound jumbled or "muddy." The tone of the celesta is a surprisingly sweet, delicate, bell-like sound, which may even be described as celestial.

The Xylophone

The xylophone is played like the glockenspiel, but it usually has a greater range. In addition, the instrument is equipped with bars which are made of wood instead of steel. These bars are often supplemented with metal sounding-tubes which increase the resonance of the tone.

The Chimes

These instruments are steel tubes of various lengths which hang from the top of a frame. The player strikes the upper ends of these tubes with a mallet. The solemn sounds produced are like those of a carillon, or church bells.

The Triangle

The triangle, which derives its name from its shape, consists of a triangular steel bar which is open at one apex. When struck, it gives a piercing, ringing sound. Its bright, metallic quality frequently penetrates through great climaxes in the orchestra.

The Snare-Drum

This is a drum which has no musical pitch. It consists of a wooden cylinder which is closed at both ends by sheepskin "heads." The name is derived from the gut strings, or "snares," which are stretched across the lower head. The upper head is beaten with two drumsticks, and the sound produced is brisk and exciting. The snare-drum is frequently used in military music, or for dramatic orchestral effects.

The Tambourine

The tambourine is a tiny drum with a wooden frame and a single "head." Little metal plates are fastened to the frame; these jingle merrily when the tambourine is struck or shaken with the hand. The gypsies use the tambourine to accompany their dancing. This instrument is very old, but it has remained unchanged in appearance throughout the thousands of years of its existence.

Courtesy Chicago Symphony Orchestra

THE CHICAGO SYMPHONY ORCHESTRA . . .

The Bass Drum

This, the giant of the drum section, is a side-drum type which produces a low resonant sound of power or suspense.

The Castanets

These are little wooden clappers which serve when knocked together to emphasize gay rhythms in dance music. The castanets are very popular in Spain, where playing them is an art.

The Gong

This instrument came from the Orient. It is a great, convex disc made of bronze which is struck with a hammer or stick. Like the drum, it is used at times for orchestral excitement.

The Cymbals

Like the castanets, the cymbals are struck together. Since they are made of metal, however, they come together with a sharp crash which is much more exciting. Sometimes one of them is beaten with a pair of drumsticks when a continuous roll or crash is desired.

Photo by Kaufman & Fabry

. . . ORCHESTRA HALL, MARCH 18, 1936

Photo by Photography, Inc.

FREDERICK STOCK
Conductor, Chicago Symphony Orchestra.

Courtesy Music Division, Library of Congress, Washington, D. C.

FACSIMILE OF ORIGINAL SYMPHONY MANUSCRIPT BY LA VIOLETTE

SYMPHONY NO. 5 IN C MINOR, OPUS 67

Ludwig van Beethoven (Dec. 16, 1770—March 26, 1827)

BEETHOVEN began the composition of his *Fifth Symphony* in 1804 and completed it in 1807. However, material and sketches for the first three movements are to be found in his sketchbooks dating from the years 1800-1801. For some unexplained reason Beethoven interrupted his work on the C minor symphony in 1806, devoting his time instead to the composition of a work subsequently published as his *Fourth Symphony.* The first performance of Opus 67 took place in Vienna on December 22, 1808, and the work was published the following year.

First Movement: Allegro con brio, C minor, 2/4 time.

The principal theme is announced without introduction by the strings and clarinets, in a challenging, defiant fortissimo. The rhythmic figure which is so prominent in this movement is employed not only as a framework for the first theme, but also as an accompaniment for the second subject. The four-note motive (Ex. 1) which is the essence of the principal theme has been

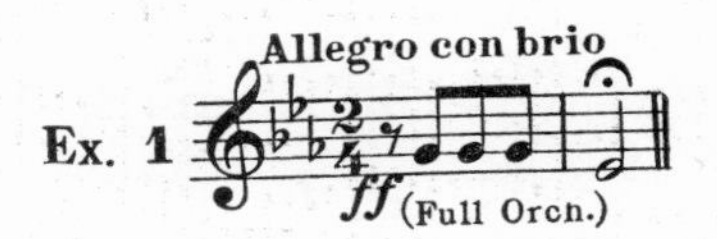

the subject of various interpretations. One of these discovers in the motive a symbolic representation of "Fate knocking at the door"; another, the masculine Beethoven by way of contrast with some particular (or generic) woman, the latter being symbolized in the second theme. A remark by the composer himself gives some foundation to the former interpretation, but the latter is undoubtedly the brain child of some overly romantic nineteenth century mind.

The second theme is introduced by a fortissimo passage in the horns, based upon the familiar four-note motive. The second subject itself is a lovely, gracious melody, tranquilly announced in the key of E flat major by the strings, and in sharp contrast to the rugged masculinity of the first theme (Ex. 2).

The opening portion of the development section deals first with the principal subject, and then elaborates on the horn passage which introduced the second theme. The succeeding portion of the development is a beautifully expressive section, during which there is a temporary respite from the four-note motive and its rhythmic equivalent. It is interesting to note that this rhythmic "motto" is present on all but a few of the thirty-odd pages which comprise the score of the first movement.

The recapitulation of the principal subject is accompanied for fourteen bars by a melodic line played by the oboe. At the climax of a crescendo, the oboe is left suddenly to sing alone with an inexpressibly profound pathos that reveals a depth of emotion granted but rarely to most humans. The second subject returns, this time in C major, and the movement is concluded by a long closing section based on the opening theme.

Berlioz found in this first movement "the painting of disordered sentiments which overthrow a great soul, a prey to despair . . . ." "Sentiment," Beethoven wrote in a letter, "suits only women. Music must strike fire from the soul of man." The first movement of the fifth symphony accomplishes this, and the sparks are those that come from the impact of a challenged fate on a great and unyielding soul.

Second Movement: Andante con moto, A flat major, 3/8 time.

The lyrical second movement is cast in the form of free variations on two themes. The first theme (Ex. 3) opens in the 'celli

and violas. The second subject is then stated by the clarinet and bassoon (Ex. 4). After a transition to C major, the second theme

is restated, this time in an almost military guise. This is succeeded by a sustained bridge passage for strings and bassoons that is breathtaking in its beauty. A set of three variations then follows, the third of which omits the second subject. The last variation is followed by a closing section, in which the bassoon sings against a syncopated accompaniment in the strings. It is of interest to point out, in bars 224-226, an anticipation of that nostalgia which was later to distinguish much of the music of Brahms.

Third Movement: Allegro, C minor, 3/4 time.

For the first time in symphonic music, the scherzo (which had replaced the minuetto) is fraught with emotional implications usually reserved, even in Beethoven's own previous works, for either the first or second movements. The opening subject conveys an impression of terror in suspense (Ex. 5). The sudden

appearance of a fortissimo theme in the horns suddenly shatters the previous mood. This subject is clearly derived from the rhythmic "motto" in the first movement. A lengthy development of the foregoing material leads to a trio, which consists of the fugal treatment of a scale figure, the subject being announced in the lowest strings. At the time of its first performance, this passage was branded by the bass players as unplayable. After a long decrescendo the scherzo theme returns, to lead with an irresistible drive into the final movement.

Fourth Movement: Allegro, C major, 4/4 time.

The first theme, a triumphant, aspiring subject based on the simple chord C-E-G, is announced fortissimo, by the full or-

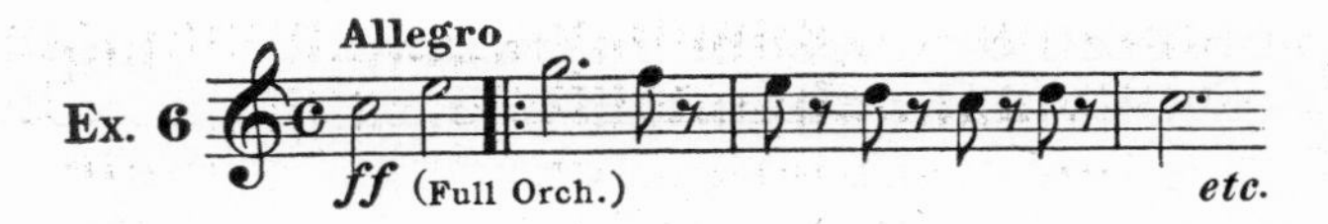

chestra (Ex. 6). This is succeeded by a transitional passage which leads to the second subject (Ex. 7), played by the strings in the

key of G major. The development section which follows is devoted to the second theme. In the midst of the development, the fortissimo horn subject of the scherzo is suddenly heard, reinvoking past fears even in this moment of triumph. The recapitulation of the first and second themes takes place in the usual manner, and the movement is brought to a close by a lengthy coda, which employs the first theme and material from the bridge passages in the expositions.

* * *

Several innovations may be remarked in this composition. For the first time in the development of the symphony, a portion of one movement had reappeared in another. This type of treatment, which is known as cyclic form, was developed further by later composers, and it achieved a high point of perfection in the works of César Franck. In the field of orchestral writing, virtually the first instance may be here found of the use of the piccolo, the trombone, and the contrabassoon in a symphonic movement. Gluck and Mozart had used the piccolo and trombone respectively in their operas, and Handel made use of the contrabassoon in the Coronation Anthem. However, it was not until the time of Beethoven that these three instruments achieved positions of importance in the orchestra.

Although the C minor symphony is not the greatest of Beethoven's works, it easily ranks as one of the most popular of his symphonies. It has an elemental power and an essential simplicity which make it readily intelligible on the one hand, and emotionally profound, as well as moving, on the other.

Courtesy German Railroads Information Office, N. Y.

BEETHOVEN'S PIANO IN BEETHOVEN HOUSE, BONN, GERMANY

SYMPHONY NO. 6 ("PASTORAL") IN F MAJOR, OPUS 68

Ludwig van Beethoven

Beethoven's *Sixth Symphony,* also called the *Pastoral Symphony,* was completed in 1807. Both it and the *Fifth Symphony* were performed for the first time in Vienna on December 22, 1808. On the program at that time the Sixth was called the Fifth, and the Fifth, the Sixth. With publication of both works, however, the sequence was established in the now familiar order.

The *Sixth Symphony* has been the point of departure for a great deal of discussion on the value, the merits, the scope, and the justification of "program" music. Much of the discussion has served to cloud, rather than clarify, both the issue and the work. Some critics have professed to find the work cheap in its attempt to "imitate the sounds of nature"; others have gone to the other extreme in their attempt to prove that the direct imitation is of negligible importance from the point of view of conception. It is best to accept the work as it is without any antecedent judgments, in the spirit in which it was written. We have Beethoven's own explicit statement that the symphony is "more an expression of feeling, than painting." Beethoven deliberately set himself the task of reflecting, not the outward aspects, but the state of mind induced by contact with nature in its various guises. The two exceptional instances are the fourth movement, "Thunderstorm," and the bird trio at the end of the second movement. The descriptive phrases at the head of each movement are Beethoven's own.

First Movement (subtitled "Awakening of Happy Feelings Upon Arriving In the Country"): Allegro ma non troppo, F major, 2/4 time.

A simple theme (Ex. 1), rustic in character, is heard in the strings. The transition to the second theme is characterized by alternate woodwind and string passages. The second theme in C major consists of a descending figure which passes through the dominant and tonic harmonies respectively. It is noteworthy that the harmonic structure throughout this work is of the simplest. Moreover, the element of repetition, which is so characteristic of Beethoven, is nowhere more congruous with the spirit of a work than in this symphony. The rhythm of the second measure of the theme is repeated over and over as the development opens. The D major and B flat major sections are early suggestions of impressionism, for here the melodic values are less important than the color value, or sheer sound of the total effect. After recapitulation of the principal subjects, the movement is brought to an end by a closing section which begins as did the development and then pursues its way independently.

Second Movement (subtitled "Scene By the Brook"): Andante molto mosso, B flat major, 12/8 time. Here the feeling of relaxation, a relaxation, however, never devoid of the suggestion of strength, is at its utmost. The fragmentary but delightful

principal theme (Ex. 2) is presented by the violins. The accompanying figure in the two muted 'cellos, as the movement opens, is an always surprising modernism. The murmur of the brook, the rustle of the forest, the semi-somnolence of a soul that is passive in the sense that it is being acted upon, active in the sense that it feels itself as one with the endless quiet—all this is implied in the movement. At the end of the movement, after a moment of sudden silence, as though someone had whispered "Listen," the songs of the nightingale, the quail, and the cuckoo are heard. It is interesting that this bird-passage, together with the principal motive which follows, makes a perfect four-bar phrase—an indication of how the bird-themes had become integrated with the music in the composer's mind. A short dialogue between the wind instruments concludes the movement.

Third Movement (subtitled "Merry Gathering of the Country-Folk"): Allegro, F major, 3/4 time. (Ex. 3).

This "scherzo" is a rustic dance, frankly descriptive, including even a caricature of the local bassoon player, who has just three notes with which to assert himself. There are two subsidiary sections, or "trios," in this movement. The scherzo returns after the first. The second trio is interesting for the use made of the trumpet, which crowns the festivities on the note of a C major chord. The recurrence of the scherzo theme is shortened, as the sudden rumble of distant thunder disperses the gathering.

Fourth Movement (subtitled "Thunderstorm"): Allegro, D flat major, 4/4 time.

Despite the fact that since Beethoven the orchestral palette has been enriched by the addition of new colors, this movement is still an effective representation of crashing thunder, swirling rain, howling winds—even lightning is heard, represented by the piercing piccolo. The flute passage at the end of this section has been aptly compared to the sun rising from the clouds.

Fifth Movement (subtitled "Shepherds' Song. Happy and Thankful Feelings After the Storm"): Allegretto, F major, 6/8 time.

From the calls of the shepherds' pipes, with which the movement opens, there emerges the principal theme (Ex. 4), which is

a hymn of thanksgiving. The first subordinate theme resembles somewhat the subordinate theme of the first movement. After the recurrence of the first theme, more richly scored, a second subordinate theme follows. The first theme is then heard again in a varied form. Near the end of the long closing section, the first theme receives a final statement, this time by the muted horn (the only instance in which Beethoven employed this effect). The movement is brought to its conclusion by abrupt, final chords.

BIRTHPLACE OF BEETHOVEN AT BONN, GERMANY

Courtesy German Railroads Information Office, N. Y.

SYMPHONY FANTASTIQUE IN C MAJOR, OP. 14A

Hector Berlioz (December 11, 1803—March 8, 1869)

The *Fantastic Symphony*, subtitled *Episodes in the Life of An Artist*, was written when Berlioz was twenty-eight years of age. Three external influences had a most pronounced effect on the composition of this work. The first of these is discernible in the principal theme, which is a somewhat modified form of a melody composed by Berlioz at the age of twelve, and inspired by his love for Estelle Gautier. The second influence may be attributed to Goethe's play, *Faust*. However, while we have Berlioz' own assertion to substantiate this, most of the material written under the sway of *Faust* was incorporated in the dramatic legend entitled *The Damnation of Faust*. The third factor was Berlioz' hectic, disordered, and fantastic relationship with Harriet Smithson prior to their unfortunate marriage.

The program, which forms the plot-outline of the work, may be considered as an expression of Berlioz' infatuation for this Irish actress. However, it must be remembered that external events in the life of Berlioz were simply means for the release of those caprices and passions which constantly sought outlet, much as molten lava continually strives to escape from the mouth of a volcano. The following quotation, which explains the program of this composition, is a part of the subtitle as it is printed on the score:

"A young artist in love, tired of life, takes opium; the dose, too weak to kill, intoxicates him, and in his fevered dream he reviews his own imaginary love history, which culminates in a fantastic and dreadful ending."

Paul's Photos, Chicago

HECTOR BERLIOZ

The work is in five movements, co-ordinated by the frequent use of a fixed idea or "motto" theme which represents the beloved one. The first performance took place on November 14, 1830, and the symphony was eventually published in 1845, with a dedication to Nicholas I, Tsar of Russia.

First Movement (subtitled "Reveries, Passions"): Largo, C minor, 4/4 time; Allegro agitato ed appassionato, C major, 4/4 time.

In this movement the moods of "somber longings, depression, joyous elation, jealousy, love, and religious consolation" alternate with one another. The melody which opens the work is the "motto" theme, heard throughout the symphony in various guises (Ex. 1).

Second Movement (subtitled "The Ball"): Waltz, A major, 3/8 time.

At a ball, amidst the tumult of the dance, the young artist suddenly finds his beloved. The orchestration, which is the only distinguishing feature of most of Berlioz' music, is particularly effective in this movement.

Third Movement (subtitled "Scene in the Country"): Adagio, F major, 6/8 time.

Against a background of whispering trees, two shepherds play a pastoral duet. The peace is disturbed by vague premonitions and forebodings; the ominous rumble of distant thunder is heard, followed by silence. Berlioz experienced some difficulty in the writing of this movement, which required three weeks for its completion, whereas the following movement was completed in one night.

Fourth Movement (subtitled "March to the Scaffold"): Allegretto, G minor, 4/4 time.

The young man dreams that he has murdered his beloved, and now, condemned to death, he is being led to the execution. A march, alternately somber and wild, brilliant and solemn, accompanies the procession. The recollection of the beloved one returns, only to be blotted out as the death blow falls.

Fifth Movement (subtitled "Walpurgis Night's Dream"): Allegro, C major, 4/4 time.

Witches and devils have come to the execution. The orchestra plays a distorted version of the hymn "Dies Irae" (or "Day of Wrath"), and the "motto" theme of the beloved one is degraded and vulgarized. At the time he was writing this movement, and in spite of the fact that he was not the recipient of Miss Smithson's affections, Berlioz was jealously tortured upon hearing some false rumor concerning her. He confided to a friend that he had pictured her as a courtesan in this last movement. However, the program of the first performance makes no mention of this metamorphosis of the theme. It is nonetheless obvious that he avenged his injured feelings by mistreating the "motto" theme.

* * * *

Berlioz is not considered a great composer. He did not possess the gift of great musical expression, but he developed the resources of the orchestra to such an extent that he is often referred to as "the father of the modern orchestra." Berlioz was also a very excellent music critic, and a pioneer in the use of the "cyclic form," a technical term for that type of composition form which employs "motto" themes or motives.

SCHELOMO, HEBREW RHAPSODY FOR VIOLONCELLO AND ORCHESTRA

Ernest Bloch (July 24, 1880-)

The composition *Schelomo* is one part of the so-called "Jewish Cycle" of Bloch's works. This cycle includes the *Trois Poèmes Juifs* for orchestra (1913), *Psalm 114* for soprano and orchestra (1913-1915); *Psalm 22* for baritone and orchestra; symphony, *Israel* (1913-1916) and *Schelomo.*

The *Hebrew Rhapsody* was composed at Geneva, Switzerland, in January and February 1916, and was written for Alexander Barjansky, Russian cellist. Its first performance was given May 3, 1917, by Hans Kindler under the auspices of the Society of the Friends of Music, in New York.

Concerning nationalism in his music, Bloch declared in an interview: "I do not propose or desire to base my works on melodies more or less authentic. It is rather the Hebrew spirit that interests me—the complex, ardent, agitated soul that vibrates for me in the Bible." Bloch had been making sketches for a setting of Ecclesiastes, but his unfamiliarity with Hebrew, which he believed was the proper language for the setting, had delayed completion of his composition. Then on hearing Barjansky's 'cello tone, he felt he had found the ideal medium for the communication of his feelings, and *Schelomo* was written.

"Schelomo" is the Solomon of the Ecclesiastes of the thousand wives and concubines, the Solomon of the multifarious slaves and warriors, the wise, the passionate, the sensual.

As its name indicates, the composition is rhapsodic in form, at one moment superbly lyric, at another declamatory or dramatic. Conflicting rhythms, chromatic passages, huge melodic leaps—all these have a literary analogue in the Ecclesiastes.

The word "Shlaymeh" is a closer phonetic equivalent to the Hebrew pronunciation of Solomon than is "Schelomo." Although the music, as such, is not affected one way or another by the fact, authorities are quite generally of the opinion that the Ecclesiastes is not the work of Solomon or, for that matter, of any single person.

SYMPHONY NO. 1 IN C MINOR, OPUS 68

Johannes Brahms (May 7, 1833-April 3, 1897)

Brahms, who had been prophetically hailed by Schumann when he was only twenty-one years of age, and who in his early thirties had already done much to fulfil the latter's prophecies, was forty-three years old when he gave his first symphony to the world. It is indicative, not only of the seriousness with which this most self-critical of all composers went about his work, but also of the responsibility he felt when attempting symphonic expression, that fourteen years elapsed between the sketching of the first movement and the completion of the last. This does not mean, however, that he had not made earlier attempts to write a symphony. In January, 1855, he wrote to Schumann: "I have been trying my hand at a symphony. I have even orchestrated the first movement and composed the second and third." This work later underwent two transformations. First it was recast as a sonata for two pianos. Dissatisfied with the latter, Brahms used the first two movements in his *D Minor Piano Concerto;* the last movement was incorporated in the *German Requiem.* It must be remarked also that at the time the first symphony was completed Brahms had already composed the truly symphonic *Serenades,* Opus 11 and Opus 16, three large works for chorus and orchestra, and the *Haydn Variations* for orchestra, Opus 56a.

In 1862 Brahms sent Clara Schumann the first movement of his *C Minor Symphony.* At that time it began abruptly, without the present introduction. The next two movements were written within the following three years. Ten more years elapsed before he added the last movement, much of which was written while he was in Switzerland. The symphony was completed at Lichtenthal in September, 1876, and the first performance took place at Carlsruhe on November 4, 1876. The symphony was none too warmly received at performances in Vienna and Munich, although the Viennese critics accorded the work a good measure of praise. Brahms received the sum of five thousand thalers from the publisher for the work.

First Movement: Un poco sostenuto—Allegro C Minor, 6/8 time.

This is the only symphony by Brahms which is provided with an introduction. In this opening section there occurs a "motto" theme (Ex. 1), which is used throughout the work. The introduc-

tion also presents material used later in the main body of the movement, including the first theme (Ex. 2). The last few bars

of the introduction are a passionate setting for the principal subject which follows. Later the second theme (Ex. 3) is presented,

and the exposition closes stormily. In the development section which follows, virtually all thematic units are treated with a skill and dexterity fully matched by a profound and moving emotional content. The main themes are restated, and the movement ends somberly.

Second Movement: Andante sostenuto, E major, 3/4 time.

This movement is characterized by a sustained beauty and a serene lyricism. The "motto" motive may be discerned in the fifth and sixth bars of the principal subject (Ex. 4). Florid pas-

sages in the woodwinds and solo violin lead eventually to the closing section, in which the solo violin makes a final reference to the "motto" theme.

Third Movement: Un poco allegretto e grazioso, A flat major, 4/4 time.

Instead of the conventional scherzo, or other dance-derived movement, which would ordinarily be expected at this point, Brahms introduces a type of composition entirely characteristic of him—a quiet, intimate movement, in whose restraint one senses more power and latent energy than in many a cataclysmic fortissimo by lesser composers. The principal subject (Ex. 5) is an-

nounced by the clarinet and is then repeated by the strings. This is followed somewhat later by a contrasting middle section. Then the main subject is recapitulated, and the movement closes with material from the middle section. This movement, as well as the preceding one, has occasioned some disapproval. An eminent conductor of Brahms's time voiced the opinion that "however beautiful, they (the second and third movements) seem to be more appropriate for a serenade or suite than for a symphonic composition of such large proportions."

Fourth Movement: Adagio, C minor, 4/4 time. Allegro ma non troppo, ma con brio, C major, 4/4 time.

Busoni in his "New Aesthetic of Music" refers to the introduction of the final movement as one of the extremely rare instances of an ultimate and "emancipated" music. Opening in an atmosphere of dark depression, the introduction gathers momentum and works up to a tremendous climax, at the peak of which the cloud of tragedy implicit in the first movement is completely dissolved. A theme of salvation (Ex. 6) is heard in the horn.

Brahms derived this subject from a Swiss shepherd horn call. A choral-like melody then paves the way for the main part of the movement.

The broadly noble principal theme (Ex. 7) is played by the

violins in the key of C major. The second theme (Ex. 8) is a

flowing melody in G major, also played by the strings. There is no development section properly speaking; in its place there is a greatly expanded restatement of the principal themes. This leads to a great climax, characterized by a literally staggering treatment of the horn theme. A closing section then follows, in which there is a final, tremendous climax. The chorale subject is thundered forth positively, assertively, with the conviction of immutable faith. The movement closes joyously, and the long tale of sorrow and conflict is ended.

SYMPHONY NO. 2 IN B FLAT MAJOR, OPUS 57

Vincent D'Indy (March 27, 1851-December 2, 1931)

Few works have come so close to greatness without achieving it as has D'Indy's *Second Symphony.* It combines the qualities of charm and elegance, seriousness and dignity, profundity without rhetoric, and it is utterly sincere in conception and execution. Such a work, it would seem, should rank with the very greatest of symphonic works. Masterly skill and consummate craftsmanship, an originality that is fresh and unhackneyed without being forced or extreme—these are but a few among the many positive qualities characterizing this very excellent work. Yet it succeeds in satisfying without leaving one with a sense of unquestioning conviction. One has the feeling, not that it "grows," but that it is synthesized. Huneker once defined music as an intuitive mathematics. In this work the balance is somewhat upset, and the resulting proportion is not in favor of the intuitive element.

The symphony is subjective but has no program. Structurally, it is developed from two generating or "motto" motives. In consequence, the work is somewhat episodic; its effect on the whole is more dependent on the approach or interpretation of a conductor than are most other large works. A slight change in shading or rhythm may destroy the continuity of the symphony, in which case one is left with a series of fragmentary impressions.

The two most pronounced musical influences on the works of D'Indy were Franck and Wagner; there are many passages in the *Second Symphony* which derive either melodically or orchestrally from one or the other. This composition was written in 1903-1904, and received its first performance in Paris, February 28, 1904.

First Movement: Extrêmement lent, 4/2 time; Très vif, B flat major, 3/4 time. The introduction, thirteen measures long, presents the two generating motives. The first of these (Ex. 1),

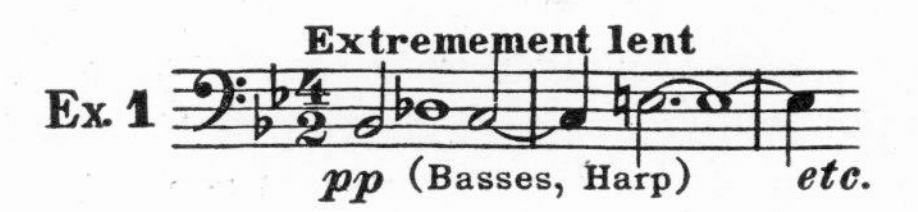

somewhat recalling the opening of Franck's *D Minor Symphony*, is heard in the basses and is followed immediately by the second motive (Ex. 2) in the woodwinds. The principal theme of the

"Très vif" which follows is sounded by horns over a reiterated-note string accompaniment. A transitional motive derived from the horn theme is presented first by itself, and later in conjunction with the first generative theme heard in the basses. The second theme, in F major and in a somewhat slower tempo, is given to the violins. The original tempo returns, and all the material previously announced is developed. A crescendo is climaxed by the return of the two principal themes. In what may be called the closing section, the transitional motive figures prominently.

Second Movement: Modérément lent, D flat major, 6/4 time.

Following a six-measure introduction, the violas, clarinets, and the English horn sing the lyric theme, a modified version of the second generative motive. Over a string pizzicato the harp plays a rather jerky motive, which becomes the accompaniment to an oboe melody, founded on the first generative motive. The oboe theme is continued in other instruments. The jerky figure recurs in the first violins, and is used as accompaniment to the principal theme of the movement, heard in the clarinet. After the preceding material is worked over, the principal subject returns for the last time in the clarinet, to close the movement softly.

Third Movement: Modéré, D minor, 2/4 time.

The "scherzo" or playful character of the movement is evidenced in the middle section. The movement opens with the principal theme, a tenderly simple, pastorale-like melody, in a solo viola. The muffled or "stopped" horn transition to the second theme is derived from the first generative motive. In a more animated tempo, the strings repeat a triplet figure for ten measures which is also based on the first generative motive. At the fourth measure, the second theme enters in the woodwinds. The dotted figure motive of the second movement is heard again, after which the woodwind theme enters in the trumpet. An animated triplet version of the solo viola theme is followed by the second theme in the brass. A sixteenth-note version of the first subject is heard and is succeeded by the opening theme, sung by the clarinet in its original tempo. The movement comes to an abrupt close with the last six measures in animated tempo.

Fourth Movement: Lent, B flat major, 4/4 time; Assez vif, B flat major, 5/4 time.

The slow first portion of the last movement is concerned with material previously heard. The two generative motives are combined in a fugal theme, the development of which leads to the faster section of the movement. Eight introductory measures in the violas precede the appearance of a flowing theme in the oboe. Material from all of the preceding movements is utilized and ingeniously combined. Toward the end of the movement, a choral version of the second generative motive is heard in the woodwinds, accompanied by the first generative motive in the capacity of bass. In this manner the symphony comes to its conclusion, leaving the listener to marvel at the masterpiece of ingenuity and technique which he has just heard, and in which may be found many of the earmarks of a great work.

SYMPHONY IN D MINOR

César Franck (December 10, 1822-November 8, 1890)

Franck's *D Minor Symphony* is one of the last and greatest of the list of superlative works written by that composer during the last twenty years of his long life. It is a remarkable fact, true of no other composer, that the works by which Franck is best known and which are, in truth, his best compositions, were written when he was past fifty years of age. The symphony, begun in 1886, was completed in 1888, when Franck was in his sixty-sixth year. However, it was not his first orchestral work; an earlier effort was an unpublished composition, *The Sermon on the Mount*, written almost forty years before. The first performance of the *D Minor Symphony* was given by the Société des Concerts du Conservatoire at Paris, February 11, 1889. According to D'Indy's account, given in his biography of Franck, the members of the orchestra were not at all well disposed toward the work, and it was only because of the uncompromising insistence of the conductor, Jules August Garcin, that the work was performed. One professor took occasion to censure, even condemn it because, said he, "who ever heard of a symphony with an English horn in it?" Gounod is supposed to have remarked that "the affirmation of impotence is elevated to a dogma," but considerable doubt exists as to whether he really did originate that critique.

While to the present-day listener the work may not seem revolutionary or so extremely different from contemporary productions as to cause any misunderstanding, certain factors affecting the symphony as well as its background must be considered. The French, who have been most consistently objective rather than subjective in the content of their music, have always leaned toward the operatic or the theatrical. Even Franck could not entirely escape this influence, as his early works indicate. He was saved from it, however, by the fact that he played the organ, an instrument which represents serenity, detachment, spirituality, and Bach. Furthermore, shy, gentle, and devout as he was, Franck became more and more a world unto himself, until in his final works we see the fruits of years of unconscious self-cultivation. It is not surprising that his works, self-contained and devoid of the kind of show to which the French concert-goer has become accustomed, were not seen in their true perspective at first. The point of view brought to bear on them was not consistent with the content of these works; until the inevitable re-orientation came about, partly as a result of his own teachings and his own works ("every great creator forms the taste by which he is to be appreciated"), it was to be expected that the popularity of his compositions should be delayed.

From a formal and idiomatic point of view, Franck's symphony, as well as the rest of his later works, is not nearly as obvious as it may seem on merely a casual acqaintance. Franck, in his chromaticism, in his disposition of the formal elements of the symphony perhaps even more than in the cyclic use of material (the utilization of the same themes or subjects throughout a work, which is analogous to the operatic *leitmotiv*), is as much the symphonic Wagnerian as is Bruckner. Characteristic of his idiom are the devices of rapidly shifting key centers, sudden and unexpected transitions, and long themes (the first phrase of his violin sonata is twenty-seven measures long). The symphony is a masterly work, wherein the craftsmanship is of the highest order throughout. The very defects spring from the virtues of the man. The traces of sentimentality, the fortissimo treatment of the principal theme of the second movement upon its recurrence in the last movement—these are the doings of a person who, removed from much worldly contact, simply fails to see that humanity at large will interpret or understand these things in a manner at variance with the composer's probable intentions. Powerfully imaginative, moving, and dramatic as it is, this symphony is deservedly one of the most popular in the orchestral repertoire.

First Movement: Lento, D minor, 4/4 time; Allegro manon troppo, D minor, 2/2 time.

The opening measures of the introduction (Lento) anticipate the principal theme of the Allegro. After the first statement of this theme, there is a literal repetition of the Lento and first Allegro sections in the key of F minor. The principal subject is based on the first (Ex. 1) of two "motto" motives which are

heard throughout the symphony. There is a transition section which leads to the key of F major, whereupon the second theme is presented. This consists of two parts, the latter of which is founded on the second "motto" motive (Ex. 2). It is this second

motive which is often referred to as Franck's "signature," because it is found so frequently in his other works. The development section makes use of both the first and the second themes. This is followed by a recapitulation of the principal subjects, and the movement ends with a closing section based on the two "motto" motives.

Second Movement: Allegretto, B flat minor, 3/4 time.

A sixteen-measure introduction, played by the harp and pizzicato strings, becomes the accompaniment for the first theme, a plaintive, haunting melody constructed from the first "motto" motive and played by the English horn. This is followed somewhat later by the first subordinate subject, which is derived from the second "motto" motive. A second subordinate subject then appears in the clarinet. Recapitulation of the principal and second subordinate themes is succeeded by a closing section which makes brief reference to both subordinate melodies. A partial statement of the second of these two themes brings the movement to a quiet and serene conclusion.

Third Movement: Allegro non troppo, D major, 2/2 time.

The principal theme is derived from the second subject of the first movement. This is followed, after a transition passage, by the second theme, which is a dialogue between the brass and the strings. The development section takes up, in order, the principal theme of the second movement and the first and second subjects of the last movement. After a pause, the orchestra embarks in a long crescendo, at the climax of which the principal theme is recapitulated. Instead of the original second subject, the first melody of the second movement is heard in a sonorous presentation which is somewhat too forced for the original content of the theme. The closing section of the movement is characterized by the return of the two main themes of the first movement. A triumphant enunciation of the principal subject of the last movement brings the symphony to its conclusion.

SYMPHONY NO. 8 IN B MINOR ("UNFINISHED")

Franz Schubert (January 31, 1797-November 19, 1828)

Probably the best known of Schubert's works is the *Unfinished Symphony,* which was written in 1822 when the composer was but twenty-five years of age. Numberless reasons have been advanced to explain why Schubert did not finish it. Some profess to see disappointment in love as the cause, but it is more probable that he put it aside either because he felt that no more was to be said, or because he intended to finish it later. At any rate, the symphony lacks a final movement, ending with what would ordinarily be the second movement. Schubert left one hundred and thirty measures of a third movement, but opinions differ sharply over the value of the fragment.

Unfinished as it is, the symphony was never heard by Schubert, for the first performance did not take place until thirty-seven years after his death, at which time one of Schubert's closest friends gave the manuscript to the eminent conductor Herbeck. Since its rescue from undeserved obscurity, the B minor symphony has become a standard and popular orchestral work.

First Movement: Allegro moderato, B minor, 3/4 time.

The first movement, which runs the gamut of musical emotion, opens with the first part of the first theme (Ex. 1), a low,

gloomy subject played by the basses and 'celli. After a few measures of interlude in the strings, the oboe and clarinet relieve the somber aspect of the beginning with the second part of the first theme (Ex. 2), a clear, simple melody which stands out in

bright color against the lower, repeated murmurs of the strings. A brief transition then leads to the waltz-like second theme (Ex. 3), a warmly emotional melody, which has been called the most

charming ever written. Extremely rich in feeling, this theme was used for one of Sigmund Romberg's best known songs, "Song of Love," from his light opera, *Blossom Time*.

Crashing chords break sharply into this atmosphere of love and beauty and lead to a repetition of the solemn theme heard in the beginning. This marks the beginning of the development section. Growing in color as instrument after instrument takes up the principal theme, the movement progresses to a flashing climax for the whole orchestra. This is followed by a stately, hymnlike development in the trombones. Recapitulation of the themes follows, and the movement ends on a note of infinite sadness as the strings mournfully intone the haunting melody of the principal theme.

Second Movement: Andante con moto, E major, 3/8 time.

Lovely, eloquent lyricism characterizes this movement. A descending line in the lower strings introduces the first subject (Ex. 4), a tender melody sung by the violins. This is interrupted

after a few bars by the opening idea, after which it continues serenely on its way. But sorrow and sadness return as sustained notes in the violins usher in the plaintive second subject (Ex. 5),

played by the clarinet against a syncopated string accompaniment. The oboe then takes up the theme, which develops into a loud, vigorous statement by the entire orchestra. The light and graceful first theme then returns, to be succeeded in due course of time by the second subject. Effective and touching use is made of the sustained tones which introduce the latter, as the movement ends in an atmosphere of intense emotion.

Throughout the entire work there is a consistency of inspiration, a pathos of utterance, that even the brilliant genius of Schubert could but rarely achieve, and never surpass. His *C Major Symphony* may be a more noble and austere work, but the deep, personal, and elevated emotion of the *Unfinished Symphony* always thrills its listeners.

SYMPHONY NO. 1 IN B FLAT MAJOR, OPUS 38

Robert Schumann (June 8, 1810-July 29, 1856)

Although the B flat symphony was published as Schumann's first, it was not his initial effort in this form. In the years 1832-1833 he had written a *Symphony in G minor*, the first movement of which was performed a number of times. The *B Flat Symphony* was begun in Leipzig, January, 1841, the first movement being completed February 4, the second and third, February 13, and the last movement, February 20. The work, Schumann tells us, was written with a steel pen which he had found lying on Schubert's grave in Vienna. The first performance of the work was a piano version played by Schumann at his home in Leipzig, February 14, 1841. At the first rehearsal, March 28, under Mendelssohn's direction, the opening two measures in the trumpets and horns were altered, because the original notes did not sound well on the valveless instruments of that time. The first performance was given March 31, 1841, at a concert given by Clara Schumann for the Gewandhaus Orchestral Pension fund. It was extremely successful. The orchestral parts were published in 1841, the score in 1853.

Three factors greatly influenced the conception of this work. The first was Schumann's happiness with Clara Schumann, the second was the very feeling of spring, and the third was a poem by his friend Adolf Böttger.

Concerning the first, Schumann had by 1840 overcome the obstacle of Wieck's objection to his marriage with Clara, and the naturally joyous reaction contributed to the happiness and lightness found in the symphony. As for the second influence, he wrote in a letter to a friend: "During the last two days I have finished, in sketch at least, a labor which has filled me with joy, which has almost exhausted me. Just think of it, a whole symphony, and what is more, a 'Spring Symphony'." The work was written, to quote Schumann again, "in the vernal longing which influences men until they grow aged, an emotion which surprises them every year."

The poem of Böttger is somber until the last line, wherein the poet exclaims: "O turn, O turn thy course, in the valley blooms the Spring." On Schumann's picture, presented to the poet by the composer, the latter had written under the opening measures of the symphony: "Beginning of a symphony, suggested by a poem of Adolf Böttger. To the poet in remembrance of Robert Schumann."

First Movement: Andante un poco maestoso, B flat major, 4/4 time; Allegro molto vivace, B flat major, 2/4 time.

Thirty-eight measures of introduction lead through a gradual increase in volume and speed into the main body of the movement. The principal theme (Ex. 1) is derived from the opening

measures of the introduction. It is worked over, and is then followed by the light, graceful second theme in the clarinet and bassoon. The development is concerned with the first part of the principal theme. Particularly effective use is made of the triangle. After the recapitulation, the movement concludes with a closing section which utilizes new material in the last portion.

Second Movement: Larghetto, E flat major, 3/8 time.

The violins sing a serenely beautiful lyric, (Ex. 2) which is

in turn taken up by 'cello, oboe, and horn, each reappearance of the theme being more richly orchestrated. This slow movement passes without pause into the scherzo, the theme of which is anticipated by a somber phrase in the trombone.

Third Movement: Scherzo, Molto vivace, D minor, 3/4 time.

The first theme (Ex. 3) begins, not in the principal key of

the movement, but in G minor. It is a virile but heavy, typically German theme which embodies the composer's characteristic syncopations. There are two subsidiary sections, or "trios." The first, in D major, is characterized by alternate passages in the woodwinds and strings. The second begins with soft woodwind chords above an ascending passage in the strings. Each trio is preceded and followed by the scherzo theme. A closing section, or "coda," based on the scherzo theme and the first trio, concludes the movement.

Fourth Movement: Allegro animato e grazioso, B flat major, 4/4 time.

This vivacious, cheery movement is a joy from first to last. A fortissimo passage for the whole orchestra opens the movement. The rhythm of this passage is used much later in the composition. The principal theme is a light, airy melody in the first violins (Ex. 4). The transition to the second theme, a combina-

tion of woodwinds and pizzicato strings, is reminiscent of the "Canzonetta" of Mendelssohn's string quartet, Opus 11. The second theme, in F major, is given to the clarinet and bassoon, and is continued by the oboe until a fortissimo by the full orchestra is reached. The rhythm of this "tutti" is that of the introduction which opens the movement. The same phrase is made much of in the development. A frank and unashamed flute cadenza conducts this lovely and lively work to a "happy ending."

Conductors have attempted to remedy Schumann's obviously inexpert orchestration, and sometimes with good effect. Where, however, some have gone to the length of a complete reorchestration, the result is frequently one that contradicts the nature of Schumann's original content. For that reason the original, with all its defects of instrumentation, is much to be preferred.

DEATH AND TRANSFIGURATION, OPUS 24

Richard Strauss (June 11, 1864-)

Death and Transfiguration, one of Strauss's most popular works, was written in 1889, when the composer was only twenty-five years of age. The first performance of this "tone-poem" was given at Eisenach, and was conducted by the composer. The published score is prefaced by a poem written by Alexander Ritter. It was the latter who influenced Strauss to divert his energies in the direction of program music, a course which Strauss eventually found most compatible with his genius. The poem, which was written *after* the music had been composed, faithfully offers a tangible index not only of the mood pervading the work, but also of the details of its development.

The story is as follows: "A sick man lies alone on his bed. The fever throbs and pulses through his veins. A moment of suspended tranquillity, and suddenly the dim vision of Death appears and struggles with the fevered mortal, attempting to wrest from him his final breath. Exhausted, on the threshold of a new existence, the man falls back. There pass before his recollection the innocent days of childhood, the youth come to man's estate, the yearning and the aspiration toward some vaguely felt ultimate, seeking ever, one against a heartless world—seeking ever and in vain. Suddenly, Death's hammer strikes, and the soul takes leave of its corporeal vestment. It ascends to the Empyrean, and in its transfiguration finds what it had vainly sought before."

The music can be clearly followed with the poem as a guide. The throbbing fever is represented by the irregular pulsating rhythm in the violas as the work opens. The joys of childhood, the pleasures of manhood, the struggle, the ceaseless, yearning aspiration—all these are clearly delineated. The theme of trans-

figuration (Ex. 1), a triumphantly ascending motive, is the subject on which the last portion of the work is based.

The thematic material of this tone-poem, in common with that of the majority of Strauss's works, does not equal in quality the breadth of imagination and conception, the truly marvelous instrumentation which characterize his best compositions. Nevertheless, *Death and Transfiguration* is among his best works, for it is clearer and better organized than many of his later, more complex compositions.

EIN HELDENLEBEN (A HERO'S LIFE), OPUS 40

Richard Strauss

Despite Strauss's assertions that his *Hero's Life* is generic rather than personal or individual in conception, representing the idea and ideal of heroism striving against inner and outer obstacles to elevation, three facts would seem to indicate that the "Hero" of this particular story is none other than Strauss himself. These facts are the following: (1) The organization and content of the work not only lend themselves to, but demand biographical interpretation; (2) there are quotations in the closing section of this composition of passages from Strauss' own preceding works; and (3) a program has been provided for the work by Wilhelm Klatte, a student of Strauss. This program follows the music so closely that one is very much tempted to accept the assertion that Strauss himself may have inspired it. The following summary is founded on Klatte's analysis.

The score consists of six sections. The first part, "The Hero," opens with the horns, violas and 'cellos presenting an upsurging

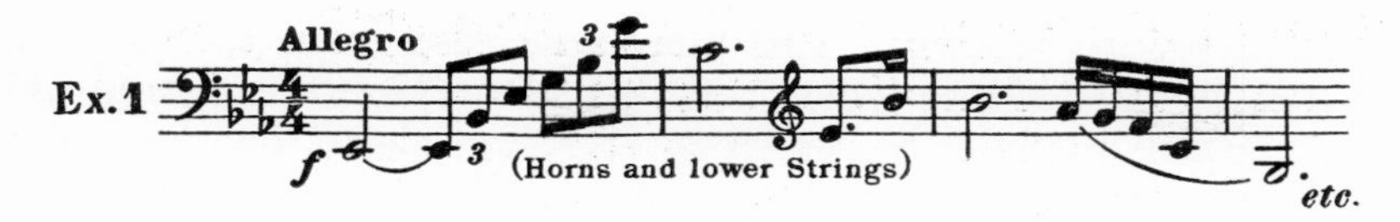

theme (Ex. 1) of gigantic span and range. Subsidiary portions of the theme, given considerable development, represent, according to Klatte, various positive qualities of the Hero.

In the second section, "The Hero's Adversaries," are represented those individuals who, lacking in greatness themselves, fail to comprehend that quality in the Hero. The spiteful, biting, satirical passages in the woodwinds serve the double purpose of delineating and scathingly denouncing the small-souled enemies of the Hero. Strauss has neither admitted nor denied that the "enemies" herein referred to are the critics who had condemned and attacked his music. Certain rule-book violations in the tubas indicate the sullen vindictiveness of the "enemies." The Hero, however, successfully overcomes his adversaries.

"The Hero's Companion," his loved one, is introduced in the third section of the poem. She is delineated by a coquettish theme in the solo violin. At first she coyly eludes the Hero's advances. The music develops in passion and intensity, and the oboe sings a tender melody to which the violin responds. The Hero has found his companion, and even the distant ominous sound of the adversaries cannot disrupt this new-found happiness.

By reason of its content, the fourth section, "The Hero's Battlefield," is almost inevitably naïve throughout, and at times it is even banal. Drums and trumpets and all the trappings of war are here. Even after the Hero's victory in battle, the sluggish tuba rumblings, recollections which plague the Hero's soul, are heard. But a promise of happier moments is brought forward by a subject in the violas and clarinet.

The maturing of the Hero's soul is represented in the fifth section, "The Hero's Mission of Peace." As happens when one embarks on a new course, the Hero looks back in retrospect, and there pass before his recollection his earlier achievements—"Macbeth," "Zarathustra," "Don Juan," "Death and Transfiguration," "Guntram." One is led to infer either that the references are irrelevant, or else that the work is frankly autobiographical.

In the sixth section, "The Hero's Release from the World," the indifference of the world which had previously angered him now awakens in the Hero an elevated resignation. Thematic material associated with past sections returns. Calmly and severely, the "Hero" theme in augmented form ascends in the trumpets, and in this mood of calm serenity the movement closes.

SYMPHONY NO. 5 IN E MINOR, OPUS 64

Peter Ilyitch Tschaikowsky (May 7, 1840-November 6, 1893)

Tschaikowsky composed his first four symphonies between 1868 and 1877. During the next eleven years he devoted his time chiefly to the composition of operas, and it was not until 1888 that Tschaikowsky again undertook the composition of a symphony. In June of that year he wrote to his generous friend, Nadezhda von Meck: "I am anxious to prove to others as well as to myself that I am not yet finished as a composer. Have I not informed you that I intend to write a symphony? Though the beginning was not easy, now inspiration seems to have come. We shall see." The *Fifth Symphony,* to which this letter refers, was completed on August 26, 1888. Friends to whom he showed the work were all very favorably impressed.

The first performance of the *E Minor Symphony* took place in St. Petersburg on November 17, 1888, under the direction of the composer. The work was immediately acclaimed by the public, and unanimously condemned by the critics. On March 11th of the following year, Tschaikowsky went to Hamburg during the course of a concert tour. His *Fifth Symphony* was to receive its first performance in that city on the 14th. Brahms happened to be visiting the city at the time, and he delayed his departure in order to attend the first rehearsal of the new work. The two composers had luncheon together after the rehearsal, and each took advantage of the opportunity to express, politely but honestly, a mutual dislike for the other's music. At this, their first and last meeting, both parted in a friendly manner. Two temperaments so diverse could scarcely have been expected to understand each other's music to the extent of liking it.

The symphony, dedicated to Theodore Ave Lallement, Committee Chairman of the Hamburg Philharmonic Society, was published in 1889. Although Tschaikowsky at no time indicated as much, there can be no doubt that some program for the work existed in his mind. The "motto" theme, which frequently jars incongruously with the other textual material, offers some corroboration for this supposition. Implications of tragedy, of an inescapable destiny, are indicated in this work. However, the transformation of the "motto" theme into the major key at the close may be interpreted as the triumph of Will over Fate. This music demonstrates the possibility of a destiny that, despite earlier conflicts, may assume a positive guise rather than, as in the *Sixth Symphony*, a hopelessly negative one.

First Movement: Andante, E minor, 4/4 time; Allegro con anima, E minor, 6/8 time.

The opening subject of the introduction is the "motto" theme (Ex. 1), a morbidly solemn motive, present in every movement of

the symphony. The principal subject of the movement proper (Ex. 2) is derived from a Polish folk song. After a climax, the

second theme (Ex. 3), in B minor, is played by the strings. The

development section which follows makes use of both the first and the second themes. These themes are heard again in recapitulation, and the movement concludes with a lengthy closing section based on the principal theme.

Second Movement: Andante cantabile, con alcuna licenza, D major, 12/8 time.

Dark, sustained chords in the strings introduce a beautiful horn solo (Ex. 4), a melody that is one of Tschaikowsky's finest

expressions. Two new themes are stated by the woodwinds, and the movement ends somberly with a quiet reference to the second subject.

Third Movement: Valse; Allegro moderato, A major, 3/4 time.

Although it might at first seem inappropriate to replace the customary scherzo movement of a symphony with a waltz, the substitution is here accomplished with a saving restraint and taste. The first theme (Ex. 5) is presented by the violins. This is soon

followed by a contrasting middle section, which eventually leads to a restatement of the first subject. The foreboding "motto" theme is heard again near the end of the movement.

Fourth Movement: Andante maestoso, E major, 4/4 time; Allegro vivace, E minor, 2/2 time.

The introduction, which leads directly into the final Allegro, utilizes the "motto" theme in the major key. The vigorous first subject (Ex. 6) is then presented by the strings. After some

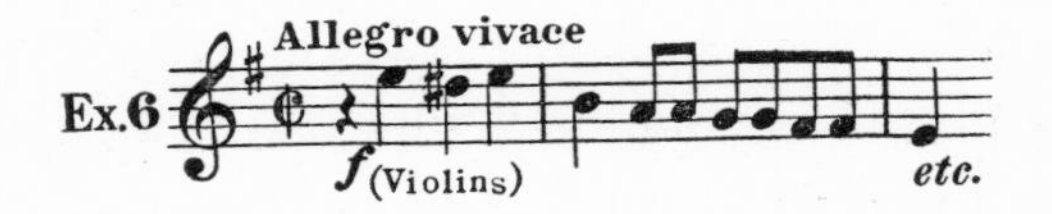

transitional material, the lovely second theme (Ex. 7) is introduced by the wind instruments, in the key of D major. The "motto" theme abruptly interrupts the mood, and the development of the two main themes of the movement follows. The first and second subjects are eventually recapitulated. During the course of this section the "motto" theme assumes more and more importance, finally bursting forth in a broad major utterance, first in the strings and then in the brass. The symphony closes triumphantly with a reference to the principal theme of the first movement.

SYMPHONY NO. 6 ("PATHETIC"), IN B MINOR, OPUS 74

Peter Ilyitch Tschaikowsky

Tschaikowsky was convinced from the very first that his *Sixth Symphony* represented his finest work. In this he was not mistaken, for it is without question the best organized of his works, and the dramatic and imaginative qualities which distinguished his compositions are here most consistently and congruously utilized. In December, 1892, while on a journey to Paris, the idea of the symphony first occurred to him. He outlined in his mind the plan of the whole composition. In a letter to his nephew, Vladimir Davydov, to whom the extremely devoted uncle dedicated this symphony, Tschaikowsky emphasized the fact that the last movement would not be the conventional Allegro, but an Adagio. The first movement was finished in four days; the remainder, however, did not come so easily and occasioned the composer considerably more effort than did this first portion. The work was completed in October, 1893, at Klin, where Tschaikowsky had taken a country house.

The first performance of the symphony was given at a program of the Imperial Russian Musical Society on October 28,

1893, under Tschaikowsky's direction. The composer was considerably disappointed by the lack of enthusiasm with which the new work was received by both the orchestra and the public. That there was at first a lack of that profoundly moved feeling and great enthusiasm with which the work was subsequently greeted may have been due in great part to Tschaikowsky's own diffident conducting, for his powers as a director were scarcely commensurate with his abilities as a composer. The day after the performance the work was to be sent to the publishers, and even then Tschaikowsky was undecided as to the title. Among those considered were "Tragic Symphony" and "Program Symphony." Suddenly the word "Pathetic" occurred to Modeste, the composer's brother; his suggestion was enthusiastically accepted by Peter, who immediately affixed the title by which the work is usually known (although the English prefer to call it the "Suicide Symphony"). Nine days after the first performance, Tschaikowsky died of cholera. He had written his own requiem.

First Movement: Adagio, E minor, 4/4 time; Allegro non troppo, B minor, 4/4 time.

The Adagio introduction opens, not in B minor, but in E minor. Over chords in the lower strings, the bassoon anticipates the principal theme of the Allegro. The key shifts to B minor and the Allegro opens with the questioning main theme (Ex. 1)

in the violas and immediately after in the flute. This material works up to a climax, which is followed by alternate passages in the strings and winds. Under somber, foreboding chords in the tuba and trombones, the cellos mutter darkly. The second theme in introduced in D major by the violins and cellos, and is repeated after a dialogue between the flute and the bassoon. Softly, the clarinet sings part of the theme again. The development opens with a sudden, crashing chord, which is followed by agitatedly rushing passages in the strings. Material derived from the first and second themes is worked over. At the climax of a great crescendo, the principal theme returns. The striking transition passage to the second theme which follows has been termed by D. F. Tovey "the climax of Tschaikowsky's artistic career as well as of this work." Recapitulation of the second theme is followed by an effectively simple closing section. A solemn chant in the brass over a descending pizzicato passage closes the movement.

Second Movement: Allegro con grazia, D major, 5/4 time.

The theme (Ex. 2) in the cello provides the material for the whole first section. The subsidiary section in B minor opens with a new theme in the violins over reiterated "D's" in the drums and bass instruments. After several anticipatory passages in the winds, the principal theme is again heard in the strings.

Third Movement: Allegro molto vivace, G major, 12/8 time.

This splendid movement opens with a bustling but quiet triplet figure in strings and woodwinds; on its second appearance, this theme accompanies a distinctive motive (Ex. 3) which anticipates

the subject of the march to follow. The march theme appears first in the clarinet, with the triplet accompaniment in the strings. The first portion of the movement is then repeated and extended in an intensified crescendo which culminates in a tremendous restatement of the march theme by the full orchestra.

Fourth Movement: Adagio lamentoso, B minor, 3/4 time.

The desperately tragic first subject (Ex. 4) appears in the

first and second violins, which play alternate notes of the melody. Over a syncopated triplet figure in the horns the second theme, in D major, is given to the violins and violas. This material is worked up to a climax, after which the first despairing theme returns. It, too, is developed to an intense climax, and then the music quietly dies away as the softly ominous knell of a gong is heard. The strings bring forward material derived from the second theme. This finds ultimate rest as the basses intone a repeated "B," and the music despairingly and wearily comes to a close.

PRELUDE TO "DIE MEISTERSINGER VON NÜRNBERG"

Richard Wagner (May 22, 1813-February 13, 1883)

Wagner first considered the subject of *Die Meistersinger* as potential operatic material in 1845. Gyrawetz and Lortzing had both written operas centered about Hans Sachs, and it is not improbable that Lortzing's work, in particular, had some influence in determining Wagner's choice of subject in this instance. In 1861 he began to work on the libretto while in Paris. Composition of the music was begun the following year, and the opera was completed in 1867. The first performance of the work took place in Munich on June 21, 1868. Although the performance lasted five hours, the opera was enthusiastically welcomed.

The prelude, however, had been performed as an independent composition at a concert in Leipzig, six years before the opera was produced. The two compositions of Wagner on this program, the prelude to *Die Meistersinger* and the overture to *Tannhäuser*, were directed by the composer. Although, as Wagner writes in his autobiography, "The public stayed away *en masse*, apparently in response to a sign from the leaders of the regular subscription concerts," the work was so well received that it was repeated there and then.

The overture opens with the pompous, assertive *Meistersinger* subject. After this material is worked over in a rather lengthy passage, the energy of which never flags for a moment, there is a sudden transition to a more lyric mood, established by presentation of the theme associated with the romance of Walther and Eva. This is played in turn by the flute, oboe, and clarinet. A brilliant unison passage in the violins introduces the "Banner" theme, a march-like melody. Introduced by a restless, syncopated figure in the strings (the "Longing" motive), the violins play a part of the Prize Song. A syncopated motive derived from the latter is used to build up a climax which, at its height, suddenly breaks off in a sharp chord, and the woodwinds present a humorous version of the *Meistersinger* theme. The strings enter and work up to the remarkable passage wherein three themes are presented simultaneously: the *Meistersinger* theme, the "Banner" theme, and the lyric *Prize Song*. In spite of their contrasting natures, each of these themes maintains its own distinct and characteristic individuality. The "Banner" theme heard in the brass is developed to a tremendous climax, at which point the whole orchestra thunders forth the *Meistersinger* subject, which, with the addition of a short peroration, concludes the work.

This overture is distinguished by the masterly treatment of its interwoven melodies, by a positive assertiveness in its moods, whether these assume the guise of the lyricism of Walther or the dogmatism of the "Guild" themes, and by a superlative orchestral texture, the consequence of the complex melodic treatment. Aggressive almost to the point of brutality, it has none of that quality of decadence which Friedrich Nietzsche professed to find in it, but is, on the contrary, one of Wagner's healthiest works.

PRELUDE AND "ISOLDE'S LOVE DEATH" FROM TRISTAN AND ISOLDE

Richard Wagner

Wagner had become familiar with the "Tristan" legend at the time he was a youth living in Dresden. About the year 1854 he read and was much influenced by Schopenhauer's "World as Will and Idea," which served him as a direct stimulus. "I felt," he writes in his autobiography, "the longing to express myself in poetry." This must have been partly due to the serious mood, created by Schopenhauer, which was trying to find ecstatic expression. It was under the influence of a mood such as this that Wagner conceived his opera *Tristan and Isolde*. Wagner's attention was further attracted to the subject by a poem founded on the "Tristan" legend and submitted to the composer by Karl Ritter, a young poet friend of his.

However, more personal influences were to affect Wagner's selection and treatment of the "Tristan" plot. In 1852, while in Zurich, Switzerland, he met Mathilde Wesendonck, the wife of a wealthy merchant. Wesendonck owned a good deal of land in Zurich, on which he had erected a large villa. Wagner rented a small cottage nearby from the merchant, and the friendship between the composer and Mme. Wesendonck ripened into something far more significant. The increasingly strained relationship between Otto Wesendonck, his wife, Wagner, and the latter's wife Minna, suddenly came to an issue when Minna intercepted a note Wagner had written to Mathilde. Wesendonck averted scandalous complications with admirable tact, and Wagner moved to Italy to work on his opera.

The prelude was orchestrated immediately after the first act of the opera had been sketched. The third and final act was completed at Lucerne, Switzerland, in August, 1859. Wagner had gone to this city with Wesendonck's permission, and he remained on at least outwardly friendly terms with the family. In a letter written to Mathilde in 1861, he said: "The main object of my ambition remains to produce *Tristan.* Once that is accomplished, I have little left to do in this world. I owe the fact that I have composed *Tristan* to you; and for that I thank you from the depths of my heart for all eternity."

The opera was first produced under the patronage of Ludwig II, King of Bavaria, in Munich, June 10, 1865, and it was enthusiastically received. However, as in the case of *Die Meistersinger,* the prelude, in conjunction with the final scene of the third act (the "Love Death"), had previously been performed at Prague, March 12, 1859, under the direction of Hans von Bülow. The title "Liebestod" had first been applied to the last scene of the act by Liszt, in his piano transcription of that portion of the opera. Wagner himself had used this term in connection with the prelude, but it is Liszt's meaning of the expression which has endured. Wagner's programme for the prelude and final scene, as he himself described it at a concert in Vienna in 1863, was as follows: "*Tristan and Isolde*—(a) Prelude (Love Death). Tristan, as bridal envoy, conducts Isolde to his uncle, the King. They love each other. From the first stifled moan of quenchless longing, from the faintest tremor to overflowing avowal of a hopeless love, the heart goes through each phase of unvictorious battling with its inner fever, till, swooning back upon itself, it seems extinguished as in death. (b) Conclusion (Transfiguration). Yet what Fate divided for this life, in death revives transfigured; the gate of union opens.

Above the corpse of Tristan, dying Isolde sees transcendent consummation of their passionate desire, eternal union in unmeasured realms, nor bond, nor barrier, indivisible."

The prelude utilizes the principal leading motives of the music drama, particularly the "Desire" theme (Ex. 1), which opens the

work, and the motive representing Isolde's magic powers (Ex. 2).

The dynamic plan of this prelude, like that of *Lohengrin,* is one long, unbroken curve, which begins quietly, rises to a great climax, and then subsides. It may be added that the dynamic pattern in *Tristan* is one of emotion as well as of acoustics. The opening bars are literally flesh-quivering in their sensuousness. The musical material of the "Love Death," which usually follows the prelude in concert performances, is drawn principally from the love duet in the second act. The opening theme (Ex. 3) has an abstract mean-

ing which has not been definitely deciphered. This material is in turn derived from the song "Träume," the text for which had been written by Mathilde Wesendonck in 1857. In the "Love Death," Isolde sings her impassioned, ecstatic song over the lifeless body of Tristan, who had died in her arms. Beginning quietly, the music gradually rises to greater and greater heights, finally achieving that "transcendent consummation" wherein life and death become absorbed in, and are conquered by, the tragic and fateful love of two mortals whose passion had first bound them, and had then brought them release.

Courtesy The Art Institute of Chicago

CROSS SECTION AND PLAN OF THE STUTTGART OPERA
(From an 18th Century French Dictionary of the Theater.)

OPERA: UNION OF MUSIC AND DRAMA

ORIGINS OF OPERA

ITALY WAS THE BIRTHPLACE of the earliest known opera, *Dafne*. The text was written by the poet, Rinuccini, and the music by the composers Peri and Caccini, in 1597. In 1600 the same three men collaborated in producing *Euridice*, which was first performed in Florence. The name "opera," however, was not at that time applied to this art form.

These men endeavored to revive, in a way, the form in which ancient Greek tragedy had been produced. It was really recitative, (singing in a speaking style), accompanied by music. To accompany *Euridice* only four instruments were used. In 1607, however, *Orfeo*, by Claudio Monteverdi, was given at Mantua, with forty accompanying instruments.

The first public opera house was built in Venice in 1637. Up to that time opera had been for the nobility and aristocracy only. When the opera was made available to the general public, the libretto ranked first in importance. As people became more and more interested in display and sensational spectacles, dramatic values became less and less important, and the accompanying music became more and more a miscellaneous collection of popular melodies. The chorus decreased in importance until it finally disappeared and the opera became a series of vocal solos.

ITALIAN OPERA BECOMES DOMINANT

In Italy the public was content with operas in which vocal display was their sole reason for being. However, when Handel in 1711 took Italian opera to London, the reaction of the English was quite different. Its absurdities were ridiculed and the use of the Italian language on an English stage was protested.

Meanwhile, in Italy, the composer Alessandro Scarlatti (1659-1725) was writing operas in which he sacrificed dramatic values to the music. He is sometimes called the originator of the *da capo* aria. In this form of aria we have a first melodic section followed by a second section, and then the first repeated. Da

Capo means repeated "from the beginning." The type of opera that Scarlatti wrote became popular with succeeding Italian composers, and became more fixed in form as time went on. It was called *Opera Seria,* and since its chief aim was to display the technique of the singers, it consisted of a succession of arias of set form. For about a century, Italian opera composers wrote in this style.

OPERA BUFFA

At the same time Opera Seria was developing, a lighter, gayer type called *Opera Buffa* was gaining in popularity. It contained much humorous dialogue, which at first was spoken, but which later became recitative, with light accompaniment.

The orchestra began to have more importance at the beginning of the nineteenth century in the operas of Gioacchino Rossini (1792-1868). His arias were brilliant and florid, and were so well written for all types of voices that many famous singers were brought forward during his time. His successors, Gaetano Donizetti (1797-1848), and Vincenzo Bellini (1801-1835), wrote in his style. *Il Barbiere di Siviglia* (The Barber of Seville), Rossini's masterpiece, was first given in Rome in 1816.

Courtesy *Musical Leader*

LAWRENCE TIBBETT AS "RIGOLETTO"

VERDI AND ITALIAN OPERA

Before the passing of Donizetti, Giuseppe Verdi (1813-1901) had written several operas. His career was a long one, his last opera, *Falstaff,* having been written when he was eighty years old. Although he produced *Oberto* in 1839, and *Ernani* in 1844, *Rigoletto* (1851) was his first important work. Within two years it was followed by *Il Trovatore* and *La Traviata,* and in 1862 *La Forza del Destino* was performed. Verdi's masterpiece, however, was *Aïda,* produced in 1871.

Verdi was still writing in the old Italian forms when Wagner was beginning to make drastic reforms in German opera. His last opera shows the influence of Wagner's changes without losing any of the melodic beauty of his earlier works. His form is free, and his melody rich and spontaneous, but he did not neglect the orchestra, which comes in for its full share of importance. Verdi's fine sense of balance makes his works sincere and strong.

MODERN COMPOSERS OF ITALIAN OPERA

As in some of the operas of Verdi, realism came to the fore in the operas of Mascagni (1863-) and Leoncavallo (1858-1919). These were sordid presentations of real life, with poignantly expressive music. Illustrative of this type are *Cavalleria Rusticana* (1890) by Mascagni, and *I Pagliacci* (1892) by Leoncavallo.

Giacomo Puccini (1858-1924), who is best known for his opera *Madam Butterfly,* has given us colorful and melodic music which is very effective dramatically, and the tradition of improving operatic technique in Italian opera has been carried on by such composers as Giordano, Alfano, Montemezzi, and Respighi.

THE DEVELOPMENT OF THE OPERA IN FRANCE

The earliest form of French opera was derived from the ballet, from which it takes its spectacular and scenic characteristics. Lully (1633-1687), who had come from Italy to the French Court in the time of Louis XIV, was the first composer of prominence in the new field of French opera. With his librettist Quinault, he produced a number of grand operas which accorded perfectly with the taste of the French people. The style was formal, but his works show progress in the use of the orchestra. From his time until that of Gluck, his form of overture was used.

Rameau (1683-1764) built upon the style of Lully, but lent importance to the orchestra and to the use of harmonic variation.

GREAT CHANGES

By far the greatest reform in French opera was brought about by Christoph Willibald Gluck (1714-1787). Starting his musical career in Italy, he early realized the necessity for a change in the style of Italian opera. He believed that the music should be related to the text to effect more dramatic expression. He made little progress with these changes either in Italy or in Vienna, where opera was under Italian influence. After collaborating with the poet Calzabigi in the production of *Orfeo, Alceste*, and *Paride e Elena*, he left Vienna and went to Paris. Here there was open conflict between him and the followers of Puccini, a strict Italian formalist brought to Paris by Gluck's adversaries.

Gluck was so successful in his improvements, however, that even Puccini imitated him, and Paris became the focal point for operatic progress. Many foreign composers sympathetic to Gluck's type of opera went there to make their contributions to the progress of opera in France. Among the men who followed in Gluck's footsteps were Spontini (1774-1851) and Halévy (1779-1862). The *Opéra Comique* was also enlivening Paris at this time.

MEYERBEER

However, the next great contributor to the operatic field was Giacomo Meyerbeer (1791-1863). His works show much dramatic variety and require great skill on the part of the performers, but, because of technical weaknesses, he was not able to make the most of his ideas. His best-known operas are *Robert le Diable* (1831), *Les Huguenots* (1836), *Le Prophète* (1849), *Dinorah* (1859) and *L'Africaine* (1863). So important was Meyerbeer's contribution to opera in France that he is sometimes called the "Father of Modern French Opera."

Stress upon the importance of the text was continued by Gounod whose *Faust* (1859), with its heart interest in an age-old human problem, still holds a prominent place in operatic repertoires. Bizet's *Carmen* (1875) is an opera of similar type.

Increased stress on human problems is noted in Charpentier's *Louise* (1900) and in Debussy's *Pelléas et Mélisande* (1902). The works of these two composers are characterized by dramatic strength, while those of their contemporary, Jules Massenet, are less dramatic and more concerned with melodic flow.

IN GERMANY

As the early opera in Germany was under Italian influence, its characteristics were much the same as those of the first Italian opera. We shall therefore begin our résumé of German opera with

Courtesy The Art Institute of Chicago

SIEVERT'S DRAWING FOR SETTING OF MOZART'S "COSI FAN TUTTE"

Wolfgang Amadeus Mozart (1756-1791). He had great skill in emotional expression and in the depiction of character. The influence of the Italian Opera Buffa can be seen in his *Le Nozze di Figaro* (The Marriage of Figaro) (1786) and *Don Giovanni* (1787), for which he used Italian libretti. However, for *Die Zauberflöte* (The Magic Flute) (1791) Mozart used a German libretto, and both libretto and plot show more influence of the old German folk theater.

After Mozart, and following his style, but also adding much from his own rich personality, came Beethoven (1770-1827). He made much use of the orchestra for expressing emotions, particularly in *Fidelio* (1805). Mozart and Beethoven together launched the romantic movement in opera. This reached its height in the works of Carl Maria von Weber (1786-1826). Supernatural subjects and stories which had their source in folk traditions were popular during the romantic periods, and the harmony and orchestration were colorful. *Der Freischütz,* produced in 1821, is an excellent example of romantic opera. In the operas composed by the inspired genius, Weber, may be traced ideas which later grew and developed in the hands of Wagner.

WAGNER, THE GREAT REFORMER

Richard Wagner (1813-1883) initiated startling changes in opera. He revolted against old traditions, and placed stress upon the orchestra's part in the plot development. Ornament which did not contribute to the opera other than as embellishment was rejected, time-worn melodic formulas were cast aside, and the libretti were made as important as the music. Fortunately Wagner had great poetic genius, and was able to carry out his ideal of having words and music created by the same brain. *Leitmotivs,* or guiding-themes, were used to identify recurring emotions, or certain characters in the story. Among Wagner's most important operas are *Rienzi* (1842) which, however, followed earlier models, *Der Fliegende Holländer* (The Flying Dutchman), produced in 1843, *Tannhäuser* (1845,) and *Lohengrin* (1850). Then came the magnificent tetralogy, *Der Ring des Nibelungen* (The Ring of the Nibelungs), on which Wagner worked from 1848 to 1876. The welding of words and music reaches its pinnacle in *Tristan* (1865), *Parsifal* (1862), and *Die Meistersinger* (1868).

Among the followers of Wagner we find Humperdinck (1858-1921) best known for his popular *Hänsel and Gretel,* the libretto of which has its source in German folklore.

TORSTEN'S DRAWING OF THE GHOST SHIP, SETTING FOR "THE FLYING DUTCHMAN"

Courtesy The Art Institute of Chicago

The most important composer of operas since Wagner is Richard Strauss (1864-). He is also one of the greatest writers for the symphony. His *Salome* (1905) and *Elektra* (1909) are examples of stark realism, but *Der Rosenkavalier* (The Cavalier of the Rose) (1911) is in a different vein, that of humor and satire.

IN ENGLAND

English opera has always been influenced by foreign traditions. Purcell (1658-1695), a native English composer, left one opera, *Dido and Aeneas*, which presaged a great operatic future, but his early demise probably deprived England of a greater place in the development of opera. Handel in 1711 (as previously mentioned) brought Italian opera to England, and it was not favorably received. In its place arose the ballad-opera, typically an English form. The first of these was Gay's *Beggar's Opera* (1728).

Notable in the nineteenth century are *The Bohemian Girl*, by Balfe, first performed in 1843, and the refreshing light operas of Gilbert and Sullivan.

IN RUSSIA

Glinka (1803-1857) was the first Russian composer to cast off the Italian style and write operas which were truly Russian in character. His *A Life for the Tsar* and *Russlan and Ludmilla* are definite expressions of national feeling. Another important Russian, who wrote in a declamatory manner, was Dargomyzhsky (1813-1837), whose style influenced later writers.

The operas most significantly Russian in character are Moussorgsky's *Boris Godounov*, first produced in 1874, which showed the influence of Dargomyzhsky, and *Khowantchina* in 1886; *Prince Igor* (1890) by Borodin, which is more lyrical in character, and two outstanding operas by Rimsky-Korsakov, *Sadko* (1898) and *Coq d'Or*, first performed in 1910. Both the lyrical and declamatory styles are used by Korsakov.

IN THE UNITED STATES

In the United States few outstanding native operas have been produced although opera performances have been given since early in the eighteenth century. Some of the most recent American operas produced have been *The King's Henchman*, by Deems Taylor, first given in 1927, *The Emperor Jones* by Gruenberg (1933), *Merry Mount* by Hanson (1933), and Walter Damrosch's *The Man Without a Country* (1937).

SOME POST-WAGNERIAN OPERA

In the stress and change going on in all music the opera has suffered most. Ever since Wagner its very existence has been threatened, artistically as well as economically. Artistically this influence springs from increased appreciation of music which is supposed to be deeper as well as "purer" or more "absolute." There are many who look upon the union of music, words, and action as illegitimate, and as being unworthy of a great art which is supposed to be the most expressive. Most musicians, however, admit that music can be a medium for corporeality, for the sensuous, for the palpable. Some composers abandon the love-duet as an unnecessary device. Others attempt to make opera, whose literature, acting, poetry, and music, make it the most universal art, an absolute, or abstract, medium, robbed of all objectivity.

The practical problem of the union of action and words is being approached in many ways. Since the contemporary trend in music is to make it nonsensuous, opera is bound to suffer, for it cannot be made completely spiritual. Much use is made of what are called "spoken melodies": in the recitative the rhythmic details are not noted. As the singer comprehends and feels the poetic phrase, he has to create the rhythm on a tune the pitch of which is approximated by a half-note. A new artistic expression is being developed in the passing from song into rhythmic speech. Much Negro influence can be traced in many of these new efforts.

SCHÖNBERG

A most curious, but also a most notable example of this new "spoken song" is Schönberg's *Pierrot Lunaire*, a cycle of poems of Albert Giraud, translated by Otto Erich, and set by Schönberg for recitation or declamation to music (the German "Sprechgesang"). The inflections of human speech are followed, and they reveal a true speech-melody. This is unlike anything preceding which can be called music, but it is an individual, powerful exposition of its story of a moon-struck Pierrot. In his score, Schönberg marks with square notes the pitch and duration of tone; but, within this duration, the voice is its own guide. This scheme of song adds a color palette that brings out characteristic emotional expression, and introduces a brilliant play of light and shadow in all the infinitesimal subdivisions of tone.

It was also Schönberg who originated the short opera. His *Erwartung* brings only one person on the stage, a woman. In the darkest night, in the forest, she comes to a rendezvous with her lover and stumbles over him, murdered by another woman. This "monodrama" is Schönberg's first opera. His *Die Glückliche Hand*, Prague, 1924, Metropolitan, League of Composers, 1930, goes far beyond his first attempt. Here action is stripped of all realism; one moves in the sphere of poetry, of symbols, or visions.

TENDENCIES

We find two opposing tendencies in opera today. One is based on the belief that words and action are a hindrance to spiritual expression in a pure art; the other reflects the convictions of those who consider them an aid to music. Subtler natures react to the former, and simpler natures uphold the latter belief. The strongest obstacle to the absolute spiritualization of opera is the human voice. It is so intimately connected with the body and its limitations that it becomes a perpetual advocate for the expression of the senses.

DEBUSSY

Debussy's solution was a renunciation of the union of music and action, rather than its acceptance, and he departed at the same time from any sensuous interpretation of words in music. There is no trace of melodrama in his *Pelléas et Mélisande*. It is filled with recitative which excludes every trace of passionate speech by rigorously avoiding extremes of pitch or tone duration. It is here, however, that the demand for unity of feeling between words and music finds complete satisfaction. The orchestration reaches the limit of restraint. It lacks rhythmic vitality, and achieves no real development even though Debussy uses "leitmotif." The opera has no definite outlines, yet it attains unity by perfect adaptation of means to an end.

Harmonically, *Pelléas et Mélisande* is a field of ninths, successive sevenths, and parallel motion, with the polyphonic phrase discarded. Debussy stands, by and large, in much the same relation to us today as Wagner stood to our immediate predecessors. Essentially he is the personification of a certain definite cultural and musical moment, representative of an attitude of mind, a phase of thought or feeling which we have all experienced at some time or other.

In *Pelléas et Mélisande,* Debussy succeeded so thoroughly in subordinating the musical interest to the dramatic needs of the moment that at times there is practically nothing left of the music. There is little doubt that the opera is too long: practically nothing happens until the third act. (There are five.) The music is invertebrate, and it lacks rhythmic life and vitality, or leaping pulse.

Pelléas is probably much nearer to the Wagnerian ideal of the preponderance of the dramatic interest than are even Wagner's own music-dramas. There are few opposing forces, however, in *Pelléas,* and opera in all forms must depend on the sensuous effect of a combination of such opposing forces. Some look upon Debussy's one opera as the beginning of a new operatic art; others think it is an end. Possibly nearer the truth is that *Pelléas* stands alone in operatic literature and will have its staunch admirers and caustic critics for years to come.

RECENT ITALIAN OPERA

In the Italian school we find several composers attacking the problems of opera in various ways.

SETTING FOR ACT II OF MONTEMEZZI'S DRAMA, "THE LOVE OF THREE KINGS"

Courtesy Chicago City Opera Co.

Italo Montemezzi has won some fame and favor by his *L'Amore dei Tre Re* (The Love of Three Kings). This work is slightly flavored with the influence of other schools and composers. It is popular among musicians but has not won its way with the laity. Since it lacks the true classical Italian operatic aria, it may be some time before it becomes a whistler's favorite.

Francesco Malipiero, another present-day Italian composer, definitely aims at operatic expressionism. He avoids *bel canto,* is boldly experimental, and shows the influence of French impressionism and post-impressionism. To him the union of song and action in opera is a radical evil. Among his experiments is *Pantea,* a symphonic drama for a dancer and a hidden choir, which enables him to separate song from representation on the stage, and also to abolish recitative entirely. His *Sette Canzoni* is a kind of folk song accompanying pantomimic action, with the orchestra suggesting emotional atmosphere. Here the action is reduced to a few simple, disconnected scenes. It has distinct poetic charm, but lacks power in a theatrical sense.

Ildebrando Pizzetti is an Italian who seeks inspiration in seventeenth century Italian music. His opera *Fedra* completely expresses his ideals. The action has been thoroughly assimilated by the composer, and out of the drama arises the music in a truly "expressionist" manner, with the orchestra adequately supporting it. Monteverdi's ideas here find a modern version. Pizzetti's latest work, "Fra Gherado" (Metropolitan) is very effective theatre music, but marks no particular advance in the operatic literature or art.

CONTEMPORARY FRENCH OPERA

In France we find a recent operatic sensation in Arthur Honegger's *Judith,* made over from an oratorio. Encompassing great vocal difficulties, it still has many high moments. The lighting, both on the stage and in the orchestra, is all in shades of dark blue or dark purple. *Judith* reveals the usual lack of counterpoint, so characteristic of all this Frenchman's writing, and is essentially homophonic; it contains many passages of power, although not so consistently as his later oratorio: *King David.* Both of these works are examples of episodic writing, without thematic development, so much in evidence in contemporary music. Orchestrally, Honegger maintains the break from the

Wagner-Strauss tradition of large masses of neutralized tone-color, into exploitation of more highly individualized color in the solo instruments, alone or in combination.

The most exacting technique of musical composition is the operatic technique. Whether the union of music, words, and action is artistically possible is a moot question. The compromise between Italian *bel canto* on one hand, and the extreme of the German *Sprechstimme* on the other is a difficult one in which to achieve artistic unity. The problems involved have driven many composers to avoid the situation entirely by dismissing song and seeking dramatic expression through other means. Pantomine, the dance, and finally the ballet, have offered evasion.

THE BALLET

The ballet, however, cannot be a solution of the so-called operatic problem. The expression of pure emotion is found in song, and cannot be achieved in the ballet, with all its blend of mind and senses, and its vivid colors. Despite the fact, the ballet, a union of music and gesture, has proved an intellectual triumph in the hands of some of the modern French and Russian masters. It is satisfying to their "expressionist" ideals of art and art alone.

One of the outstanding French examples of ballet is Ravel's *Daphnis et Chloé*. It is a distinct and vital expression of strength and intensity from a composer whose work was largely of the salon, though it be a brilliant salon. It is the finest score Ravel achieved.

A BALLET PRODUCTION ON THE STAGE OF RADIO CITY, NEW YORK

Courtesy The Art Institute of Chicago

Probably the most popular ballet composer of the day is the Russian, Stravinsky, with his *L'Oiseau de Feu, Petrouchka, Sacre du Printemps.* ("Fire-Bird," "Petrouchka," and "Rite of Spring").

Although his first ballet, *L'Oiseau de Feu,* is in a direct line from *Le Coq d'Or* by his teacher, Rimsky-Korsakov, it is admittedly far more brilliant than its predecessor.

Considered as an art-form the ballet must be seriously criticized as being too primitive, too purely physical, and emotional. The appeal of the Russian ballet is more sensuous than aesthetic, to the emotions of life rather than of art.

The tragedy of Schönberg's *Pierrot Lunaire* is rooted in human experience, and reflects its composer's metaphysical conception of life. Much of Stravinsky's music is an effort to become objective because of his own emptiness of subjective emotions and qualities.

A GERMAN EXPERIMENT

A new operatic experiment in Germany requires brief mention. It is Alban Berg's *Wozzeck* (German State Opera, 1925), which has achieved not only first-night success, but an enduring place in the repertoire. Some consider it the most original and remarkable attempt in opera since Debussy's *Pelléas et Mélisande.* It is completely atonal in character, but its origins point back to Tristan and reflect the teachings of Schönberg.

The work is so difficult it required one hundred rehearsals. It is done on the twelve tone scale, and is the first attempt to carry "atonality" into opera.

Wozzeck is in three acts. The first act begins with an orchestral suite, and in the second scene there is a passacaglia with twenty-one variations. The five scenes of the next act are a symphony in as many parts: sonata, prelude and fugue, largo, scherzo, and rondo. The third act has six inventions, one of them an orchestral interlude. The inventions employ one theme, one rhythm, one single sonority.

Berg orchestrates in the grand manner, and his demands on the singers are excessive. The work immediately and completely won its German public.

SOME WAYS OF LISTENING TO OPERA

For so many generations opera has been the plaything of either the nobility or the aristocracy, that it is difficult to realize that at last it is becoming the property of those for whom it was written: men and women in all stations of life.

The impression is still abroad that in order to enjoy opera it is necessary to have much technical training in music, or at least a good deal of experience with it in other forms. But thousands of listeners have found in the last few years, thanks to the radio and to sponsors of opera programs, that it is possible to enjoy opera thoroughly without seeing the stage. Certainly, then, with the aid of the eye and the presentation on the stage, it can easily become material for complete enjoyment. True, as in many other experiences in life, the person who is familiar with the routine, or who has had previous experience in music, will better appreciate opera. But opera, like painting, is a form of beauty which can be enjoyed at first contact and in which pleasures will grow with widening experience.

There are two ways of listening to music: the intellectual and the emotional. The ideal way is a fusion of both. With a story being enacted on the stage, with lighting effects, frequently with a ballet added, and with an orchestra contributing to the delineation of the story by underlining and emphasizing the moods and situations, it is evident that several senses come into response when seeing and hearing an opera. For these reasons many people find opera a door to further enjoyment of other forms of music.

Also, the human voice is the most capable medium we have for the reflection and expression of human emotions. As it is the primary instrument of the opera, with the orchestra providing the background, the voice stimulates the emotional response of the listener.

READ THE STORY FIRST

Since listening to opera is a matter of emotional response, knowing the plot will aid in developing that response. So, first read the story, either in full or in résumé. The stories included here summarize the plots of those operas which are most frequently presented. It is not overly important to understand the language in which they are sung. The story is the thing. There is usually enough action and stage business to follow its development. The concern of the listener is not with the machinery of the composer in producing his effects, but only with what the composer does and says. The composer has but one guiding purpose, and that is to project, by all the varied means at his disposal, the most potent expression of the drama. He may indulge in the vocal embroidery of Donizetti or Rossini; he may project the impassioned song of Puccini; or he may use the sumptuous orchestral web of Verdi or Wagner. The means matter but little; it is the end that is important. That end is a sufficient dramatic unity, expressed powerfully enough to stir the emotions of the listener. It is this combination of theater, drama, lighting, and music, that makes opera the universal art that it has become. It is popular because it is easily understood and emotionally enjoyed.

Some of the earlier operas have plots that today dramatically often seem ridiculous, even absurd. But that does not gainsay the fact that knowing what Lucia went mad about enhances the beauty of the famous aria known as the "Mad Scene."

NOT ALL OPERA IS TRAGIC

The stories of so many operas deal with perfidy, murder, and tragedy, that the general impression is that a grand opera must include some of these baser emotions. But it is erroneous to think of all opera as being morbid. Indeed, the *Barber of Seville* and *Die Meistersinger* reach a high point in operatic comedy. Though Verdi wrote *Falstaff* when he was eighty, it is filled with the buoyancy of youth, almost an elixir of life, and it is most refreshing to hear. That it is also a most superbly made score need not concern us. It is a magnificent welding of dramatic situations and forceful music, and is delightful, emotionally, for pleasure, or, aesthetically, for beauty.

In some of the later Wagnerian operas, where the dramatic and philosophical idea generates and directs the entire tonal conception, it becomes even more important to have some knowledge of what the plot is about. Our time is so far removed from myths, fables, sagas, and allegories, that it is helpful to an understanding of most of the Wagnerian magic if the listener is somewhat prepared to know what the dragons, swans, magic fire, magic swords, and other stage business represent. The symphonic beauty of the orchestra, with its marvelous web of tonal tapestry, and the colorful effects on the stage will prove sufficiently distracting from the plot even if it is already familiar.

It would be possible to indicate some of the high points in many of the operas, but that would require a separate volume. The only way to become familiar with opera is to experience its beauty and emotional force by seeing and hearing it as often as possible. It is an aesthetic adventure each lover of beauty owes to himself. For each one it is an unexplored country where he can search for and discover new treasures, and discovering them, widen his vision anew.

ACT II, SCENE IV, OF VERDI'S "AIDA"

AIDA

Music by Guiseppe Verdi (1813-1901)
Words by Bey, Du Locle, and Ghislanzoni
First produced: Cairo, Egypt, 1871

The Characters

Aïda (Ah-ee'dah), an Ethiopian slave	Soprano
The King of Egypt	Bass
Amneris (Am-nay'riss), his daughter	Mezzo-Soprano
Rhadames (rahd'ah-maze), Captain of the Guard	Tenor
Amonasro (Ah-moh-nahz'roh), King of Ethiopia	Baritone
Ramfis (Rahm'fiss), High Priest	Bass
A Messenger	Tenor

Aïda probably represents the highest point of Italian opera, and marks a turning-point in the musical development of Verdi. At the time it was written, Wagner's reforms had already made old-style Italian operas, written in a florid manner to show off the vocal technique of the singers, seem passé. Although *Aïda* gives singers a chance to show their technical skill, it has a rich color and fine tonal effects not present in earlier Italian operas.

At the request of the Khedive of Egypt, the first performance was given in Cairo, Egypt, a very fitting place for the première of this opera with its oriental plot and music.

The prelude is characteristic of Verdi's vigor and melody. A love theme is first voiced in the violins alone: then follows a short development, after which the solemn theme of the march of the priests of Isis sounds forth. Again we hear the love song mounting in triumph and then dying away.

Act I

The scene opens in the columned hall of the palace of Pharaoh. Ramfis, the High Priest, and the young soldier, Rhadames, are in conference over an Ethiopian invasion. As the solemn music forebodes militant and heroic scenes to follow, the Priest tells the young soldier that the oracle of Isis has revealed the name of the

Captain who is to lead the Egyptians against the invaders. When the Priest goes to inform the King, his look conveys to Rhadames that he is the chosen one. While Rhadames is waiting for the return of the Priest, he rejoices in the thought that through victories he may be able to win the freedom of Aïda, with whom he has fallen in love, although she is a slave to Amneris and a captive from Ethiopia. Unknown to all, she is the daughter of the king of that country. He voices his love in the beautiful aria, "Celeste Aïda" (Heavenly Aïda).

Amneris, the Pharaoh's daughter, enters while Rhadames is rejoicing and asks the reason for his happiness. He is evasive in his replies but his confusion arouses her suspicion. Aïda, who is in love with him, enters and Amneris becomes jealous when she sees the looks that pass between the slave girl and Rhadames. The orchestral background is illustrative of her emotional state of jealousy. Amneris asks Aïda the cause of his agitation, and Aïda tells of her fears for her fatherland in the coming battle. Then follows a trio in which the singers voice their secret emotions: Rhadames sings of his hope, Amneris of her jealous suspicions, and Aïda pours forth her ardent love for Rhadames.

With military pomp the King and his retinue come upon the stage. He announces to his subjects that the Ethiopians, led by King Amonasro, are invading Thebes. Amidst cries of "Vengeance!" from the people, he informs them that Rhadames is to lead the army which is now ready. A patriotic chorus follows.

At last Aïda is left by herself. She had joined in the universal cries which were spurring her lover on to victories, but now with time to reflect, she goes through an emotional struggle. Victory for Rhadames means failure and captivity for her father, and if the Ethiopians win, Rhadames may be killed. Her doubts and fears are expressed in the well-known aria, "Ritorno Vincitor" (Return Victorious). As the curtain falls, she sinks to the ground with the cry "Now let me die!"

The scene changes and we see the large hall in the Temple of Ptah, God of War. A double row of pillars stretches into the distance, and the air is heavy with incense. An altar occupies the center of the stage. The chorus "Possente Ptah!" (Almighty Ptah) is sung by priestesses standing between the columns.

This is a ceremonial scene in which Rhadames receives the blessing of the God of War and receives from Ramfis, the High Priest, the sacred veil and sword with which he is to triumph over the Ethiopians. Ramfis and the other priests call upon the god to bless the expedition. There is a universal shout of "Almighty Ptah!" and the curtain falls.

Act II

In the first scene of this act we see Amneris upon a couch, fanned by her slaves, while she is preparing her toilette for a festival which is about to take place. She is thinking of Rhadames, and as her slaves dance before her she sings, "Ah vieni, amor mio!" (Come to me, my love).

Announced by the love-theme first heard in the Prelude, and now played softly by the cellos, Aïda enters. Amneris deceitfully sympathizes with her because of the defeat of her countrymen, and betrays her into revealing her love by telling her that Rhadames is dead. At her cry of anguish Amneris is triumphant. She tells her that she lied. Now Aïda gives thanks to heaven and further reveals her love. Angered and jealous, Amneris tells Aïda that she too loves Rhadames and that *she* is the daughter of Pharaoh. Aïda in her excitement almost reveals her noble birth.

Courtesy Chicago City Opera Co.

ROSA RAISA AS "AIDA"

Courtesy Chicago City Opera Co.

VIRGILIO LAZZARI AS "RAMFIS" IN "AIDA"

When the returning army is heard outside, Amneris haughtily leaves Aïda alone in the room to contemplate Amneris' threats of humiliation.

In the second scene, which takes place outside the city walls, where a throne has been placed, the King, court, priests and people are gathered to welcome the victorious army. First come the King and his retinue, then Amneris, attended by Aïda and her other slaves. The exultant chorus, "Glory to Egypt and to Isis who protects our sacred land!" is sung by the people and priests.

In magnificent attire, the advance guard of the army enters with blaring trumpets. Next, a dance is performed by Egyptian girls before the throne of their king.

Finally in a burst of magnificent pageantry, to the "Triumphal March" which is so well known to the opera-loving public, the victorious army comes upon the stage. Statues of the gods and their emblems are carried in by the soldiers. Last of all, the victorious Rhadames is borne in upon a canopied litter carried by officers. The King descends and embraces Rhadames, and Amneris, to the accompaniment of the theme which depicts her passion, crowns him with laurel. The King offers to grant Rhadames whatever he may wish. Rhadames asks first that the Ethiopian prisoners be brought before the King. The captives enter under guard, King Amonasro among them. No signs of his royal rank are visible. Aïda rushes to him and he warns her in a whisper not to reveal his kingship. When the King asks who he is, Amonasro tells him that he is Aïda's father and adds that the King of Ethiopia has fallen. He begs the King to have mercy upon the captives. In the ensemble that follows, the priests ask that the prisoners be put to death, while the prisoners and Egyptians are begging for mercy. Above the chorus are heard six solo voices: Rhadames singing of his love for Aïda, Amneris of vengeance, and Aïda, her father, and the High Priest trying to solve the problem of what is to be done about the prisoners.

When Rhadames goes before the King to ask his boon, he requests the pardon of the prisoners. Through his pleading the pardon is granted, with the stipulation that although all but Amonasro and Aïda might return to their country, these two should be held for hostages.

When the King tells Rhadames that as an additional reward he shall marry his daughter and inherit the throne, Amneris is triumphant.

ACT III

This act contains melodies which rise to great climaxes. The scene is laid on the banks of the Nile in the moonlight. Sounds of stringed instruments and chanting voices can be heard coming from the Temple of Isis.

Down the Nile in a boat float Ramfis and Amneris who is coming to the temple to pray all night for divine blessing upon her union with Rhadames. After they have entered the temple and the sound of the chanting has died away, the theme of Aïda's love is heard as she enters, closely veiled, to wait for her lover. She is despondent as she sings, "Oh, should he come only to take a last farewell." She asks the Nile to take her to its bosom so she may find peace. After her beautiful aria "O, Patria Mia" (My Native Land), in which she laments that she will never see her home again, her father enters and embraces her. He tells her that he has come to take her home, and that his people will come back and revenge themselves upon the Egyptians. He insists that Aïda find out from Rhadames what route the Egyptians are planning upon taking in the new campaign they are about to launch. Aïda protests that she cannot ask such a thing of her lover. Her father becomes angry and when he describes to her the horrors of war, and tells her that the dead form of her mother is cursing her for being nothing but an Egyptian slave, she succumbs to his demands. As Rhadames approaches, he hides among the palms.

Courtesy Chicago City Opera Co.

MARTINELLI AS "RHADAMES" IN "AIDA"

Rhadames tells Aïda that he is about to conduct another campaign against the Ethiopians, and tells her that, if he is again a victor, they will surely be permitted to marry. Aïda answers that neither Amneris nor the King would consent, and begs him to flee with her to

Ethiopia. At first Rhadames protests, but after Aïda's pleadings he finally consents in the aria, "Si! Fuggiam da Queste Mure" (Yes, let us go from here), and they sing a triumphant love duet. As they are about to leave the stage, Aïda asks which path will be left open, unguarded. He tells her, "The pass of Napata." At this Amonasro steps out and reveals his identity.

Rhadames is overcome with despair when he realizes that he has betrayed his country. Amonasro tries to comfort him, telling him it is the will of Fate, but Amneris has heard the conversation and rushes out on the stage, calling him "Traitor." The King of Ethiopia draws a dagger and attempts to stab her, but she is saved by Rhadames.

Amonasro and Aïda escape just as Ramfis comes in with his guards. Rhadames surrenders himself.

Act IV

The act opens with an orchestral prelude in which we hear the motive of Amneris' jealousy. The scene is the dimly-lighted anteroom of a prison. Amneris is leaning against the doors. At her request the guards bring Rhadames in. She beseeches him to save himself, telling him that if he will marry her, she will kneel before the throne and beg for pardon for him. When he refuses, he is taken back to his cell.

Again Amneris is alone, a prey to thoughts of jealousy and hatred. However, when she sees the priests in their white robes file into the hall of judgment her mood changes to one of despair. Rhadames is brought and led into the hall of judgment. Left alone again, Amneris hears the chanting of the priests and the pronouncement of the sentence: "Rhadames is to be entombed alive."

In the final scene we see two stages, an upper and a lower. Above is the interior of the Temple of Isis, where the priests and priestesses are performing a sacred dance. The priests lower into place the stone which seals the tomb of Rhadames.

On the lower stage we see the dark, sealed chamber in which Rhadames awaits his doom. He is thinking of his lost Aïda. Suddenly she appears beside him; she has stolen into the vault in order to die with him. In each other's arms, the lovers sing the final duet, "O Terra Addio" (Farewell, O Earth) while above, Amneris prays for the soul of her lost lover.

THE BARBER OF SEVILLE

(Il Barbiere di Siviglia)

Music by Gioacchino Antonio Rossini (1792-1868)
Words by Cesare Sterbini, based on the comedy by Beaumarchais
First produced: Rome, February 5, 1816

The Characters

Count Almaviva (Ahl-mah-vee'vah)	Tenor
Bartolo (Bahr'toh-loh), a physician	Bass
Rosina (Ro-zee'nah), his ward	Soprano
Basilio (Bah-seel'yoh), a music master	Bass
Figaro (Fee'gah-roh), Barber of Seville	Baritone

In *The Barber of Seville,* Rossini first used orchestral accompaniment throughout in place of long passages of recitative. Many new and brilliant effects were obtained in both the vocal and instrumental parts. At the first performance it was a failure, but it was revised and by the end of the week had found favor with the public.

ACT I

The scene is a street in Seville, Spain, before the house of Dr. Bartolo.

Count Almaviva is serenading Rosina, ward of Bartolo, whom Bartolo himself hopes to marry. He sings "Dawn, with her Rosy Mantle," and after the accompanying musicians sing a hilarious 'thank you' for his generous tips, they depart. Rosina appears upon the balcony but, hearing a guitar, retreats.

Courtesy Chicago City Opera Co.

VITTORIO TREVISAN AS "BARTOLO" IN "THE BARBER OF SEVILLE"

The Count hears someone approaching and hides. Figaro enters, singing "Largo al factotum" (Room for the city's factotum). He is the town's jack-of-all-trades. He tells of his matchmaking for all the girls and widows in town. Upon recognizing Figaro, the Count comes out of hiding, and learns that Bartolo is Rosina's guardian and not her father, as he had supposed. Figaro promises to arrange for him to meet Rosina. As the Count does not want her to know his rank, he says he will be called Lindoro.

By subterfuge, Rosina manages to drop a note to her serenader, asking his name and station. He again sings to her, this time, "Se il mio nome" (If My Name You Would Know).

Bartolo comes out of the house and gives instructions that nobody but Basilio, Rosina's music teacher, is to be admitted. Figaro helps Count Almaviva plan how to get into the house. Finally it is decided that the Count shall take the name of Lindoro and disguise himself as a dragoon. He is to say he is with the troops that have come into the town, and is to be quartered in the home of Bartolo.

The second scene is a room in Bartolo's house. Rosina is reading a note from Lindoro. In great excitement, she sings the well-known aria "Una voco poco fa" (A Little Voice I Hear). This is a typically florid coloratura song, brilliant and effective, and contains all of the embellishments which serve to display that type of voice.

When Rosina leaves the room, Bartolo enters with her music teacher, Basilio, who is acting as a matrimonial agent. Bartolo confides to him that he wishes to marry his ward, and that the Count Almaviva is also suing for her hand. (He does not know, however, that the Count and the serenader are the same person). Basilio promises to get rid of the Count by spreading a scandal about him which will force him to leave town. He sings "La Calunnia" (Slander's Whisper).

The Count, disguised as a drunken soldier, enters, and manages to slip a note to Rosina, who has come into the room with Figaro. However, Bartolo sees the note change hands, and orders the soldier out of the house. He summons officers to arrest the disguised Count, but they release him at once when he displays the insignia of his rank.

Act II

The curtain rises upon the library of Bartolo's house. A harpsichord is in the room. As Bartolo wonders whether or not the

Courtesy Chicago City Opera Co.
VIRGILIO LAZZARI AS "BASILIO" IN "THE BARBER OF SEVILLE"

drunken soldier was a messenger of Count Almaviva, the Count himself arrives, this time in a different disguise. He says he is Alonzo, a pupil of Don Basilio, who, since the music master is ill, has been sent him to give Rosina her lesson. To allay Bartolo's suspicions, "Alonzo" produces the note which Rosina wrote to "Lindoro," saying that the Count left it in an inn. He promises Bartolo to show it to Rosina and convince her by subtle means that her lover is unfaithful. This bit of intrigue wins favor with Bartolo, who says that the young man is an apt pupil of the crafty Basilio.

Now Rosina comes in for her lesson. The trio which Rossini wrote for this scene was lost, and during the lesson the singer taking the role of Rosina sings whatever she chooses.

Figaro arrives to shave Bartolo, who gives him the keys to get the shaving utensils. He thus slyly obtains the balcony key. A loud crash is heard off-stage where Figaro is searching for the soap dish. Bartolo hurries to see what has happened, and the lovers are left alone for a short time. They plan to elope. Bartolo and the barber return and the shaving begins. At this point, Basilio, the music master, arrives. He seems perfectly well and says he has never seen Alonzo. Figaro realizes that something must be done at once to get Basilio out of the house, so he rushes up and tells him he is not well enough to be out, slyly giving him a purse. The bewildered music master is hurried out of the house.

The scene becomes even more humorous when the shaving begins. Figaro gets soap in Bartolo's eyes so that he cannot see the lovers plotting their elopement. In his excitement, however, the Count raises his voice, and Bartolo realizes what is going on. He chases Figaro and the Count out of the house. Then he shows Rosina the note she had written to Lindoro, but deceives her as to how it had come into his hands. He tells her that Lindoro was planning to give her up to the Count. This evident unfaithfulness angers her, and she reveals to her guardian the elopement plans. They then arrange to have Figaro and Lindoro arrested when they arrive for the elopement. Rosina promises to marry her guardian on the following day.

We hear a stormy interlude in the orchestra portending the tempestuous scene which follows. Figaro and Lindoro enter, concealed in cloaks. Rosina greets them with reproaches because of Lindoro's supposed infidelity, but when he opens his cloak and reveals himself as Count Almaviva in all his splendor, she accepts his explanations. A duet between the lovers, "Ah, quel colpo!" (Oh, What Success), follows. Figaro looks out of the window and sees two people approaching. He and Rosina decide to leave in a hurry but discover that the ladder has been removed. Basilio and a notary arrive, bringing a marriage contract for Bartolo and Rosina. The Count takes Basilio aside and with one hand offers him a ring to let him sign the contract in place of Bartolo. In the other hand he flourishes a pistol. Basilio accepts the ring rather than be shot, and the contract is signed.

Now Bartolo rushes in upon the intruders. He is finally reconciled when the Count makes a gift to him of Rosina's dowry, which really had been Bartolo's chief object in marrying his ward.

BORIS GODOUNOV

Music by Modest Moussorgsky (1835-1881)
Words by the composer, based upon Pushkin
First produced: St. Petersburg (Leningrad), January 24, 1874

The Characters

Boris Godounov (Bori'ss Goh-doo-noff')	Bass
Xenia (Xee'nyah), his daughter	Soprano
Feodor, his son	Mezzo Soprano
Marina, daughter of an officer	Mezzo Soprano
Prince Shouisky (Shoo-is'ky)	Tenor
Gregory, novice	Tenor
Varlaam and Missail, vagabond monks	Bass and Tenor
Pimenn (Pee'men), a monk	Bass
Tchelkalov (Chel'kah-loff), Secretary	Baritone

In this masterpiece by Moussorgsky, *Boris Godounov,* the rich and colorful orchestration is used chiefly as a background to the voices and as an integral part of the dramatic expression. While there are songs, there are no formal arias which place vocal skill above dramatic portrayal. The subject matter of the plot is national and is admirably supported by typically Russian music. Moussorgsky uses a few folk tunes in the opera, but he makes more use of recitative than lyricism in the solo parts. One very unusual fact must be noted: in this opera the Russian people take the place of a hero, and the choruses given to them are very expressive. The stark realism of the plot is well supported by the Russian harmonies and modal music. The version of the opera usually performed is a revision made by Rimsky-Korsakov after Moussorgsky's death. In actual presentation the order of the scenes is often changed.

Feodor Chaliapin has so masterfully portrayed the character of Boris that the two names will always be linked together.

Courtesy Italian Tourist Bureau

FEODOR CHALIAPIN IN "BORIS GODOUNOV"

Act I

As the curtain rises, we see the courtyard of a monastery. Here Boris, privy councilor to the Tsar, has retired after the death of his master, whose only heir, Dimitri, he had previously caused to be assassinated. Although Boris is pretending that he does not want the crown himself, he has secretly arranged to have officers force the people to come to the convent and beg of him to be their ruler. They are now in the courtyard singing the powerful chorus "Ma perchè tu ci abbandoni?" (Why Hast Thou Abandoned Us?)

The second scene reveals the interior of a cell in the monastery where Pimenn, an old monk, is writing, while a younger monk, Gregory, sleeps in a corner. Gregory awakens presently and asks Pimenn, among other things, about the assassinated Dimitri, who, he learns, would have been about his own age. Upon hearing this, Gregory conceives the idea of starting a rumor that Dimitri is still alive. By this means he hopes to usurp the throne.

In the square between the two great cathedrals of the Assumption and the Archangels the populace is gathered for the coronation festivities. The colorful banners, the gaily attired people, and the glittering cathedral domes above them, combine with the rich orchestral music of the Coronation Scene to make a most impressive setting for the procession of Boyards which escorts Boris to the Cathedral of the Assumption. A cry of "Long Live Tsar Boris" comes from Prince Shouisky. The crowd responds with "Salve a te, Zar Boris Teodorovic!" (Glory to Tsar Boris!).

Act II

While singing a song to break her solitude, the hostess of a small inn on the Lithuanian border is interrupted by the abrupt appearance of two wandering friars, accompanied by Gregory, who has escaped from his monastery. Gregory is on his way to Poland, where he intends to claim that he is Dimitri, still living and escaped from Boris. He has hopes of raising an army, unseating Boris from the throne, and himself usurping it as the rightful heir of the Tsar. Varlaam, one of the friars, is singing a boisterous drinking song when soldiers come in to arrest Gregory, whose escape has been reported. He manages to evade them and get away.

In a room in the Tsar's apartments, Feodor and Xenia, son and daughter of Boris, are with their nurse, who is singing a song in an attempt to divert the thoughts of Xenia from the loss of her betrothed lover. Boris comes in and tries to comfort her. He is gratified to see that Feodor has been studying a map, for he thinks of this as preparation for the time when the boy will inherit the throne.

Boris is telling of his vain search for peace in spite of all the power he has attained, when suddenly Prince Shouisky arrives with disturbing news. A youth pretending to be Dimitri is at the border with his followers, and the people, believing that the impostor is really Dimitri, are in revolt. Sending the children out of the room, Boris asks the Prince if he is sure Dimitri is dead. The Prince says that he saw the murdered boy, and is about to go into details when Boris stops him and bids him go. There follows one of the most impressive scenes in the opera. We see the torments of the king's guilty conscience. Visions of the murdered boy rise up before Boris and he cringes back in horror. We hear the relentless ticking of the great clock while Boris struggles with his conscience. Finally he drops to his knees and prays: "Lord, have mercy on the guilty soul of Boris."

A Polish noblewoman, Marina, working in the interests of her own country, has arranged a meeting with Gregory in the moonlit garden of her palace. After the guests have departed from a banquet, she comes out to Gregory. A love duet takes place in which Marina urges Gregory to lead an attack against Moscow, take the throne, and make her his queen.

Act III

In a forest some peasants have come together. They have captured a nobleman and are making cruel sport of him as they sing "Glory to this great Boyard and his Tsar Boris!" The village fool

Courtesy The Art Institute of Chicago

SCENE FROM FEDEROWSKI'S PRODUCTION OF "BORIS GODOUNOV" AT THE MOSCOW OPERA

joins them, and Missail and Varlaam enter, denouncing the Tsar. Then two Jesuits approach singing Latin praises to Dimitri, but the people, not wishing Rome to enter into their problems, bind them and take them away to be killed. Finally the supposed Dimitri passes by with his followers. He promises to free the people from oppression, and they follow him out. In the falling snow, the village fool is left alone, musing. He symbolizes the hopeless, helpless state of the populace.

In the Imperial Palace, the Duma is discussing ways and means of quelling the uprising and destroying the usurper. Prince Shouisky relates to them how Boris is tortured by visions of the murdered boy which his guilty conscience conjures up before him. Boris enters and mounts the throne. Prince Shouisky asks him to see an old monk who is outside. Boris agrees, hoping to find comfort. The old monk, however, tells of a shepherd who was cured of blindness by praying at the tomb of Dimitri. Boris listens with growing horror, and finally falls to the floor senseless.

When he regains consciousness, he asks that his son be brought in, and dismisses the Duma. Now comes the most impressive scene of the entire opera. Boris and his boy are alone. He sings to him "Farewell, My Son, I am Dying," and bids the boy protect his sister. He begs him never to ask how he came to inherit the throne, but to rule wisely. Boris prays to heaven to protect him. He hears the portentous, solemn tolling of bells, and the praying of his subjects, and sings "Hark, 'Tis the Passing Bell." The impression of Boris' terror and excruciating mental agony is intensified by the powerful orchestration. As the priests enter in procession, Boris summons all of his remaining strength and rises to his feet, saying, "While I have life I am still Tsar." He calls upon God for mercy—then points to his son and says "Behold your Tsar." With one last cry for mercy, he falls dead upon the steps of the throne.

CARMEN

Music by Georges Bizet (1838-1875)
Words by Meilhac and Halévy, based on the novel by Mérimée
First performed: Paris, March 3, 1875

The Characters

Don José (Don Ho-zay'), a Corporal	Tenor
Escamillo (Es-ca-mee'lyoh), a Toreador	Baritone
Zuniga (Tsoo-nee'gah), a Captain	Bass
Morales (Moh-rah'-layz), a Brigadier	Baritone
Le Dancaire } Smugglers	Tenor
Le Remendado } Smugglers	Tenor
Micaela (Mee-kah-ay'la), a Peasant Girl	Soprano
Frasquita (Frass-kee'ta)	Soprano
Mercedes (Mer-chay'dayz)	Soprano
Carmen (Kar'-men), a Gypsy Cigarette Girl	Mezzo Soprano

Place: Seville, Spain
Time: 1820

Today *Carmen* is one of the most universally popular operas in the repertoire, in spite of the fact that when it was first produced, it was so unfavorably received that Bizet was extremely discouraged, and died believing that it was a failure. The story offered Bizet a splendid opportunity to show his skill in using local color. The characters are strongly drawn, and the music is melodious and rhythmic.

GEORGES BIZET

Act I

The overture which has preceded this act has prepared us, by its sparkling gaiety and infectious rhythms, giving way to music of a sinister and foreboding character, for Spain in all its excitement before a bullfight. When the curtain rises, we see a square in Seville at the noon hour. Soldiers, shop girls, and townspeople are passing to and fro. After the lively opening chorus "Sur la Place" (On the Square), a young peasant girl appears hunting for a corporal, Don José. She is told that the guard will soon change and he will come on duty. Frightened when the soldiers invite her to the guardhouse to wait, she leaves.

When the guard changes and José comes upon the stage, the soldiers tell him of the pretty girl who was inquiring for him. He says she must be Micaela, his sweetheart from home. Presently a bell rings, and the girls come out of the nearby cigarette factory and begin flirting with the soldiers.

To the accompaniment of a "fate motif" in the orchestra, the attractive and sensuous Carmen comes among them. The crowd asks her when she will fall in love again, and she replies with the ever-popular "Habanera" (Love is Like a Wood-Bird). During her song and dance she directs her words and glances to José and dances very near to him, but his thoughts dwell upon Micaela, and he seems entirely unaware of Carmen. She snatches a flower from her bodice and throws it at him as she sings "But if I love you, beware!" He starts up angrily, but encounters her eyes and stands motionless. When she is gone, he picks up the flower, inhales its intoxicating fragrance and places it in his blouse.

At this point Micaela returns and joyfully greets her lover, telling him she brings a kiss and some money from his mother. Memories of his home come back to him, and he sends her back with a tender message for his mother.

After she leaves, he is about to throw the flower away when shrieks and commotion are heard within the cigarette factory. They bring out Carmen who has stabbed another girl in a quarrel; she is arrested and left under the guard of José. When they are alone, she asks what he has done with the flower. Then in the aria "Seguidilla" (Near the Walls of Seville) she makes such passionate love to him, that he succumbs to her wiles and says he will untie the knot which binds her hands if she will give him her love. She consents. He loosens the knot, leaving it so it still seems binding. As she is being led away between guards, Carmen suddenly breaks away and escapes, amid cheers.

Act II

As the curtain rises, we find Carmen, in company with gipsy smugglers and soldiers, in the inn of Lillas Pastia. They are just finishing their repast. Soon they begin a wild gipsy dance in which Carmen joins. The rhythm and color effects in the orchestra reflect the carefree and daring life of the gypsies. Carmen has just been told by one of the soldiers that the officer who let her escape has been under arrest since he let her get away, but has now been freed.

Suddenly cries of "Long live the Toreador! Hail Escamillo!" are heard outside. The noted bullfighter, Escamillo, enters singing the famous "Toreador Song," which mirrors his bravado, conceit, and gaiety. His glittering habiliments and strong personal magnetism seem to impress Carmen, in spite of the fact that she is still intent upon winning José, and Escamillo is much impressed by her.

After Escamillo leaves, a couple of smugglers try to enlist the services of Carmen and two of her girl friends to help them in one of their adventures, but she says she is waiting for José. When he arrives, she dances for him and taunts him for not appreciating her charms. To prove his love he sings "Air de la Fleur" (Flower Song), telling how he has kept her flower all this time. As he is about to leave, Captain Zuniga, another of Carmen's admirers, enters. He is angry to find that she prefers a common soldier to him, and orders José to leave. A fight ensues and Carmen is forced to call her friends to separate the men. Zuniga is led away. Now, after having raised his hand against an officer, José has no choice but to join the outlaws.

Courtesy Italian Tourist Bureau

GABRIELLA BESANZONI IN "CARMEN"

ACT III

The smugglers' secret meeting place is a spot of woodland beauty. Here José, Carmen, and a band of smugglers are gathered. José is thinking of his mother and regretting his present life, but when Carmen suggests that they part, he threatens her with his dagger. Carmen decides to tell her fortune with cards, and draws the Death card. "First, I, then he!" she cries. The smugglers depart to take their contraband goods through the pass, leaving José on guard behind some rocks.

Unobserved by José, a guide has led Micaela into the smugglers' retreat. She sings "Je dis que rien ne m'épouvante," (I said naught should frighten me here), and prays for protection. A shot in the distance startles the company. They find that a quarrel has arisen between José and Escamillo, who has heard that Carmen is tired of her peasant lover. The smugglers separate the fighters, and Escamillo invites them to come to see him win the bullfight in Seville. Carmen shows plainly that she is pleased by the Toreador's advances. After he leaves, Micaela is brought forth from her hiding place. She pleads with José to return home to his dying mother. Carmen tells him she thinks that he should go, and he is about to leave with Micaela when Carmen, hearing the Toreador's song in the distance, seems about to go to him. José stops her, threatening her with his dagger.

Act IV

All the dazzling beauty of a Spanish festival assemblage is before us as the gaily attired crowd mills around outside the arena in Seville where the long-heralded bullfight is to take place. Amid pomp and ceremony Escamillo enters, accompanied by Carmen. As he passes into the arena, she promises that she will always love him and no other.

Carmen's friend Frasquita seeks her out to warn her that José is there and that she should guard her life. When she goes to the gates, she finds him barring the way. She tells him that all is over between them. As he pleads with her, they hear shouts announcing the triumphant victory of Escamillo. "Is it he you love?" José demands. "Yes," Carmen tells him fearlessly and he stabs her. Just at this point the people pour out of the arena, cheering Escamillo, who sees the prostrate form of Carmen before him. José gives himself up, still declaring his love for Carmen. In the orchestra is heard the solemn theme of doom.

CAVALLERIA RUSTICANA (RUSTIC CHIVALRY)

Music by Pietro Mascagni (1863-)
Words by Targioni-Tozzetti and Menasci
First produced: Rome, May 17, 1890

The Characters

Santuzza (San-toot'sah), a village girl	Soprano
Lola (Low'lah), Alfio's wife	Mezzo Soprano
Turiddu (Too-ree'doo), a young soldier	Tenor
Alfio (Al'fee-oh), a teamster	Baritone
Lucia (Loo-chee'ah), Turiddu's mother	Contralto

Cavalleria Rusticana made its composer famous in one night. It won the prize in a contest offered by a publisher for a one-act opera. Before winning this, Mascagni was a poor music teacher. Now all sorts of honors were thrust upon him, including the Order of the Crown of Italy, conferred upon him by the king.

Before the curtain rises, we hear the beautiful song of love "Thy Lips Like Crimson Berries," which Turiddu is singing to Lola.

The setting is a Sicilian village, with a tavern on one side of the street and a church on the other. Bells are ringing, summoning the people to Easter services. The music reflects the carefree happiness of the villagers, some of whom enter the church.

Santuzza comes to the wine shop and calls Lucia, who owns it. When Lucia emerges, she asks her where Turiddu is. Lucia answers evasively. Finally she says that her son has gone to Francofonte for wine, but Santuzza tells her he was seen last night in the village. While they are talking, Alfio enters and asks Lucia for some of her good, old wine. She replies that Turiddu has gone after some, but Alfio tells her she is mistaken, for he saw him near his cottage this morning.

Now Easter music is heard coming from the church. The people in the square kneel and sing. All but Lucia and Santuzza enter the church.

When the two are alone, Santuzza, in the melodious and pathetic aria "Voi lo sapete, O mama" (Well You Know, Good Mother), tells how Turiddu has been unfaithful to her. Overcome with emotion and sympathy for the girl, Lucia goes into the church to pray for her.

Now Turiddu enters on his way to church. He does not want to talk to Santuzza, but she waylays him and reproves him for deserting her for the wife of Alfio. He tells her that Alfio would kill him if he were to find out about his attentions to Lola. Santuzza is frightened and says she still loves him.

From afar Lola is heard singing a love song. Soon she comes in, and the two girls exchange sharp words. Lola passes into the church, asking Turiddu to follow. Santuzza vainly begs him not to desert her, but he repulses her and enters the church.

When Alfio comes into the square in front of the church, he finds Santuzza cursing her unfaithful lover. She tells him that it was his wife who won him from her. He is at first angry and threatens her, but finally he believes her and swears vengeance. They leave the stage and we hear from the orchestra the famous "Intermezzo," which reflects all the melodic beauty of the Easter peace as well as the turbulent emotions of the tortured lovers.

The people come from the church, among them Turiddu and Lola, happy with each other. Turiddu invites his friends to join them at his mother's tavern, where they sing a joyous drinking song. When Alfio comes in, he refuses a drink proffered by Turiddu, saying it might be poison. They challenge each other to a duel, according to Sicilian custom. Turiddu bids his mother farewell and asks her to care for Santuzza if he does not come back. In a short time people rush in, saying that Turiddu has been killed.

DON GIOVANNI

Music by Wolfgang Amadeus Mozart (1756-1791)
Words by Lorenzo da Ponte
First produced: Prague, Oct. 29, 1787

The Characters

Don Giovanni (Joh-vahn'nee), a gay young gentleman	Baritone
Leporello (Le-poh-rel'loh), his servant	Bass
Don Pedro (Pay'droh), a Commandant	Bass
Donna Anna, his daughter	Soprano
Don Ottavio (Ot-tah'vee-oh), engaged to Donna Anna	Tenor
Donna Elvira (El-vee'rah), a lady	Soprano
Zerlina (Tsair-lee'nah), engaged to Masetto	Soprano
Masetto (Ma-set'toh), a peasant	Bass
Peasants, musicians, dancers, etc.	

Don Giovanni was extremely successful upon its first presentation, and still remains a favorite. Such composers as Beethoven,

Rossini and Gounod have paid homage to the greatness of the score. The characterization is skilful and the music is melodic and brilliant.

Act I

Outside the house of the Commandant of Seville, Spain, Leporello is waiting for his dissolute master, Don Giovanni, who is inside flirting with Donna Anna. In song, the servant tells how his master keeps him up all night while he makes merry. Don Giovanni, rushes from the house pursued by Donna Anna, who is trying to snatch the cloak from his face so she may find out who he is. Her cries bring her father to her aid. While she runs for more help a duel takes place, and the Commandant is killed. When Donna Anna returns, with Ottavio, her lover, they find her father's body. The murderer and his servant have fled. The lovers vow to avenge the murder.

The scene changes. Outside the city, Don Giovanni and Leporello are walking down a lonely road. The servant is lecturing his master upon his dissolute life, when they see a lady in tears. Don Giovanni tells his servant that he is going to comfort her, and Leporello replies "As you've done eighteen hundred others." Don Giovanni is surprised to find that the lady is Donna Elvira, an old sweetheart of his whom he deserted. She reproves him for his treatment of her. He tries to explain why he left her, but becomes confused, and refers her to Leporello. As she turns to the servant, Don Giovanni disappears. Leporello sings the clever aria "Madamina!" in which he gives the list of all of Don Giovanni's conquests. After listening to this, Donna Elvira is also bent upon revenge.

Courtesy Italian Tourist Bureau

FERNANDO AUTORI IN "DON GIOVANNI"

When the curtain rises upon the next scene, we see a group gathered in the village square for the wedding festivities of Masetto and Zerlina. Don Giovanni, whose palace is nearby, walks among the merry-makers. He sees Zerlina and decides to make a conquest. To this end he invites the entire party to use his palace and gardens for the day. When the others go, he manages to detain Zerlina. She is inclined to be flirtatious, and they sing together the duet, "La ci darem la mano!" (There we will give each other our hands), in which he pleads with her to come with him to his country house. At this point Elvira comes in and warns Zerlina against Don Giovanni. Alarmed, the girl hurries off to seek her husband-to-be. Soon Donna Anna and Ottavio enter. They are acquainted with Don Giovanni, but when Donna Anna hears his voice, she recognizes him as her father's murderer, and she leaves the stage. Alone, he sings the beautiful aria, "Dalla sua pace" (On Her All Joy Dependeth), in which he expresses his love for his beloved Anna.

The festivities in the Palace Gardens are in full sway, and Zerlina and Masetto are among the dancers. When Masetto reproaches Zerlina for her flirtation with Giovanni, she sings to him the aria so popular among sopranos "Batti, Batti, o bel Masetto," in which she begs him to beat her if he is angry, and all is forgiven. They go into the palace with Don Giovanni just as three masked figures enter the garden. They are Donna Anna, Donna Elvira, and Ottavio.

Act II

An unusual musical effect is produced. In three different apartments in the palace, three small orchestras are playing at the same time, one playing a minuet, another a german, and a third a gavotte. All three blend together in a harmony which creates the effect of a large ball. During the dancing, Don Giovanni lures Zerlina into a private room, and she escapes with difficulty. Don Giovanni tries to blame Leporello, but Donna Anna, Donna Elvira, and Ottavio unmask and accuse him. He again escapes.

Donna Elvira has taken Zerlina into her house to protect her, but Don Giovanni has not abandoned the chase. He forces Leporello, his servant, to change clothes with him and lure Donna Elvira away, while he lays siege to the girl. Under Zerlina's window he, Don Giovanni, sings the serenade "Deh vieni alla finestra" (Open Thy Window).

Scarcely has he finished the song when Masetto enters with a group of armed peasants. They are hunting for Don Giovanni. Thanks to his disguise he is not recognized, and he says he will help them. After the others have gone, he engages Masetto in conversation. Under pretense of finding out if he is well armed, he gets Masetto to hand him his weapons. Then he gives him a beating and throws him in a ditch, where Zerlina finds him.

Meanwhile poor Leporello, in his master's clothes, is pursued by his master's enemies until he has to reveal his true identity and take to his heels. Don Ottavio again vows vengeance upon Don Giovanni, in a great aria "Il mi tesoro" (To My Beloved).

It is past midnight when Don Giovanni and Leporello meet by chance near the newly-erected statue of the slain Commandant. They hear an awful voice and discover the statue is speaking. It says "Laugh on until the dawn—Then—no more laughter!" Leporello is terrified, but Don Giovanni boldly invites the statue to dinner. The stone figure nods.

The scene shifts once more. In his palace, to the accompaniment of his private orchestra, Don Giovanni is dining with ladies. Donna Elvira comes in and pleads with him to change his mode of life, but he laughs at her. She starts to leave but returns in fright, and leaves by another door. Leporello is sent to determine the cause of her terror, and comes back terrified to tell his master the statue has come. The figure of the dead Commandant comes heavily into the room. Don Giovanni, undaunted, orders Leporello to serve him. The statue says that he has tasted the food of Heaven and does not desire that of earth. He then asks Don Giovanni to be his guest, and Don Giovanni clasps the stone hand of his strange visitor. "Repent in this, your last hour!" cries the statue, but Don Giovanni says, "Never!" The stone man drops Don Giovanni's hand and disappears, as the pit of Hell opens and Don Giovanni is dragged into it.

FALSTAFF

Music by Giuseppe Verdi (1813-1901)
Words by Arrigo Boito, after Shakespeare's *Merry Wives of Windsor.*
First produced: Milan, March 12, 1893

The Characters

Falstaff, a roguish old knight	Baritone
Bardolph } friends of Falstaff	Bass
Pistol } friends of Falstaff	Bass
Dr. Caius	Tenor
Fenton, in love with the daughter of Mistress Ford	Tenor
Dame Quickly	Mezzo-Soprano
Mistress Page	Soprano
Mistress Ford	Mezzo-Soprano
Anne, daughter of Mistress Ford	Soprano
Ford, a wealthy burgher	Baritone
Robin	Bass

Written when Verdi was over eighty years old, *Falstaff* is full of sparkling gaiety and shows great technical skill on the part of the composer.

Act I

Dr. Caius quarrels with Falstaff in the Garter Inn, and is ejected. After he has gone, the roguish Falstaff, with the help of his friends, Bardolph and Pistol, composes two love letters. These he sends to Mistress Ford and Mistress Page, who find that the letters are alike. They plan to get even with him, and all the men agree to help them. They scheme to have Ford introduced to Falstaff under a different name. Dame Quickly is sent to arrange a meeting between Falstaff and Mistress Ford.

Act II

Ford, under the name of Signor Fortuna, pays Falstaff to intercede for him with Mistress Ford. Shortly after Falstaff has arrived at the Ford home on his pleasant mission, Ford and the other men come in. Falstaff has just time enough to get behind a screen, before they begin to search for him. Unsuccessful in the search, the men leave. The women have previously prepared a basket full of soiled clothes. Into this they put Falstaff, cover him with the clothes, and fasten down the lid. Ford returns, remembering that he failed to look behind the screen. Anne and Fenton happen to be making love there. Ford hears them kiss, thinks it is Falstaff and his wife, and hurries out in anger. At orders from Mistress Ford, the basket containing Falstaff is emptied into the Thames. Ford returns just in time to see him clambering up out of the water, to the amusement of all.

ACT III

Though somewhat disheartened and stiff from his experience, after he returns to the Inn, Falstaff allows Dame Quickly to arrange another meeting with Mistress Ford. This time it is in Windsor Forest, at midnight, in a spot supposed to be haunted. When Falstaff begins to make love, eerie sounds are heard and Mistress Ford pretends fright and runs away. Fearing it would be fatal to look at supernatural beings, Falstaff prostrates himself on the ground. The rest of the characters come in dressed as fairies. When they chance upon Falstaff, they decide to beat him until he promises to reform.

Ford has promised Dr. Caius to give him his daughter, Anne, in marriage, but the women, knowing that Anne and Fenton are in love; so arranged the disguises in the Fairy Scene that Dr. Caius made love to Bardolph before the masks were removed. In the ensuing merriment, Ford consents to the marriage of Anne and Fenton.

THE KING'S HENCHMAN

Music by Deems Taylor (1885-)
Words by Edna St. Vincent Millay
First produced: New York, February 17, 1927

The Characters

Edgar, King of England	Baritone
Aelfrida (El-free′-dah)	Soprano
Maccus (Mock′-us), a bard	Tenor
Aethelwold (Eth′-el-wold), a warrior	Tenor
Ase, Aelfrida's serving-woman	Contralto

The composer, Deems Taylor, and the poet, Edna St. Vincent Millay, both Americans, collaborated in writing *The King's Henchman,* which is one of the most successful of American operas. The story, a variation of the Tristan legend, is based upon an early Saxon chronicle, and an approximation to the old Saxon style of speech is used in the libretto. The music, which is modern, is well orchestrated, and, in the manner of Wagner, conforms to the action.

Act I

The curtain rises on a scene of feasting and festivity at the court of Edgar, King of England in the tenth century. Maccus, a bard, is singing a song of heroes and battles. At the close of the song we learn that King Edgar, who has long been a widower, is about to wed Aelfrida of Devon, if he finds her as beautiful as hearsay pictures her. Because of a disturbance in his kingdom, Edgar dares not leave it, so he sends his foster-brother, Aethelwold, to woo his bride. According to an old Saxon rite, Edgar and Aethelwold pledge friendship and loyalty by drinking from the same wine-cup. At the break of dawn Aethelwold and his retinue depart as Maccus sings "Oh! Caesar, Great Wert Thou!" Aethelwold and the courtiers join in the refrain.

Act II

Aethelwold and Maccus are lost in a dense forest, having been separated from their men by fog. While Maccus goes in search of the others, Aethelwold lies down to sleep.

Aelfrida comes into the forest with her serving-woman, Ase. It is Hallowe'en, and Aelfrida hopes that by means of charms and incantations she may be able to avoid marrying a man her father has selected, and find one of her own choice. She sends her serving-woman away and begins the magic rites. While she sings an incantation, the fog disappears and she discovers the sleeping Aethelwold. Believing that the charm has been successful, she awakens him with a kiss. At first he thinks she is a supernatural being, but soon they realize that they are both mortal, and also that they are very much in love with each other. In the distance Ase is heard calling Aelfrida, who leaves Aethelwold's arms to answer the summons. When Aethelwold hears the name Aelfrida, he knows that this is the woman for whom Edgar has sent him. Deeply disturbed, he is about to hurry away when Aelfrida calls to him. Finally he tells Maccus to go back to the king and tell him that Aelfrida is not beautiful, but ugly, but that since she is rich, he himself, being very poor, will marry her, if the king consents.

Act III

Although Aelfrida and Aethelwold seem happy in their marriage, Aethelwold's conscience is troubled because he has not taken his bride to court, where she fully expected to go when she married the foster-brother of the king. He knows that Aelfrida has grown tired of her father's house. Finally Aethelwold consents to take her to Ghent in Flanders, where she has always longed to go.

Before they have a chance to leave, Maccus arrives saying that the king is coming with his retinue. Aethelwold is greatly alarmed and tells his wife how he has deceived the king. He entreats her to go to her room and disguise herself so she will appear ugly and crippled. Then he will tell the king that she is ill and take him to see her. At first Aelfrida is angry, thinking that the king, whom she might have married, will never know how beautiful she is. However, fear for Aethelwold's safety makes her yield. Ase, however, goes to her room with her and persuades her not to do as her husband has requested. When Aethelwold takes the king to her chamber, Aelfrida, dressed in her most gorgeous raiment and jewels, stands at the door to greet them. The king sternly reproaches Aethelwold, who, in remorse, stabs himself with his dagger. Edgar, distressed, walks over to the body of his foster-brother and sings a song of lamentation, "Nay, Maccus, Lay Him Down." As the people join in the refrain, Aethelwold's body is carried away, and Aelfrida follows alone.

International News photo

A SCENE FROM "THE KING'S HENCHMAN"

LA BOHÈME (THE BOHEMIAN LIFE)

Music by Giacomo Puccini (1858-1924)
Words by Giuseppe Giacosa, and Luigi Illica,
founded on *La Vie de Bohême,* by Henri Murger
First performed: Turin, Italy, February 1, 1896

The Characters

Rudolph (Roo′dolf), a poet	Tenor
Marcel (Mar-sel′), a painter	Baritone
Colline (Col-leen′), a philosopher	Bass
Schaunard (Shauw-nard′), a musician	Baritone
Benoit (Be-nwah′), an importunate landlord	Bass
Parpignol (Par-pi-nyol′), a vendor of toys	Tenor
Alcindoro (Al-sin-do′-ro), a state councilor and admirer of Musetta	Bass
Musetta (Moo-set′-ta), a grisette	Soprano
Mimi (Mee-mee), a maker of artificial flowers	Soprano

La Bohème is a story of the joys and sorrows in the lives of young people living in Paris in order to become artists, and of the gaiety, unconventionality, and pathos of this Bohemian life.

Act I

When the curtain rises on the first scene we see Rudolph and Marcel in their attic room. It is Christmas Eve. They have no fire and are so cold that they can scarcely work. Marcel starts to break up a chair for firewood, but Rudolph offers a play of his in its place. They burn it act by act. Just as the last act is burning, Colline comes in. Before the fire has died down, the trio is surprised by the entrance of Schaunard, their other roommate, accompanied by errand boys bringing wood, wine, and food in abundance. He says an eccentric Englishman hired him to sing to a neighbor's parrot until the parrot should die. After singing himself hoarse to no avail, he gave the bird poison. However, he was well paid.

They decide that as long as it is Christmas Eve and everyone in the Latin Quarter will be dining out, they will save the food for another time. They are all having a drink before going out to celebrate when the landlord enters, demanding his rent. They give him wine, and manage to get him out of the room.

While his three comrades start out for the merry-making, Rudolph stays alone to finish something he is writing. He finds, however, that he is not in the mood.

Courtesy Chicago Civic Opera Co.

ANTONIO CORTIS AS "RUDOLPH" IN "LA BOHÈME"

There is a knock at the door, and his young neighbor enters, asking for a light for her candle. She is seized with a coughing spell and seems about to faint. Rudolph revives her. She is about to leave when she discovers she has lost her key. As they both search for it, their candles go out. They grope in the dark for the key; Rudolph finds it, secretly puts it in his pocket, and keeps on with the search. Accidentally their hands touch. Rudolph sings the popular tenor ario "Che gelida manina" (Your Tiny Hand Is Frozen). They give up their search for the key, and Mimi sings "Mi chiamano Mimi" (My Name Is Mimi). They go out to join the others.

Act II

This act opens with a gay street scene in front of the Café Momus, where everyone is celebrating the holiday. Mimi and Rudolph join Colline, Marcel, and Schaunard at a table set before the inn. There is much activity on the stage, due to the passing of many people, among whom vendors are hawking their wares.

There is also excitement when Musetta, a former sweetheart of Marcel, comes in with Alcindoro, a rich old man. Musetta, in an attempt to let Marcel know she still loves him in spite of appearances, sings directly to him the "Valse di Musetta" (Musetta's Waltz), a sparkling coloratura aria. To get rid of her elderly admirer, Musetta sends him for shoes, telling him that the ones she has on pinch. When he leaves, she and Marcel embrace.

After they all feast together, Musetta tells the waiter that Alcindoro will pay the bill for all when he returns, and the gay party leaves.

The gay act ends humorously. Alcindoro returns and is presented with the bill. He collapses.

Act III

As the curtain rises, we see an inn near one of the toll gates of Paris. Outside the inn is hanging a signboard decorated with the painting on which Marcel was working in the first act. Tradespeople are passing through the city gate. Everything is covered with snow. Soon Mimi enters from a side street. She is racked with spells of severe coughing. She asks if Marcel is living at the inn, and, when she finds he is, sends for him. He comes out and tells her that he and Musetta are living there. Musetta is giving singing lessons and he is painting to pay for their board. Rudolph is there too, he tells Mimi, who answers that she and Rudolph have quarreled and must part. She hides when Rudolph comes out, and overhears a conversation between Rudolph and Marcel in which he says that he wants to separate from Mimi because of her fickleness. Then he gets to thinking of how ill she is, and he begins to worry. Just then Mimi coughs and Rudolph rushes to embrace her. She pushes him away and sings "Addio" (Farewell). Then, overcome with tenderness at the thought of parting, they sing a duet of the joys that will come to them when winter is over. Together again, they leave the stage.

Act IV

We see once more the attic room where the four comrades were living when the opera opened. Rudolph and Marcel are alone, trying to work. They talk of their former sweethearts, who have left them. Rudolph has seen Musetta on the street looking happy and prosperous. Marcel tells Rudolph that Mimi passed him, riding in a fine carriage. They sing a duet in which they voice their sorrows. Meanwhile Colline and Schaunard come in with food, after which they all begin to dance to enliven their spirits. In the midst of a mock duel between Colline and Schaunard, Musetta enters. She brings in Mimi who is very ill. They put her on Rudolph's bed. Musetta gives Marcel her earrings, Colline gives him his overcoat; and Colline goes out to try to get medicine and food and to bring a doctor. Left alone, the lovers sing a beautiful love duet, interrupted by Mimi's coughing.

Soon the others return. While they are preparing medicine for her, Mimi seems to fall asleep. Schaunard discovers that she is dead, and Rudolph throws himself upon the bed, sobbing.

LOHENGRIN

Words and music by Richard Wagner (1813-1883)
First produced: Weimar, August 26, 1850

The Characters

Henry the Fowler, King of Germany — Bass
Lohengrin, (Lo′-en-grin) — Tenor
Elsa of Brabant — Soprano
Duke Godfrey, Elsa's brother
Frederick of Telramund (Tel′-rah-moond) — Baritone
Ortrud (Ohr′-trood), Frederick's wife — Mezzo-Soprano
The King's Herald — Bass
Nobles, Ladies of Honor, Pages, and Attendants

The story of Lohengrin is from an old German legend which originated even earlier than the Middle Ages. In the score Wagner uses individual motives and rich orchestral colorings to identify his characters. This opera was first produced under the sponsorship of Liszt while the composer was a political exile, and it was not until fourteen years after he had finished the score that Wagner himself heard it performed.

Courtesy Chicago Civic Opera Co.

A SCENE FROM ACT I, "LOHENGRIN"
Lohengrin (René Maison) dismisses the boat which has carried him to Elsa's side.

ACT I

Henry the Fowler, King of Germany, has come to Brabant to assemble an army. He finds the people greatly disturbed over the disappearance of their ruler, the young Duke Godfrey. As the curtain rises, the king is seen sitting upon a throne which is placed under the Oak of Judgment on the banks of the river Scheldt. On one side of him are his nobles; on the other side are Frederick of Telramund, his wife Ortrud, and the nobility of Brabant. Frederick outlines the circumstances attending the disappearance of the young Duke. Upon the death of the old Duke of Brabant, his two children, Elsa and Godfrey, had been left under the care of Frederick. One day Elsa had come home from the forest alone, saying she had lost her brother. Frederick, who had intended to marry her, believed that she murdered her brother in order to inherit her father's property and married Ortrud instead.

Upon hearing Frederick's story, the king has Elsa brought in. She moves as if in a dream, and is accompanied by women attendants. Announcing that the trial shall be an ordeal by battle, the king asks Elsa to name her champion. At first she is too timid to speak, but finally she begins to tell of a strange dream she has had. She sings "Elsa's Dream," in which she describes a handsome knight in glittering armor, who, she says, will be her champion.

At the command of the king four trumpeters blow, in four directions, a summons for Elsa's champion, while the herald calls, "Who will do battle for Elsa of Brabant?" When there is no reply, Elsa explains that her knight is coming from a distance. A second call is sounded, and still no knight appears. Elsa drops to her knees and prays.

Presently those nearest the river see in the distance a boat drawn by a swan, with a warrior in radiant armor standing on the prow (Ex. 1). When the boat reaches shore, he dismisses the

swan and announces himself as Elsa's heaven-sent defender. He offers himself as her champion and asks if she will be his bride if he wins. She tells him that all she has and all she is will be his. The stranger-knight asks her to promise that if he becomes her husband she will never ask his name, his rank, or whence he came, and Elsa promises.

Frederick of Telramund engages in battle with Elsa's champion, and is soon struck to the ground, but the strange knight, Lohengrin, spares his life. While Ortrud and Frederick lament their defeat and swear vengeance, the others join in a chorus of praises to the victor.

Act II

Ortrud and Frederick are sitting on the cathedral steps, brooding over Frederick's defeat. Their despondency is accentuated by the gloom of the night, and emphasized by the sounds of gaiety coming from the citadel. Frederick blames Ortrud for causing his disgrace, because it was she who had told him that Elsa was guilty. Ortrud replies that Elsa's champion gained his victory by sorcery, and she tells Frederick that if he can find out the strange knight's real name and rank, his power will be broken, and Frederick can fight him again and be victorious. She adds, however, that only Elsa can get the secret from her lover.

As they talk, Elsa comes out on the balcony of the women's quarters and sings the beautiful lyric known as "Elsa's Song to the Breezes." After telling Frederick to leave her alone with Elsa, Ortrud pretends she is repentant and asks Elsa to protect her.

Courtesy Chicago Civic Opera Co.

SCENE FROM ACT II OF "LOHENGRIN"
Lohengrin leads Elsa in to the minister for their marriage rites.

She is taken by Elsa into the palace, where she proceeds to fill the mind of her benefactress with suspicions regarding her betrothed.

When day dawns, the people begin to gather for the wedding of Elsa and Lohengrin. A herald announces that Frederick is to be banished and that Lohengrin is to rule in his place. Frederick says that he will prove Elsa's champion to be an imposter.

As Elsa comes out, the nobles sing in chorus, "May ev'ry joy attend thee." When she reaches the church steps, Ortrud stops her and bursts out in a tirade, jeering at Elsa for not knowing the name of her betrothed. Frederick steps forth and accuses the unknown knight of sorcery, as evidenced by his swan-drawn boat. He demands Lohengrin tell his name. The knight refuses, the king has Ortrud and Frederick driven away, and the bridal procession continues.

ACT III

(Ex. 2) As the curtain rises upon the bridal chamber, the chorus of nobles sings the famous "Bridal Chorus" to which so many brides in all lands have marched (Ex. 3). The doors in the

back of the room are opened and the bridal procession enters. The singers march around the room, salute the bride and groom and leave them alone.

When Lohengrin calls Elsa by name, she says:

> "How sweet my name as from thy lips it glided!
> Canst thou deny to me the sound of thine?"

It is evident that Ortrud's carefully planted suspicions have begun to bear fruit. As Lohengrin reminds her of her promise and begs her not to ask his name, she becomes more insistent. Suddenly Frederick rushes into the room, sword in hand. Elsa gives Lohengrin his sword and he kills his enemy.

The scene changes, and again we see the banks of the Scheldt. It is dawn and the army is gathering. When the king arrives, he notices that the leader, Lohengrin, is missing. Now four men enter, bearing the body of Frederick. Elsa follows.

At last Lohengrin comes in and tells of the slaying of Frederick. While music symbolic of the Holy Grail comes from the orchestra (Ex. 4), Lohengrin sings "In Distant Lands," which he

says is his answer to Elsa's question. He tells of the Castle of Montsalvat where the Holy Grail is kept; and of the Knights of the Grail who go afar to fight for God and the right, but who retain their power only while they keep secret their names and origin. As soon as they are discovered, they must return. Lohengrin says that his father, Parsifal, whose knight he is, reigns at Montsalvat.

Now the swan is again seen in the distance. Lohengrin turns to Elsa and tells her that had she kept her promise for a year, he could have disenchanted her brother and returned him to her. As he goes toward the river bank, Ortrud comes forward and reveals the fact that the swan is Elsa's brother, whom she had enchanted. At her words Lohengrin kneels and prays. The dove of the Grail descends and hovers over him, as the swan sinks into the water. In its place rises Elsa's brother, the young Duke Godfrey. Lohengrin helps him from the water and cries out, "Behold the ruler of Brabant!" As the boat, now drawn by the dove, and carrying Lohengrin, disappears in the distance, Elsa falls dead into the arms of her brother.

LOUISE

Words and music by Gustave Charpentier (1860-
First produced: Paris, February 2, 1900

The Characters

Louise	Soprano
Julian, a poet	Tenor
Father	Baritone
Mother	Contralto
Irma	Soprano

This opera is one of interest to the sociologically minded listener. It deals with the gay street life of Paris and with the painful breaking of family ties. The name of Mary Garden, the famous American soprano, will probably always be linked with that of *Louise*, for it is was in this opera that she made her debut, and her interpretation of the title role has never been excelled.

Act I

When the curtain rises, Louise is in the living-room of her humble home. Strains of song are coming from outside. Julian, the poet, is serenading Louise. She goes to the window and joins him in a duet. So absorbed are they in each other, that Louise's mother enters the room unobserved. She reprimands Louise for disobeying her and makes unkind remarks about Julian, whose letter asking for Louise's hand has been ignored. In the midst of their argument Louise's father enters, holding a second letter from Julian. The father is willing to investigate the character of the young man, but the mother is violently opposed to Julian.

Act II

In the first scene of this act we see a street at the foot of the Hill of Montmartre. The strange characters who people the city by night slink away as daylight approaches. Workers begin to pass by enroute to their daily tasks. Presently Louise appears, accompanied by her mother. When the mother leaves her at the door of the work-shop, Julian appears and tries to persuade her to elope with him. Although she loves him, Louise is afraid to go with him, and enters the shop.

Courtesy Chicago Civic Opera Co.

VANNI-MARCOUX AS THE FATHER IN "LOUISE"

Courtesy Chicago Civic Opera Co.

MARIA CLAESSENS AS THE MOTHER IN "LOUISE"

Inside, the girls are singing and making merry. They make fun of Louise because she is quiet, and accuse her of being in love. Soon music is heard coming from the street. Julian is again serenading Louise. The other girls begin to flirt with him, much to her annoyance. Presently, she says she is ill, and puts on her hat to go home. Suspicious, the girls look out of the window after she leaves the shop. They see her going away with Julian.

ACT III

In a section of Paris known as the Hill of Montmarte is a rustic cottage with a picturesque garden in front of it. Julian is sitting in a chair in the garden; Louise is behind him. She is very happy as she sings to him of her joy in their love. Her song is the lyrical "Depuis le Jour" (Ever Since the Day), an aria that has become a favorite on the concert stage.

Soon their tranquillity is interrupted by a band of Bohemians. They crown Louise Queen of Montmartre, and decorate the little garden with lanterns.

The merry-makers are suddenly silenced as Louise's mother appears. She is dressed in black. The revelers leave and she is left alone with her daughter and Julian. The sorrowful mother tells Louise that her father is very ill, and begs her to return to see him. Julian is suspicious, but his fears are lessened when the mother promises that she will let Louise return to him. The lovers bid each other a touching farewell.

ACT IV

Louise is again in her old home. Her father is still weak, but has partially recovered. Louise is discontent, and her father tries to comfort her by pulling her down upon his knee and singing a lullaby as to a child. But Louise is still unhappy; her promised freedom is refused her. Her father does not understand why he cannot make her happy. Her mother comes in and tells her that they do not intend to let her return to Julian. Louise says excitedly that all she wants is Julian and her freedom. Angry, her father orders her to leave the house, and she rushes out. Too late, he realizes what he has done and tries to recall her, but in vain. He goes to the window and looks out over the city, which he holds responsible for his grief. With his despairing cry, "Oh, Paris!" the curtain falls.

MADAMA BUTTERFLY (MADAME BUTTERFLY)

Music by Giacomo Puccini (1858-1924)
Words by Giuseppe Giacosa and Luigi Illica,
founded on a play by David Belasco
First produced: Milan, February 17, 1904

The Characters

Madame Butterfly (Cho-Cho-San)	Soprano
Suzuki, Cho-Cho-San's servant	Mezzo-Soprano
B. F. Pinkerton, Lieutenant in United States Navy	Tenor
Sharpless, United States Consul at Nagasaki	Baritone
Kate Pinkerton, the Lieutenant's American wife	Mezzo-Soprano
Goro, a marriage broker	Tenor
Prince Yamadori, Suitor of Cho-Cho-San	Baritone
The Bonze, Uncle of Cho-Cho-San	Bass

Because the Japanese setting and Japanese melodies which Puccini had put into the score of *Madame Butterfly* were strange to the audience at Milan when the opera was first produced, the première was a failure. After some revision, the opera was presented again at Brescia a few months later, and was hugely successful. The pathetic appeal of the plot, the charm of the settings, and the melodic beauty of the music, combine to make this one of the world's favorite operas.

MARY McCORMIC AS "MADAME BUTTERFLY"

ACT I

Pinkerton and Goro, a marriage broker, are examining a little Japanese house which Pinkerton is leasing for the duration of his stay at Nagasaki. Goro has arranged for him a marriage according to Japanese fashion—it will last for nine hundred and ninety-nine years, but may be annulled any time. His bride is to be the charming little geisha girl Cho-Cho-San, known as Butterfly. Sharpless, United States Consul, comes in and Pinkerton tells him what a convenient temporary arrangement the marriage will be. Sharpless cautions him that the little bride may take it seriously, but Pinkerton brushes his admonitions aside and asks him to drink a toast to the time when he shall have a real wedding in America.

Now Goro announces the approach of Butterfly with her friends. When the girls have all assembled in their colorful kimonos, Sharpless and Butterfly begin to talk together. She tells him that her family once had money but had become so poor that she was forced to become a geisha girl. He asks her about her father, and there is evident embarrassment as she replies that he is dead.

Now Butterfly's relatives and the other wedding guests arrive. The little fifteen-year-old bride introduces them to the man she is about to marry. Then she takes Pinkerton aside and pulls from her sleeve all sorts of girlish treasures to show him. Among them is one of a sinister character—a knife in a sheath. This, she tells him, is precious because it was sent to her father by the Mikado. Knowing what it implied, her father obeyed by killing him-

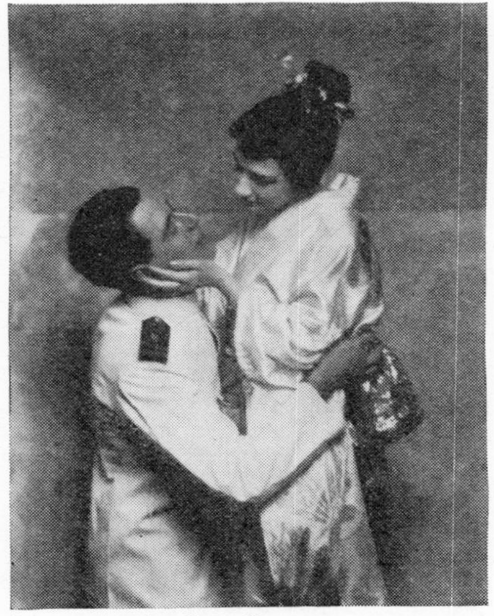

Courtesy American Opera Co.

CHARLES HEDLEY AND CECILE SHERMAN AS "PINKERTON" AND "BUTTERFLY" IN "MADAME BUTTERFLY"

self (hara-kiri). She also reveals to Pinkerton that she has gone to the Mission and accepted his faith, deserting that of her ancestors. She throws away her little idols.

Finally the marriage ceremony is over and the feasting is in progress when Cho-Cho-San's uncle, the Bonze, High Priest of Buddha, rushes in, cursing her for forsaking the ancient faith. All turn against her now, and there is much confusion until Pinkerton drives them out.

Left alone, the lovers sing of their love for each other, and Butterfly is comforted by Pinkerton: "O quant' occhi fisi" (Oh Kindly Heavens). Butterfly beseeches him to love her as he would a baby. He tells her how appropriate the name Butterfly is for her, but she has been told that in his country men pierce the hearts of butterflies and leave them to die. The thought terrifies her.

Act II

Three years later we find Butterfly and the faithful maid Suzuki alone in the little house. Suzuki is praying before an image of Buddha. In the three years of waiting, they have used up the money left by Pinkerton. Butterfly is still hopeful that he will return when the robins nest, as he promised. She plans to surprise him with the fine baby son whose existence he does not know about. To Suzuki she sings "Un bel di" (One Fine Day), in which she describes the arrival of the ship and Pinkerton's return to them.

Goro and Sharpless now come into the garden. Sharpless has with him a letter from Pinkerton. He tries to tell Cho-Cho-San something, but she is so overjoyed at the prospect of the return of her loved one that he hardly knows what to say. Finally he asks her what she would do if Pinkerton never returned. She replies that she might become a geisha again, but that it would be better to die. Sharpless and Goro, the match-maker, plead with her to marry the rich Yamadori who has long desired her. Butterfly refuses, however, and has Suzuki bring in the child. With pride she shows Sharpless the blue eyes and golden hair of an American. Greatly troubled, the consul leaves.

Now Butterfly and Suzuki rush about, decorating the house with flowers, for she is sure that Pinkerton is coming. She hears the boom of a cannon, and looking through a telescope sees the "Abraham Lincoln," the ship on which Pinkerton is an officer. Her wait for him begins, as she makes three peepholes in the paper wall where Suzuki, the baby, and she may look out. First the baby and then the maid fall asleep, but Butterfly, standing erect, keeps her lonely vigil.

Act III

It is now morning and Butterfly is still watching. She awakens the baby and the maid. Suzuki tries in vain to persuade her to rest, but finally Butterfly goes into another room with the child. After she is gone, Sharpless and Pinkerton arrive. They motion Suzuki to be still so that Butterfly will not hear them. Then Sharpless tells Suzuki she must prepare Butterfly for the sad news that Pinkerton has married an American woman, who has come to adopt the boy. Pinkerton is unable to face Butterfly, and leaves Sharpless to break the news. Butterfly, hearing his voice, rushes in happily, but is disappointed when she sees only Sharpless and the American woman. She sees Suzuki crying, guesses the truth, and asks only if he is alive. When Mrs. Pinkerton has sympathetically revealed her identity and promised to care for the child, Butterfly tells her that if Pinkerton will come for him in half an hour, she will let him have the boy.

After they are gone Butterfly bids the child goodbye, blindfolds him, and gives him a doll and an American flag to play with. Then she kills herself with her father's dagger. As she is dying, she embraces the child once more. Just at this point Pinkerton rushes in. After kneeling beside Butterfly and sobbing out his shame and grief, he takes up the child and leaves the room.

Courtesy Italian Tourist Bureau

A SCENE FROM "MANON"

MANON

Music by Jules Massenet (1842-1912)
Words by Meilhac and Gille, after a novel by Abbé Prévost
First produced: Paris, January 19, 1884

The Characters

Chevalier des Grieux (Shev-al-yay′ day Gree-uh′)	Tenor
Count des Grieux, his father	Bass
Lescaut (Les-koh′), Manon's cousin	Baritone
Guillot Morfontain (Jwee-yo′ Mohr-fon-ten′) Minister of France	Bass
De Brétigny (Duh Bray-tee-nyee′), a nobleman	Baritone
Manon (Ma-non′), a schoolgirl	Soprano

To prevent confusion in the reader's mind, it may be well to mention that Puccini wrote an opera with a libretto also based on Prévost's novel, *Manon Lescaut.* Both versions are popular. Puccini's, called *Manon Lescaut,* is typically Italian in treatment, while Massenet's shows all the characteristics of the French school.

Act I

In front of an inn at Amiens, a gay crowd is awaiting the coming of the stagecoach from Arras. One of the men in the crowd is Lescaut, a guardsman. He is there to meet his cousin, Manon, whom he is to take to a convent.

When the coach stops in front of the inn, Lescaut sees among the arrivals a shy young girl. Guessing that she must be his cousin, he introduces himself. In the charming aria "Je suis encore étourdie" ("I am still dazzled"), she sings of her joy in all the new experiences she is having. The coach departs, and likewise the crowd of people. Leaving Manon alone, Lescaut goes to see about her baggage.

An old roué, Guillot, sees Manon, and begins to make advances. He has gone as far as to ask her to elope with him, when her cousin returns and warns her against talking to strangers.

His advice is futile, however, for when he leaves Manon a second time, the Chevalier des Grieux, a charming young gentleman, appears, and he and Manon fall in love immediately. (A theme is heard in the orchestra that may be called Des Grieux' love motif.) Manon tells her new lover that she is on her way to a convent, but he says they must never part. A carriage which has been ordered by Guillot comes into the court, and the two young people decide to elope in it.

When Lescaut and Guillot come back and find the carriage gone, they begin to quarrel, and each accuses the other of being to blame for the elopement.

Act II

Manon and Des Grieux are living in an apartment in Paris. As the curtain rises, he is writing a letter asking his father to permit their marriage. The letter finished, he is about to take it out and mail it, when he sees a beautiful bouquet. He asks Manon who sent it. She says she has no idea, for it was thrown in through the window.

At this point the maid announces that two guardsmen wish to see Des Grieux. She says one is Manon's cousin, and whispers to Manon that the other is "a wealthy lord, who adores you!" Manon, by her immediate exclamation "De Brétigny!" tells us who sent the bouquet.

The two visitors enter. Lescaut inquires of Des Grieux whether or not he intends to marry Manon, and is shown the letter in answer. Lescaut, pretending that he wants to read the letter in a better light, succeeds in leading Des Grieux over to the window, thus leaving De Brétigny alone with Manon. De

Courtesy Italian Tourist Bureau

BENIAMINO GIGLI AS "CHEVALIER DES GRIEUX" IN "MANON"

Brétigny offers her many luxuries if she will leave her lover and come with him. He also tells her that a servant of Des Grieux's father is coming to take the Chevalier away that very night.

When the two visitors have gone, Manon keeps the plot secret. She is sorry to leave Des Grieux, but her desire for riches is greater than her love.

The supper table is set for two, and while Des Grieux is out mailing his letter, Manon sings a farewell to the little table where they are about to eat their last meal together. When he returns she is crying, and he sings to her of a dream he has of her in a cottage. The song is rudely interrupted by a knocking at the door. Though filled with sorrow, Manon finally lets Des Grieux answer it. He is captured by his father's servants. She looks from the window as he is being carried away and then falls into a chair, overcome with grief.

Act III

Manon, richly dressed, is with De Brétigny at a festival in the streets of Paris. They meet the Count des Grieux, who is an old friend of De Brétigny. Manon hears the Count tell De Brétigny that his son, the Chevalier, is about to enter the priesthood at St. Sulpice. The father tells Manon that his son has forgotten her, but she leaves immediately for St. Sulpice.

The second scene shows us the seminary at St. Sulpice, where young Des Grieux is trying to free himself from the memory of Manon. He sings "Fuyez, douce image" (Flee, sweet image). His father has been to see him and has tried to persuade him not to enter the priesthood, but his entreaties are in vain. Now Manon comes. Her persuasions are more than he can withstand, and he leaves the priesthood to be with her.

Act iv

Lescaut and his friends are in Paris, in a fashionable gambling house. The typical crowd of gay ladies and gentlemen about town is present. Into the casino come Manon and Des Grieux. He is uneasy but Manon urges him to venture, in the hope that he may increase their rapidly diminishing money. He finally starts to play against Guillot, and wins so much that the old man has them arrested as sharpers. Just as the arrest is made, Des Grieux's father comes in. His intervention secures Des Grieux's release, but Manon is to be deported to the West Indies.

In the next scene, we see the road to Le Havre. Des Grieux is hiding in a lonely place by the roadside where he can see the convict gang pass on their march to the ship. Lescaut was supposed to bring a body of men to help Des Grieux rescue Manon, but his men have failed him. Des Grieux hears that Manon is dying. Desperate, he bribes one of the guards to leave her behind until evening. In his arms once again, she speaks of their past joys. Des Grieux tries to tell her that there is still much happiness ahead of them, but Manon realizes that she is dying. Finally she kisses him, and dies in his arms.

GREAT STAIRCASE OF THE PARIS OPERA

DIE MEISTERSINGER VON NÜRNBERG (THE MASTER-SINGERS OF NUREMBERG)

Words and music by Richard Wagner (1813-1883)
First produced: Munich, June 21, 1868

The Characters

Hans Sachs, cobbler	Bass
Pogner, goldsmith	Bass
Beckmesser, town clerk	Bass
Sir Walter von Stölzing, a knight	Tenor
David, apprentice to Hans Sachs	Tenor
Eva, Pogner's daughter	Soprano
Magdalena, Eva's nurse	Soprano
Vogelsang, furrier	
Nachtigal, buckle maker	
Kothner, baker	
Zorn, pewterer	
Eisslinger, grocer	
Moser, tailor	
Ortel, soap boiler	
Schwarz, stocking weaver	
Folz, coppersmith	
Burghers, journeymen, apprentices, girls, and people.	

Wagner based this opera upon historical realities instead of the usual legendary tales. The Mastersingers were members of the trade guilds of Nuremberg in the sixteenth century. At first, these groups were formed to create and maintain interest in the fine arts. As time went on, however, the guilds came to be governed by strict rules, upon which their members placed undue importance (Ex. 1 and 2).

ACT I

In a back row in the Church of St. Catherine sit Eva and her nurse Magdalena, who join the congregation in the singing of a fine old hymn. Walter von Stölzing, impatient for the service to conclude, watches Eva from a distance. When the congregation begins to leave, he approaches her and, while her nurse is absent for a moment, asks her if she has promised to marry anyone. Before she can reply, Magdalena returns and answers for her. Eva is betrothed, she says, but nobody knows to whom, because the winner of the song contest to be held on the morrow will also win Eva as a bride.

Walter, a stranger in town, is bewildered at this statement, but Magdalena's sweetheart, David, who has just entered, tells him of these traditional festivals, and explains to him that only a Master of the guild may compete. David, an apprentice of Hans Sachs, who teaches him both shoe-making and music, decides to become a Master also in order to enter the contest.

The Mastersingers arrive for a trial hearing, preparatory to the contest on the following day. Walter asks for a test and is given an opportunity to sing. He starts to improvise "Fanget an" (Now begin), but this song of love and spring time is so free and unbound by the strict rules of the Guild that Hans Sachs, alone of all the Masters, is willing to let him go beyond the first verse. Hans thinks there is real worth in the song, but when Walter finishes, he can hardly be heard above the wrangling and taunts of the others.

ACT II

The apprentices are busy closing their masters' houses on the eve of the contest, of which they talk as they work. Hans Sachs sits down beside his door and begins distractedly to work at his cobbling. He thinks of the beauty of Walter's song and muses upon his own lack of ability.

Eva comes in and questions him about Walter's failure in the trial for the contest, but Hans answers evasively. He is a widower, much in love with Eva, and it saddens him to realize that she has already lost her heart to Walter. Soon Eva sees Walter and crosses the street to talk to him.

Hans hears Beckmesser, the town clerk, arrive to serenade Eva. He begins his song, but Hans also begins to sing, so lustily that he drowns out the discomfited serenader. Magdalena appears at Eva's window, and Beckmesser, thinking she is Eva, wants more than ever to have his song heard. The shoemaker says he will listen and act as "Marker," hammering on the shoe whenever Beckmesser makes an error. As the song proceeds, Hans hammers more and more on his shoe and Beckmesser becomes furiously angry. He sings on to the discordant noise of the hammering, but finally the shoe is finished and Hans sings a song of triumph. A crowd has gathered, and David comes in and sees his beloved Magdalena being serenaded by Beckmesser. Not knowing that the clerk thinks she is Eva, he immediately begins a fight with him. Soon the horn of the night watchman is heard and the crowd vanishes.

Act III

It is the morning of the contest, and Hans is seated in his home, reading. David comes in to apologize for his actions on the night before, and then leaves him alone. As Hans sits and meditates he sings "Wahn! Wahn! Überall Wahn!" (Mad! Mad! The Whole World Is Mad!). Walter enters as he finishes, and tells him of a beautiful poem and melody which have come to him in a dream. Hans persuades Walter to sing it for him while he writes it down. The two then leave to prepare for the contest.

Beckmesser comes into the empty room, sees Hans's copy of the song, and puts it in his pocket. When the cobbler enters, Beckmesser charges him with composing a song for the contest and accuses him of having started the happenings of the previous evening in order to get rid of himself as a rival. Hans retorts by claiming that Beckmesser has stolen the song, but surprises the clerk by offering it to him. Beckmesser accepts it eagerly, not knowing as Hans does what a failure he will make of it.

Eva enters, dressed for the contest. Walter, who comes in soon after, is delighted to see her, and sings a third verse to the song which he had sung to Hans. So moved is Eva by it that she falls sobbing into Hans's arms. Filled with emotion, Hans sings again his cobbler's song, "A Shoemaker's Life."

David and Magdalena now enter and the five sing as a quintet: "Selig wie die Sonne" (Brightly as the Sun).

In the second scene, a great assemblage has come together for the contest, which is to be held in a field along the banks of the river Pegnitz. The crowd increases as processions of journeymen

Courtesy Chicago Civic Opera Co.

RUDOLPH BOCKELMANN AS "HANS SACHS" IN "DIE MEISTERSINGER"

Courtesy Chicago Civic Opera Co.

OSCAR COLCAIRE AS "DAVID" IN "DIE MEISTERSINGER"

and apprentices march in with their various guilds. At last, announced by a herald, the Mastersingers enter and take their places on the platform. Sachs, after being greeted by a beautiful chorus, gives the rules for the contest and Beckmesser, oldest of the contestants, is called upon to sing first.

Beckmesser makes a miserable failure of Walter's song. He blames Hans for having written it to make him ridiculous, throws the paper down, and leaves.

After he is gone, Hans picks up the song and declares that he is not the author. He calls for a volunteer to give the song its deserved interpretation, and Walter comes forward. When he first begins to sing, the Masters busy themselves trying to catch him in an error, but soon they are carried away by the beauty of his melody. At the end of the song, all the Mastersingers rise and pronounce Walter the victor. Eva places the wreath of victory on his head, and the people join in a final chorus of joy that rises to a noble climax as the curtain closes on the scene.

OTHELLO

Music by Giuseppe Verdi (1813-1901)
Words by Arrigo Boito, after Shakespeare
First produced: Milan, 1887

The Characters

Othello, a Moor in the Venetian army	Tenor
Iago, his ensign	Baritone
Cassio, his lieutenant	Tenor
Roderigo, a Venetian gentleman	Tenor
Montano, ex-governor of Cyprus	Bass
Ludovico, ambassador from Venice	Bass
Desdemona, wife of Othello	Soprano
Emilia, wife of Iago	Mezzo-Soprano

Verdi wrote *Othello* when he was seventy-four. To it he brought a lifetime of experience in the composition of operas. The influence of Wagner's operas on his work is strong. There are few separate arias, and the opera is less melodic than his others. Its maturity of style gives it a high place in Verdi's works.

Act I

A group made up of citizens and soldiers has assembled to greet Othello, the new Governor of Cyprus, when he returns from fighting a war against the Turks. Anxiously they watch a storm-tossed vessel in the harbor. Finally the wind subsides and Othello is able to land. He tells the crowd about the success of his expedition, and then he goes into the castle, leaving his soldiers to celebrate the victory.

To Roderigo, Iago, Othello's ensign, expresses his hatred of Othello, and also his bitterness toward Cassio, whom Othello has made Captain, when he, Iago, should have had the office. He engages Roderigo's help in getting Cassio intoxicated. Under the influence of the liquor, Cassio quarrels with Roderigo and Montano, the ex-governor, and a street riot begins. The commotion causes Othello and Desdemona to come out of the castle. Othello blames Cassio for the disturbance, and as punishment takes from him his rank of Captain. Thus Iago has been successful in his evil designs.

The end of the Act is a love duet between Othello and Desdemona. In it Othello recalls how Desdemona fell in love with him when she heard his accounts of his romantic exploits in battle:

> She loved me for the dangers I had pass'd,
> And I loved her that she did pity them.

Courtesy Chicago Civic Opera Co.

CHARLES MARSHALL AS "OTHELLO"

Act II

Iago, covering his hypocrisy with assumed sympathy, is with Cassio in a room overlooking the castle garden. He suggests that Desdemona might be prevailed upon to intercede with Othello in his behalf. As Cassio leaves to follow his suggestion, Iago sings his famous creed, which reveals his thoroughly evil character.

In accordance with his suggestion, Cassio goes to Desdemona and lays his case before her. Iago sees them together, and when Othello comes out, begins to sow the seeds of jealousy. He asks if Cassio was not acquainted with Desdemona before her marriage. Then he warns Othello of the dangers of jealousy.

Now Desdemona, accompanied by fisher-folk and children, comes from the garden. Othello is charmed by her beauty. When the people finally leave, Desdemona begins to plead for Cassio. As she becomes more persistent, Othello's jealousy increases. His actions make Desdemona think he is ill. She attempts to wipe his forehead with her handkerchief, but he seizes it and throws it on the ground. Emilia, Desdemona's maid, picks up the fallen handkerchief, but Iago, her husband, manages to snatch it from her. Meantime, Desdemona is trying to placate Othello. Her efforts are in vain, and Othello dismisses her.

When Iago is alone with Othello, he sows more suspicion in the mind of the enraged husband by telling him that he has seen Desdemona's handkerchief in Cassio's room. Beside himself, Othello joins Iago in a vow of vengeance.

ACT III

Othello and Iago are together in a room in the castle. Iago goes to get Cassio.

Soon Desdemona appears in all her loveliness. She looks so innocent that Othello's faith is about to revive, until she again starts pleading for Cassio. Then Othello demands her handkerchief. She hands it to him, but he says that it is not the one he wants; he refers to one which he had given her. She replies that it is in her room and she will get it for him. With recriminations, which she cannot understand, Othello violently pushes her away.

When she has departed, weeping, Iago tells Othello to hide behind some pillars and listen, for Cassio is coming.

Skilfully Iago leads Cassio on to talk of his love affairs. Although he names the woman who is his sweetheart, calling her Bianca, Othello is so overcome with jealousy that he does not hear. Finally Cassio takes the fatal handkerchief from his pocket and shows it to Iago, saying that he does not know who put it in his room. Othello recognizes the handkerchief, and is wild with jealousy.

When Cassio leaves, Othello tells Iago of his determination to kill Desdemona. Iago advises him to suffocate her, and promises that he will get rid of Cassio.

An embassy from Venice arrives, and Desdemona comes to help Othello welcome the visitors. She seizes another opportunity to plead with Othello for Cassio, and he silences her.

The ambassador brings word that Othello is to be recalled to Venice, and Cassio appointed Governor in his place. Othello seems so distressed that Desdemona begins to weep. Blinded by jealousy, Othello thinks she is weeping over the coming separation from Cassio. Before the whole company, he throws her to the ground, saying "Lie there and weep." The assembled people join in a chorus of sympathy, while Desdemona pleads for mercy. Othello in an insane rage gives a wild cry, and all the others rush from the stage. Exhausted by his rage, Othello falls to the ground unconscious.

ACT IV

As Desdemona is preparing for bed, assisted by Emilia, she sings "Salce, Salce" (The Willow Song), the story of a girl who died because she had loved too well. Then, kneeling before an altar, she sings "Ave Maria," one of the loveliest arias in musical literature. Trustingly she goes to sleep.

Othello enters and looks at his sleeping wife. He kisses her, presses a pillow down over her face. Emilia is clamoring for admittance, and soon the room is filled with people. Othello tells them that Desdemona was unfaithful to him. Emilia, however, discloses the treacherous use her husband made of the handkerchief, and proves the innocence of Desdemona.

Filled with remorse, Othello kisses his dead wife and then stabs himself. Iago tries to escape, but is caught and given the punishment he deserves.

I PAGLIACCI (THE PLAYERS)

Words and music by Ruggiero Leoncavallo (1858-1919)
First produced: Milan, May 21, 1892.

The Characters

Canio (Kan'nee-o), owner of the troupe	Tenor
Nedda, Canio's wife	Soprano
Tonio (Toh'nee-oh), the clown	Baritone
Silvio (Sil'vee-oh), a young farmer	Baritone
Peppe (Pep'pay), a player	Baritone

Into this opera Leoncavallo introduced two innovations. One was having one of the characters come out before the curtain rises and sing a prologue after the manner of the old Greek theater. The other was the use of a play within a play.

Prologue

Tonio, the clown, comes out in front of the curtain and explains to the audience that the actors are real like themselves, and the story that is about to unfold is true. He tells them that sometimes the actors have to play the part of clowns when their hearts are breaking. He sings "Up with the curtain," and disappears.

Act I

It is afternoon in an Italian village. A theater has been set up in a field for a wandering theatrical troupe. Tonio, the hunchback and one of the actors, has been left to guard it. The villagers have assembled to greet the rest of the players when they arrive.

Soon the approach of the troupe is heard. Canio, the owner of the show, is playing the drum. Nedda, his wife, in real life and on the stage, is riding in a cart drawn by a donkey. Canio passes out handbills, and invites all the people to attend the play. He is to play the part of Pagliaccio, Nedda the part of Columbine, and Peppe, that of Harlequin.

When Canio goes to help his wife from the cart, Tonio is already there. Canio boxes his ears and helps Nedda out himself, much to the amusement of the peasants, who think it is all part of the entertainment. Nedda, however, is alarmed by the expression on her husband's face, and Tonio goes away muttering.

One of the villagers suggests that they go to a tavern for a drink. Canio invites Tonio to go with them, but the clown refuses, pretending he must rub down the donkey. Canio's suspicion increases when a villager intimates that Tonio may be staying to make love to Nedda.

When Nedda is alone she sings a song to the birds, and then Tonio, who has been hiding, comes out and makes love to her. She mocks him and laughs at his ardent wooing, but he is so persistent she strikes him with a whip. Crazed with anger, he swears vengeance as he leaves.

When Nedda is alone once more, her lover, Silvio, appears, and we see that Canio has grounds for his jealousy. The lovers arrange an elopement to take place at midnight.

In the meantime Tonio has gone for Canio and brings him in just in time to hear Nedda pledge her love. Canio pursues his wife's fleeing lover, but Silvio escapes. Returning, Canio demands that Nedda tell her lover's name. She refuses and he tries to stab her but Peppe and Tonio prevent the rash deed. The clown tells Canio that it is best to wait for his revenge until the show is over. He says that the lover will undoubtedly be among the audience, and will probably betray himself in some way. The others leave to dress for the play, and Canio sings of his grief in the heart-rending song, "Vesti la giubba" (On with the Play). He tells how he must amuse the people while his heart is breaking.

Act II

Tonio beats his drum to summon the people to the theater. All is now in readiness, and when the villagers are finally seated, Nedda goes around to collect the money. As she comes to Silvio, seated in the front row, he reminds her of their appointment.

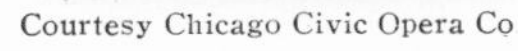
Courtesy Chicago Civic Opera Co

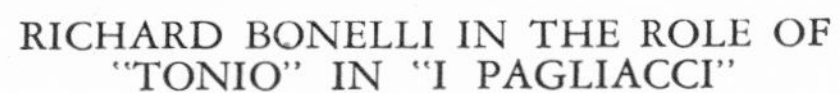
RICHARD BONELLI IN THE ROLE OF "TONIO" IN "I PAGLIACCI"

Courtesy Chicago Civic Opera Co.

CHARLES MARSHALL AS "CANIO" IN THE OPERA "I PAGLIACCI"

The play begins with Nedda, in the role of Columbine, dancing about the stage to a minuet. Soon a guitar outside the window is heard; Harlequin (Peppe) is singing a serenade. Taddeo (Tonio) comes in with a basket of provisions. He begins to make ardent love to Columbine, but Harlequin enters and marches him out, holding him by the ear.

In turn, Harlequin is forced to make a hurried departure by jumping from the window when Columbine's husband returns unexpectedly. Canio, taking the part of Columbine's husband, comes in just as his wife is saying the same words to her fleeing lover that he had heard her say to Silvio that afternoon. It is in his part to ask her the name of her lover. This is too much. He sings "No Pagliaccio, non son!" (No, Punchinello, No More!).

The audience is delighted with the apparent reality of the acting, but Silvio is alarmed, for he sees it is too genuine. With his dagger, he endeavors to go onto the stage but is held back by the others. Nedda tries to flee into the audience, but Canio's revenge is not to be denied, and he plunges his knife between her shoulders. Dying, she gasps the name of Silvio. Canio rushes from the stage, stabs her lover, and then turns to the audience and says, "The Comedy is Ended."

DER RING DES NIBELUNGEN (THE RING OF THE NIBELUNGS)

Words and Music by Richard Wagner (1813-1883)
First complete production: Bayreuth, 1876.

The entire work consists of a Prologue, *Das Rheingold,* and three complete operas, *Die Walküre, Siegfried,* and *Die Götterdämmerung,* through which runs a connected story. Wagner started work on the score while he was still a political exile. When it was partially written, he laid it aside for more than ten years. By this time King Ludwig of Bavaria had become interested in Wagner, and had built a theater at Bayreuth for the production of the *Ring.* The first performance of the *Ring* took place in the Bayreuth Theater in 1876.

The instrumentation of the operas is for a very large orchestra. Wagner invented for it four new instruments called either "Bayreuth tubas" or "Wagner tubas." These are very large brass horns which play the bass parts in the orchestra.

Courtesy The Art Institute of Chicago

THE WAGNER THEATER, BAYREUTH

DAS RHEINGOLD (THE RHINEGOLD)

Words and music by Richard Wagner (1813-1883)
First produced: Munich, September 22, 1869

The Characters

GODS	
Wotan (Vo'tahn)	Baritone
Donner (Dohn'er)	Bass
Froh	Tenor
Loge (Loh'gah)	Tenor
GIANTS	
Fasolt(Fah'zohlt)	Bass
Fafner (Fahf'ner)	Bass
NIBELUNGS	
Alberich (Ahl'ber-ik)	Baritone
Mime (Mee'mah)	Tenor
GODDESSES	
Fricka (Frik'ah)	Soprano
Freia (Fry'ah)	Soprano
Erda (Air'dah)	Contralto
RHINE MAIDENS	
Woglinde (Vog-lin'dah)	Soprano
Wellgunde (Vell-goon'dah)	Soprano
Flosshilde (Floss-hill'dah)	Contralto

(Ex. 1) *Das Rheingold* is the introductory story which serves as a Prologue to other operas in the *Ring*. When the curtain rises, we see, in the translucent depths of the Rhine River, three Rhine Maidens swimming. Suddenly Alberich, the Nibelung dwarf, appears. His home is deep in the earth, but he has come up and is trying to catch the elusive Rhine maidens (Ex. 2). A ray of

sunlight reveals the gleaming Rhine gold on a high rock. As the maidens swim about, they sing that, if the gold is made into a ring, it will bestow upon its owner the power to rule the world (Ex.

3). In order to forge the metal, however, one has to give up forever the joys of love (Ex. 4). Alberich, who has been listening

greedily to their tale, climbs up and secures the gold. He swears an oath to give up love, and disappears into his underground home.

Now the scene changes and we see a clearing high in the mountains. In the background can be seen Valhalla, a castle which has just been completed by the giants, and which is to be the home of the gods. In the clearing, lying asleep, are Wotan, the father of the gods, and his wife, Fricka (Ex. 5).

When Wotan awakes, his wife reminds him that he has promised to give Freia, the goddess of youth and beauty, to the giants, as payment for the castle. She is to be turned over to them as soon as the castle is finished (Ex. 6).

Just at this point, Freia rushes in, pursued by the two giants, Fasolt and Fafner (Ex. 7). Wotan is worried because Freia has the

golden apples, which keep the gods young. Of course, if she takes these with her, the gods will grow old (Ex. 8). However, Wotan

must keep his word, and the giants are dragging Freia away when Loge the firegod enters. He tells Wotan about Alberich's theft of the gold. He also says that the dwarf has made a Ring of it, endowed with magic power. Hearing this, the giants promise to release Freia if they are given the Ring instead, but they demand to keep her as hostage until they receive it. As the giants depart with Freia and her golden apples, the gods become grey and bent. Wotan sends for Loge to help him secure the Ring.

Now Wotan, led by Loge, descends to Nibelheim, the home of the dwarfs (Ex. 9). Amid the clanging of anvils, they arrive in

an underground workshop. With the power of the Ring, Alberich has made slaves of the other dwarfs. He is making them dig costly metal for him, and make it into various objects of beauty (Ex.

10). Among these is a helmet which Alberich has forced his brother Mime to forge for him, and which has the strange power of making its wearer invisible, and also of changing him into whatever form he wishes. He calls the helmet the Tarnhelm (Ex. 11).

When Loge and Wotan enter, they persuade Alberich to illustrate its powers for them. Unsuspectingly, the dwarf changes himself into a dragon, and after that into a toad. Quickly Wotan puts his foot upon him, and takes the Tarnhelm from his head. Then the two gods bind him and carry him away.

In the last scene we are again above the earth. Wotan and Loge, who have forced Alberich to turn over his treasure to them, call forth the dwarfs by means of the Ring and order them to bring the gold. It is piled high and on top is put the Tarnhelm. The two gods then seize the Ring from the raging Alberich, who puts upon it a curse of death to whomever shall own it.

Now the giants, Fasolt and Fafner, come for the promised Ring, but with it they demand a pile of gold high enough to hide Freia. The giants then insist that the Tarnhelm and the Ring be placed on top of the heap. Wotan refuses to release the Ring until Freia is freed. Just then Erda appears and warns Wotan that death and destruction will come to the holder of the Ring, so he throws it on the treasure pile. The deadly curse begins to take effect (Ex. 12). The giants quarrel, and Fafner kills Fasolt and

escapes with the treasure. As the gods watch him in dismay, Donner, the god of thunder, climbs on a high rock and summons a storm. Lightning and thunder break upon the scene. Then a rainbow bridge appears, leading to Valhalla. Over the bridge pass the gods to the towering battlements of their now home, as from the river the Rhine maidens cry out for their lost gold.

DIE WALKÜRE (THE VALKYRIE)

Words and music by Richard Wagner (1813-1883)
First produced: Munich, June 25, 1870

The Characters

Brünnhilde (Bruen-hill'dah)	Soprano
Sieglinde (Zeeg-lin'dah)	Soprano
Siegmund (Zeeg'moond)	Tenor
Wotan (Voh'tahn)	Baritone
Hunding (Hoond'ing)	Bass
Chorus of Valkyries	

An orchestral prelude vividly pictures a fierce storm which subsides as the curtain rises.

Act I

We see the living room of Hunding's woodland home. Into this dwelling comes Siegmund, and falls on the floor, exhausted (Ex. 1).

Soon Sieglinde enters, and, discovering the stranger, she brings him water, and they begin to talk to each other with ever-increasing sympathy and interest (Ex. 2).

Presently Hunding, Sieglinde's husband, returns, and the three partake of the evening meal, during which Siegmund tells them of his life. When he was a lad, he and his father had returned from a hunt to find his mother killed, and his twin sister abducted by their enemies, the Neidungs. Later, his father also disappeared. Now, and for some time past, Siegmund has been a wandering outlaw. He tells his listeners that on this very day he had come upon a young girl who was to be given as bride to a man whom she did not love. He attempted to rescue her but was overpowered by her enemies, who broke his sword.

As Siegmund relates his story, Hunding becomes aware of the fact that this is the man whom he has been pursuing. According to the laws of hospitality, however, a host may not harm even an enemy while he is a guest in the house. Before Hunding and Sieglinde leave their guest for the night, Hunding warns his enemy what the morning will bring forth (Ex. 3).

After they have gone Siegmund bewails his misfortune, as he thinks of the beautiful woman, Sieglinde, who has befriended him, and who is married to a man she does not love (Ex. 4 and 5). He

recalls how his father promised to send him a weapon when he most needed it. In his anguish he cries to his father, "Wälse, Wälse, where is thy sword?" As he utters this cry, the blazing firelight shines upon the hilt of a sword driven into the trunk of the tree around which the house is built. He wonders what it is that shines so brightly (Ex. 6).

Scarcely has he lain down to sleep when Sieglinde enters; she tells him that she has given her husband a sleeping potion in order that she may recount without interruption the story of the sword which projects from the tree. She says that at her wedding feast a strange man, who kept his face hidden, appeared and thrust the sword deep into the tree, saying that only one man would be able to withdraw it. That hero, Sieglinde hopes, will rescue her from Hunding. Siegmund embraces her and tells her that he is the one who will withdraw the sword and take her with him as his wife. As they sing together a beautiful duet, the door suddenly opens. There is no one at the door, and Siegmund tells Sieglinde that the spring had entered the room. Sieglinde then sings the famous "Spring Song" (Ex. 7). Suddenly, while looking at her

lover, she notices how much he looks like the image of herself she has seen in the water. She asks if his father's name was Wälse. When he says that it was, she tells him that now she knows that the sword was left for him, for she, too, is a Wälsung. Siegmund rushes to the tree and draws out the sword, which he names "Needful." Then the two lovers flee from the house of Hunding.

Act II

The prelude to this act is descriptive first of the flight of the lovers, and then of the Valkyries as they ride their galloping horses (Ex. 8).

As the curtain rises we see Brünnhilde, Wotan's favorite daughter, arrayed in armor, standing upon a rocky cliff. She is one of the nine Valkyries who are daughters of Wotan by the goddess Erda, and whose duty it is to carry to Valhalla the bodies of warriors killed in battle. Wotan is sending Brünnhilde to aid Siegmund in his approaching fight with Hunding.

Courtesy Chicago Civic Opera Co

THEODORE STRACK AS "SIEGMUND" IN "DIE WALKÜRE"

Courtesy Chicago Civic Opera Co.

RUDOLPH BOCKELMANN AS "WOTAN" IN "DIE WALKÜRE"

Siegmund is really the son of Wotan, whose desire it is to regain the possession of the Ring of the Nibelungs and return it to the Rhine maidens. According to his own laws he may not himself steal that which he has given in payment of a debt. Therefore, some time before, he had disguised himself as a warrior, Wälse, and had gone to earth and had a son and daughter by a mortal woman. By means of the race he thus founded, he hoped some day to regain the Ring.

Now we hear Brünnhilde's famous war cry, as she warns her father of the approach of Fricka, the Goddess of Marriage.

Fricka comes in raging because the Wälsung couple have sinned against the laws of marriage (Ex. 9). She demands their

punishment. Wotan pleads with her, explaining why he became father of Sieglinde and Siegmund, but she is firm and he promises to withdraw his aid from his son.

Now Brünnhilde comes back and, as she can read what is really in her father's heart, protests when he tells her that Siegmund must perish. Wotan is angry, however, at her defiance, and leaves her, demanding that she obey him.

When she is alone, Brünnhilde goes into a cave to await the coming of Siegmund. Soon she sees the lovers. Siegmund is trying to soothe his beloved, who is so weary that she faints in his arms. When he looks up, he sees Brünnhilde, who tells him that she has come to take him to Valhalla (Ex. 10). When he asks if Sieglinde

is to accompany him, Brünnhilde tells him that he must go without her. Rather than leave his sweetheart and their unborn child, he is about to take her life, when Brünnhilde decides to defy her father and cause Hunding to die instead of Siegmund. After telling this to Siegmund, she vanishes. He kisses Sieglinde and goes to seek his adversary.

Sieglinde awakens and hurries to the fray. A flash of lightning stops her, and by its gleam we see Brünnhilde hovering over Siegmund as he fights Hunding. Soon we see Wotan's form above Hunding. As Siegmund is about to run his enemy through, Wotan stretches forth his spear and the sword of Siegmund is broken. Then Hunding drives his sword into Siegmund's breast. Brünnhilde retrieves the bits of broken sword, then picks up Sieglinde, and hurries away with her. When Hunding and Wotan are left alone, Wotan bids Hunding go and tell Fricka that she has been avenged, but so contemptuous is the god that Hunding falls dead.

Act III

As the curtain rises, we hear the music of the famous "Ride of the Valkyries" with its vivid description of galloping and neighing horses. The Valkyries are hurrying to their meeting place on the top of a mountain. We hear their warcry, "Ho-jo-to-ho" as they signal to each other. Soon all the sisters are assembled with the exception of Brünnhilde. In a short while she enters, bringing Sieglinde.

Brünnhilde tells her sisters what has taken place and asks them to lend her a horse, so that she and Sieglinde can escape from Wotan, who is pursuing them in wrath. Afraid, her sisters refuse to come to her assistance, and Sieglinde begs to be allowed to remain where she is and die, but Brünnhilde tells her that she must save herself for the sake of her child, for he will be a great hero. In obedience to Brünnhilde, Sieglinde flees to the forest, wherein the giant, Fafner, who has changed himself into a dragon by means of the Tarnhelm, is guarding the Ring and the rest of the treasure of the Nibelungs. Brünnhilde says that her father seldom goes into that forest.

Brünnhilde remains to meet her father, Wotan. When he arrives he bids her sisters leave them alone. He then tells her that for her disobedience she shall be chained to a rock, doomed never to see his face again. She pleads for mercy, telling him that, by saving the pieces of the sword and the unborn child who might some day overcome the enemy and recover the Ring, she had fulfilled his real wish (Ex. 11 and 12). Failing in her entreaties, she

asks that she be surrounded with fire to protect her from the chance passer-by. Wotan grants this request (Ex. 13). After

singing a beautiful song of farewell to his favorite daughter, he kisses her, lays her down upon a rock, and covers her with her shield. Loudly he summons Loge, the fire-god and strikes his spear upon the rock three times. Flames spring up, and she is surrounded

by a ring of fire (Ex. 14). She is to sleep, thus protected, until a hero free from fear shall awaken her and claim her for his bride, for she has lost her immortality and will awaken a mortal. Higher and higher mounts the ring of fire as Wotan sorrowfully departs.

SIEGFRIED

Words and music by Richard Wagner (1813-1883)
First produced: Bayreuth, August 16, 1876

The Characters

Siegfried (Zeeg'freed)	Tenor
Mime (Mee'mah)	Tenor
Wotan (Voh-tan)	Baritone Bass
Alberich (Ahl'ber-ik)	Baritone Bass
Fafner (Fahf'ner)	Bass
Erda (Air'dah)	Contralto
Brünnhilde (Bruen-hill'dah)	Soprano
Forest Bird	Soprano

ACT I

(Ex. 1) The scene opens in the forest dwelling place of the Nibelungen dwarfs, Mime and Alberich. With the two brothers live Siegfried, young son of Wotan's children, Sieglinde and Siegmund. Both of Siegfried's parents are dead, Sieglinde having died in giving him birth shortly after Siegmund had been killed in combat. Their son is now a brave and handsome youth of eighteen or twenty.

As Mime, the smith, works at his forge, we learn that he hopes that the boy, Siegfried, will be able to overcome the dragon and obtain the treasure. It is necessary, however, that he have a sword, and Mime has been unable to forge one strong enough to suit Siegfried. Mime knows that only one sword exists that is strong enough: the sword called "Needful," the pieces of which were bequeathed to Siegfried by his mother. But the dwarf is not able to forge these mighty pieces together.

Preceded by the sound of a hunting horn, Siegfried enters (Ex.

2). He is leading a wild bear which he has captured in the forest. When Mime hides in fear, the boy drives the animal back to the woods. He now asks Mime for his sword, and the dwarf hands him the one he has just made. Siegfried strikes the anvil with it and the weapon is shattered.

Then Siegfried asks Mime to tell him who his parents were. The dwarf tries to make the boy believe that he is his father, but Siegfried knows better. Finally, after almost beating the dwarf, Siegfried forces him to tell the truth. Mime tells him of his mother, Sieglinde, but does not tell him that his father's name was Siegmund. The pieces of broken sword reveal this. After again bidding Mime forge the sword "Needful," Siegfried leaves for the forest.

While the youth is gone, Mime has a strange caller, an old man with one eye hidden (Ex. 3). The stranger, who is Wotan in dis-

guise, asks Mime for shelter, and although the dwarf refuses, he will not leave. He sits down and tells Mime that he will answer three questions and will forfeit his head if he fails. Wotan answers the three questions put to him by Mime, and then says he will ask one in his turn. He asks who will forge the pieces of the sword. To this Mime is unable to reply. The stranger rises to leave, but before going he answers his own question, saying that the sword "Needful" will be forged by one who has never known fear. He bids the dwarf beware, for he will forfeit his head to the man who forges the sword. Then the stranger leaves. His visit has put Mime into a nervous state. He fears that Fafner, the giant, is after him.

When Siegfried returns, he finds the dwarf hiding behind the anvil. Soon Mime begins to talk about fear. Siegfried does not seem to understand what Mime is talking about, but agrees to go with him to the dragon's den where he may learn the meaning of fear. First, however, the sword must be forged (Ex. 4). When

Mime confesses his inability, Siegfried disdainfully says that he himself will forge it, which he proceeds to do. Seeing that Siegfried is going to be successful, Mime begins to fear that he will gain possession of the Ring. The crafty dwarf prepares a poison, which he plans to offer Siegfried as a drink, as soon as the dragon is killed.

At last the sword is finished. With it, Siegfried strikes the anvil, splitting it to the ground.

Courtesy Chicago Civic Opera Co.

HARRY STEIER IN THE ROLE OF "MIME" IN "SIEGFRIED"

Act II

The theme of the giants is heard as the curtain rises. The scene is dark; we are outside the dragon's cave. Alberich is watching the dragon guard the treasure. Suddenly Wotan appears, disguised as a wanderer. He informs Alberich that Fafner is about to be killed by Siegfried, and suggests that Alberich wake the dragon, give him warning, and try to persuade him to give up the Ring. The dragon, however, it not afraid, and the wanderer disappears, riding away upon a storm cloud. Alberich hides in a space between the rocks.

Soon Mime comes in leading Siegfried. He is promising the boy that the meaning of fear will soon be clear to him. Siegfried shows his contemptuous loathing of the dwarf, and Mime leaves him alone.

As the orchestra plays the beautiful music known as the "Forest Murmurs," (Ex. 5) Siegfried thinks of his mother. He at-

tempts to imitate a bird call, and when he is unsuccessful tries his horn instead of the reed which he has been using. The sound of the horn awakens the dragon, who comes from his cave and, in the ensuing fight, is mortally wounded by Siegfried. Dying, the dragon warns his brave slayer to beware of Mime.

When Siegfried pulls his blade from the dragon's body, a burning drop of blood falls on his hand. To ease the pain he lifts his hand to his mouth. As soon as he has tasted the dragon's blood he is able to understand the singing of the birds. One of them, which had been singing to him before the fight, now tells him about the Tarnhelm and the Ring.

While Siegfried is in the cave searching for the treasure, Alberich and Mime emerge and begin to quarrel. When Siegfried comes out, Alberich leaves and Mime tries to get the boy to accept a drink. But the dragon's blood has given him power to see through the dwarf's designs. Just as Wotan had foretold, he cuts off Mime's head and puts the body of the dwarf in the dragon's den.

Now Siegfried is alone, and he begins to weary of his solitude. The bird sings to him of the sleeping Brünnhilde, who is surrounded by flames which only a man without fear may pass. He asks to be shown the way to her.

Act III

First we see Wotan, who comes to the foot of a mountain, at the summit of which is visible the Rock of the Valkyries. He summons the Earth Goddess, Erda, and asks her for her advice. She inquires why he does not consult his daughter Brünnhilde, and Wotan explains to her that Brünnhilde is no longer a goddess. Erda feels that he is wrong in having punished his daughter for doing what he wished, and, refusing to console him, she goes back into the earth.

Soon Siegfried appears and inquires the way to Brünnhilde's Rock, saying that the bird which was leading him has flown away. The wanderer is about to help him, when Siegfried makes some rude jokes about the appearance of the stranger. This so angers Wotan that he stretches out his spear to obstruct the path. Siegfried breaks it into fragments with his sword, and the wanderer leaves.

The scene changes, and we hear the Fire Music. Brünnhilde is seen sleeping on the Rock, encircled by flames. When Siegfried comes upon her, he thinks that she is a sleeping knight, but when he removes the helmet and shield he finds that she is a beautiful woman. He tries to awaken her but does not succeed until he kisses her. Then Brünnhilde opens her eyes and inquires the name of her deliverer. When he tells her that he is Siegfried, she is filled with rapture, and they join in a beautiful song of love. As he embraces her, she, who has never before known mortal love, becomes frightened. She tries to evade him, but gradually she is moved by his ardor, and comes back into his arms. The opera ends with their beautiful duet, "The Decision to Love."

DIE GÖTTERDÄMMERUNG (THE TWILIGHT OF THE GODS)

Words and music by Richard Wagner (1813-1883)
First produced: Bayreuth, August 17, 1876.

The Characters

Brünnhilde (Bruen-hill'da)			Soprano
Siegfried (Zeeg'freed)			Tenor
Gunther (Goon'ter), Chief of Gibichungs			Bass
Alberich (Ahl'be-rich), the Nibelung			Baritone
Hagen (Hah'gen), son of Alberich			Bass
Gutrune (Goot-troon'a), Gunther's sister			Soprano
Woglinde (Vo-glin'da)			Soprano
Wellgunde (Vell-goon'da), Rhine Maidens			Soprano
Flosshilde (Floss-hill'da)			Soprano
Three Norns	Contralto	Mezzo-Sporano	Soprano

Prologue

The scene is the Rock of the Valkyries. It is night, and Brünnhilde and Siegfried are resting in a cave. In the gloomy darkness sit the Three Norns, or Fates, spinning the rope of destiny. As they spin, they discuss the story of Wotan. They say that his downfall is near; it will be caused by the Ring which Alberich has cursed. Suddenly the rope that the Norns are weaving breaks. Their work on earth is finished, and they go back into the earth to their mother, Erda.

When morning breaks, Brünnhilde and Siegfried come out of the cave. It is time for Siegfried to go out into the world and accomplish heroic deeds.

Before leaving, he gives Brünnhilde the Ring which he has taken from the dragon. In return for this pledge of his love, Brünnhilde gives Siegfried all the knowledge that she had when she was a goddess. She also presents her lover with her horse, "Grane," which is still endowed with unusual strength and fortitude, although he lost his supernatural powers at the same time his mistress lost hers.

Leaving Brünnhilde guarded by the ring of fire, Siegfried departs.

ACT I

In the home of the Gibichungs sit Gunther, the chief, Hagen, his brother, and their sister, Gutrune, discussing family affairs. Hagen, expressing regret that both Gunther and Gutrune are still unmarried, suggests that the sleeping Brünnhilde, of whom he has heard, would be an ideal bride for Gunther, and that Siegfried, the brave youth who killed the dragon, Fafner, would be a good mate for Gutrune. Both Gunther and Gutrune are filled with enthusiasm, but Gunther says he could never pass the protecting wall of fire around the sleeping Valkyrie. Hagen tells him that Siegfried will be able to brave the flames for him, but he withholds from his brother the knowledge that Siegfried has already won Brünnhilde. He says that in return for Siegfried's services in winning Brünnhilde for Gunther, they will give him Gutrune for a bride. In case her charms do not win Siegfried, Hagen says he knows of a secret love potion that will.

While they are planning, Siegfried himself enters. He has come to their kingdom in search of adventure. He is cordially greeted by the Gibichungs, and Hagen asks him if it is true that he is in possession of the Nibelungs' treasure. Siegfried replies that he has kept only the Tarnhelm, whose magic power he does not know how to use, and a Ring which he has left with a beautiful woman.

Soon Gutrune, who has taken the opportunity to leave the room to prepare the love potion, returns and offers Siegfried a drink, as a token of hospitality. He drinks it as a toast to Brünnhilde. Soon, however, the potion begins to work its magic, and Siegfried, forgetting Brünnhilde, becomes completely enamored of Gutrune.

When Hagen tells Siegfried of a beautiful, sleeping woman whom they wish to win as a bride for Gunther, he readily agrees to help them, if in return for his services he may marry the fair

Courtesy Chicago Civic Opera Co.

ALEXANDER KIPNIS AS "HAGEN" IN "GÖTTERDÄMMERUNG"

Gutrune. Hagen explains the use of the Tarnhelm. Then, after a vow of blood brotherhood, Gunther and Siegfried depart together to seek Brünnhilde. When Hagen is left alone, we learn from his broodings that the real object of his plotting is not to get mates for his brother and sister, but to gain the Ring for himself.

The scene changes and we again see the Rock where Brünnhilde is guarded by the magic fire. Waltraute, one of Brünnhilde's sisters, comes to her and tells her how her father and the rest of the gods are unable to withstand their enemies, and are doomed to destruction unless the Ring is returned to the Rhine Maidens. Brünnhilde refuses to give up the Ring because it was given to her by Siegfried as a love token, and Waltraute sorrowfully leaves.

By the brightening of the surrounding flames, Brünnhilde knows somebody is approaching. Believing it is Siegfried, she prepares to give him a joyous greeting, but is startled to see a stranger. Siegfried, by means of the Tarnhelm, has assumed the external form of Gunther, so that he may woo Brünnhilde for him. He tells Brünnhilde that he is Gunther of the Gibichungs, and has come to woo her for his bride. Brünnhilde tries to defend herself by means of the Ring, but its magic power does not operate against him to whom it really belongs. After a short struggle, the visitor succeeds in pulling the Ring from her finger, and she is forced to go with him into the cave.

Act II

As the curtain rises we see Hagen on the shore outside of the hall of the Gibichungs. Alberich, the dwarf, is with him. We learn from their conversation that Hagen is the son of Alberich, who, although he forswore love in order to forge the Ring, had been able to marry a woman interested only in his gold. The father urges his son to be ruthless in his efforts to recover the Ring so that it may become their joint possession.

As Alberich departs at dawn, Siegfried returns, and relates his experiences in winning Brünnhilde for Gunther. He tells how, as they descended the mountain in a dense fog, he was able to change places with Gunther. Gutrune is inclined to be a bit jealous, but Siegfried soon convinces her that he has wooed Brünnhilde only for his blood brother, Gunther.

Soon Gunther's followers are summoned to take part in a feast of greeting to him and his new bride. Brünnhilde is surprised to find Siegfried there, but when she sees on his finger the Ring which she believed Gunther had taken from her, she begins to suspect that it was he who came to her in the guise of Gunther. She declares that Siegfried is her husband, but he denies it, and swears with his fingers upon the point of Hagen's spear that he has not betrayed his blood brother. Brünnhilde knocks his hand away from the spear and declares that he has sworn a false oath. She prays that he may die by the point of the spear upon which he has sworn.

Act III

Again we see the three Rhine Maidens of the Prologue *(Das Rheingold)*. Siegfried, having strayed from his hunting party in search of his lost quarry, reaches the bank of the river in which the Rhine Maidens are sporting. They offer to show him the way to his quarry if he will give them his Ring. He is about to give it to them, when they mention the curse Alberich has put upon it. They hope to frighten him into giving it up immediately, but he refuses, for he does not want anybody to think that he has succumbed to fear. The Rhine Maidens prophesy that he shall die on the same day, and they feel confident that when Brünnhilde inherits the Ring, she will gladly return it to them.

Soon the other members of the hunting party enter. While they sit down by the river bank to refresh themselves, Siegfried tells them of his adventures. As he talks, they are leading him on to his downfall. They know that because of the power of the Ring there is only one way to kill him and gain possession of it, and that is to stab him in the back with the spear upon which he has sworn his false oath. Meanwhile Hagen drops into Siegfried's drinking horn a potion which counteracts the one which made him forget Brünnhilde. Immediately he begins to tell the story of his finding and wooing her. Gunther becomes enraged at what he is saying. As two ravens fly over Siegfried, Hagen asks him to prove his statement that he understands the language of birds by telling the company what the ravens are saying. When Siegfried turns to look, Hagen drives the spear into his back, declaring that he has punished falsehood. Siegfried dies with Brünnhilde's name upon his lips.

The scene changes and we see Gutrune awaiting Siegfried in the Hall of the Gibichungs. Hagen enters and tells her that Siegfried has been killed by a boar. When Siegfried's body is carried in, however, Gunther tells Gutrune that Hagen killed her husband (Ex. 1). Hagen admits the deed and asks for the Ring in

payment, but Gunther also claims it and the two begin to fight. Hagen is victorious and kills his brother, then goes to take the Ring from the finger of the dead Siegfried. As he approaches the body, the dead hand is raised in protest, and Hagen shrinks back.

Through the frightened crowd comes Brünnhilde, who has been told by the Rhine Maidens of the treachery of the Gibichungs. She says that she has come to avenge the wrongs that they have brought upon her and Siegfried. She tells of Hagen's plot, and Gutrune faints.

Brünnhilde tells the vassals to make a pyre and place Siegfried's body upon it. She takes the Ring from his finger, promising that the Rhine Maidens shall soon have their gold again, free of its curse. She puts the Ring on her finger, and she throws a flaming torch upon the pyre. Then, turning to her horse, Grane, she mounts him, and rides into the flames which are blazing on the pyre. Suddenly, at this moment, the Rhine overflows its banks and covers the pyre. The Rhine Maidens are seen swimming where the pyre has been. Hagen plunges into the water demanding the Ring, which is already in the possession of one of the Maidens, but he is dragged by them into the depths.

All the heavens seem ablaze, and we see in the sky Valhalla with all its Gods and heroes. Suddenly all is consumed by fire. The Gods are destroyed. Now indeed is finished the strand of fate woven by the three Norns, and the age of Wotan and his mighty cohorts passes from the earth.

ROMEO AND JULIET (ROMÉO ET JULIETTE)

Music by Charles Gounod
Words by Barbier and Carré, after the play by Shakespeare.
First produced: Paris, April, 1867

The Characters

Juliette, daughter of Capulet	Soprano
Stéphano, page to Roméo	Soprano
Gertrude, the nurse	Mezzo Soprano
Roméo	Tenor
Duke of Verona	
Tybalt, nephew to Capulet	Tenor
Benvolio } friends of Roméo	Tenor
Mercutio } friends of Roméo	Baritone
Paris	Baritone
Grégorio	Baritone
Capulet	Bass
Friar Laurence	Bass

The libretto of *Roméo et Juliette,* based on Shakespeare's well-known play, needs little introduction to the average reader. Romeo and Juliet are among the greatest lovers in literature.

In the opera a prologue, preceding the first act, tells us of the feud existing between the families of the two lovers. As the libretto is in French, we use the French versions of the names in the story.

ACT I

Great festivities are in progress in the home of the Veronese nobleman, Capulet. His daughter, Juliette, is making her debut into society. There is much dancing and gaiety. After the guests have left the dance hall, Juliette sings her aria, "Dans ce rêve que m'énivre" (In this dream which inflames me).

A group of gay young men come in wearing masks. One of them proves very attractive to Juliette, but her new lover is discovered by her cousin Tybalt to be a member of the house of Montague, with whom the Capulets have had a feud for years. A fight is prevented only by Juliette's father who, not wanting the gaiety of the occasion to be spoiled, lets the young man and his friends depart.

ACT II

Roméo comes to sing under Juliette's balcony in the evening. He serenades his new-found love with "Ah, lève-toi soleil!" (Arise, Fairest Sun). Then Juliette comes out upon the balcony and sings a beautiful love duet with Roméo. Finally the lovers bid each other good night.

Courtesy Chicago Civic Opera Co.

CHARLES HACKETT AS "ROMEO"

ACT III

To the cell of Friar Laurence, the two lovers have come to be secretly married. Gertrude accompanies Juliette, and with Roméo and the Friar, they sing a quartet. Then Juliette returns to her home.

The scene changes. In a street in Verona, a fight starts between Roméo's page, Stéphano, and Gregorio, a servant of the house of Capulet. While it is in progress, Roméo and Tybalt, Juliette's cousin, come upon the scene. Tybalt tries to engage Roméo in a duel, but, for the sake of Juliette, Roméo does not accept the challenge. But his friend, Mercutio, challenges Tybalt, and is killed. This incenses Roméo, who now enters the fight and takes the life of Mercutio's slayer. In punishment for his deed, Roméo is sentenced by the Duke of Verona to banishment.

ACT IV

Roméo succeeds in getting into Juliette's room in spite of the guards about the palace of the Capulets. With tenderness and sorrow they bid each other farewell.

After Roméo has taken his departure, Juliette's father and Friar Laurence come in. Her father tells her she must prepare to marry Count Paris at once. Then he leaves her with the Friar. The Friar tells her to pretend to comply with the wishes of her father, but says he will give her a potion to drink just before the wedding ceremony. This potion will put her into a trance for forty-two hours. After the time has passed, she will awaken and can go with her lover.

She carries out the plot suggested by the Friar, and when her father arrives with the bridegroom of his choosing she falls as if dead into his arms.

Act v

Supposedly dead, Juliette lies amid the bones of her ancestors in the ghostly tomb of the Capulets. The message from Friar Laurence has not reached Roméo, who hurries to the tomb of his beloved, believing her to be dead. He rushes to the bier, and embraces Juliette, who sleeps cold and motionless in the light of the flickering torch he holds over her. After a passionate farewell to the body of his beloved, he drinks poison so that he may join her in death. Then he perceives that the apparently lifeless form is breathing. Soon Juliette opens her eyes and Roméo tells her what he has done. They kiss each other farewell, and he dies in her arms. Since he had taken his life to die with her, Juliette stabs herself and falls lifeless beside the body of her lover.

EDITH MASON AS "JULIET"

Courtesy Chicago City Opera Co.

DER ROSENKAVALIER (THE CAVALIER OF THE ROSE)

Music by Richard Strauss (1864-)
Words by H. von Hofmannsthal
First produced: Dresden, January 26, 1911

The Characters

Baron Ochs von Lerchenau	Soprano
Octavian, Count Rofrano	Mezzo-Soprano
Baron Ochs von Lerchenau	Bass
Sophie von Faninal	Soprano
Herr von Faninal, her father	Baritone
Marianne, her duenna	Soprano
Valzacchi } Italian adventurers	Tenor
Annina } Italian adventurers	Alto

The dramatist who wrote the libretto of *Der Rosenkavalier* shares honors with the composer. While the story is a comedy, it is filled with touches of poetic beauty. The music is sympathetically adapted to the various changes in mood and much use is made of delicate and sparkling waltz music.

Act I

We see the boudoir of the Princess von Werdenberg, in her palace in eighteenth-century Vienna. As she rests upon a sofa, young Octavian sits at her feet and tells her of his love. In the midst of his avowals, they think they hear the Princess' husband coming in, and Octavian hides. The new arrival, however, turns out to be the Baron Ochs von Lerchenau, a cousin of the Princess. Although uncouth and pompous, he thinks himself attractive to the fair sex. He tells the Princess that he is about to be betrothed to the daughter of the rich von Faninal. It is customary to send a silver rose to one's fiancée, as a symbol of the love of her betrothed, before he presents himself, and the Baron has come to ask the Princess whom he shall send as its bearer.

Meantime, young Octavian has come back into the room disguised as a maid named Mariandel. The Baron flirts with the supposed maid, until "Mariandel" is sent to procure for him a picture of a relative to whom the Princess may entrust the rose. The maid, Mariandel, comes back with a picture of himself, Count Octavian Rofrano. Satisfied with the ambassador chosen by his cousin, the Baron departs.

Now a crowd of petitioners comes in and the Princess gives audience while her hairdresser is busy with her coiffure. When they finally leave, she thinks first of the Baron, and feels disgust at his marriage to a young girl. Then she begins a soliloquy bemoaning her own vanishing youth.

When Octavian, dressed once more in his own clothing, comes back, he leaves her without his usual kiss. He has forgotten also the silver rose which he was to deliver, so she has it sent after him, hoping that it will express her love for him as well as serve its purpose as a message to the Baron's fiancée.

Act II

The members of the household of Herr von Faninal are awaiting with excitement the bearer of the silver rose. Herr von Faninal is pompous in his importance, and Sophie, his daughter, is overcome with joy at her impending marriage with a real nobleman. However, when Octavian, attired in white and silver, comes in with the rose, her elderly suitor is forgotten. The two young people immediately fall in love, but sing a duet about the approaching marriage, which Sophie is certain will be a happy one.

Courtesy Chicago Civic Opera Co.

ALEXANDER KIPNIS AS "BARON OCHS" IN "DER ROSENKAVALIER"

Courtesy Chicago Civic Opera Co.

MARIA OLSZEWSKA AS "OCTAVIAN" IN "DER ROSENKAVALIER"

Her optimism, however, is short-lived, for soon the Baron arrives with his retainers. His uncouthness and coarse mannerisms disgust her, and his compliments seem to her proper to the purchaser of a fine horse. Octavian becomes more and more incensed, and trouble is avoided only by the arrival of Faninal and the notary, who take the Baron into the other room. When the duenna also leaves to ascertain the cause of a commotion which she hears, Octavian and Sophie are alone, and confess their love for each other in a beautiful duet "Mit Ihren Augen voll Tränen" (With Your Eyes Full of Tears). Unseen, two adventurers, Valzacchi and Annina, have come into the room, and when the two lovers are in each other's arms, they seize them and summon the Baron. The Baron is not inclined to take the episode seriously, but Octavian forces him to draw his sword and wounds him in the hand. When Sophie tells her father that she will not marry the Baron, her father says she will either marry him or she must take the veil. She leaves the room, her lover having previously departed.

Now Faninal goes out to get wine for his future son-in-law. Annina comes in and gives the Baron a note from the maid "Mariandel" to whom he was so attracted upon his visit to his cousin. It contains an appointment to meet him at an inn on the following night. The baron is so filled with pleasurable anticipation that he makes the grave mistake of forgetting to tip Annina, the bearer.

Act III

The inn is dimly lighted, and we know by the stealthy preparations being made by Annina and Valzacchi that some plot is under way. Octavian, disguised as Mariandel, comes in and gives some money to Valzacchi. Then all depart, leaving a table set for two.

Soon the Baron and Mariandel arrive. When he begins to make

Courtesy Chicago City Opera Co.

FRIEDA LEIDER IN THE ROLE OF THE PRINCESS IN "DER ROSENKAVALIER"

love to her, all sorts of queer things begin to happen. Faces appear and disappear; a man apparently vanishes through the floor. Finally Annina comes in, disguised, wearing black, and followed by several children who greet the Baron with "Papa!" She says the Baron is their father and her husband. The landlord is distressed at the danger of scandal, and excitement grows. Finally the police come in and begin to question the Baron who says that Mariandel is his fiancée, Sophie von Faninal. At this moment, in response to a secret summons from Octavian, Herr von Faninal arrives. He is made aware of the cause of the Baron's arrest and is very angry. Sophie, who has accompanied her father and has been waiting outside, now comes in, and Octavian throws off his disguise. The excitement increases as the Princess, to whom the Baron's servant has appealed, comes in and rescues him. She tells him, however, that he had better forget his desire to marry Sophie, and leave Vienna. After the Baron has left the stage, the Princess, still in love with her boy admirer, Octavian, tells him to follow the dictates of his heart. She joins the young couple in a trio, "Hab' mir's gelobt ihn lieb zu haben" (I have pledged to love him ever), and then leaves them alone, having promised to reconcile Sophie's father to the match.

LA TRAVIATA

Music by Giuseppe Verdi (1813-1901)
Words by Francesco M. Piave, founded on
"La Dame aux Camélias" by Dumas *fils*
First produced: Venice, March 6, 1853

The Characters

Violetta Valery (Vee-oh-let'tah Val-lay-ree)	Soprano
Flora, her friend	Mezzo-Soprano
Alfredo Germont (Ahl-fray'do Zhair-mon')	Tenor
Giorgio Germont (Jor'jo)	Baritone
Baron Douphol (Doo-fohl')	Baritone
Gaston	

Place: Paris. Time: Middle nineteenth century

Verdi showed his originality in *La Traviata* by presenting contemporary society. His audience was not pleased, however; it preferred the rich and glamorous costumes of the past. It was not until the nineteenth century became history that the opera received the popularity the music deserves.

ACT I

A lively crowd of friends are assembled in the drawing-room of Violetta, a young Parisienne. She has just recovered from a serious illness, and is bothered by a persistent cough.

A young man by the name of Alfredo is introduced to Violetta, and she learns that he has long been an ardent admirer of hers, and that during her recent illness he had inquired about her daily. She gives him champagne, and the two drink together and sing a duet, after which Violetta invites all into the next room to dance. Just as she is about to follow, Violetta is seized with faintness and a coughing spell. She catches sight of herself in the mirror and is shocked by her appearance, for she fears that she is becoming tubercular. Alfredo returns in search of her, and is alarmed by her condition. He begs her to let him take her away from her gay and exciting life and gain back her health in the country. She laughs at his concern. He sings to her the charming aria "Un di felice" (One Happy Day), and she tells him it would be best for him to forget her. But this only makes his avowal of love more insistent. As they part, she gives him a flower, and he promises to come back for a fresh one each day. Now the guests take their leave.

When Violetta is alone, she debates with herself whether or not she should accept Alfredo's offer, and go away with him to start life anew. As she meditates, she sings "Ah, fors' è lui" (The One of Whom I Dreamed). For the first time, she has found sincerity in one of her lovers. Finally, however, she begins to feel her hopes are futile, and as she feigns gaiety, the song turns into a florid coloratura aria, symbolical of her gay and frivolous life.

ACT II

Violetta and Alfredo have been living for some time in the country. However, Violetta has so long been accustomed to an expensive mode of living that her money is now exhausted. She has sent her companion, Annina, to sell some of her property and jewelry. When Alfredo realizes for the first time that he has been living at the expense of Violetta, he hurries to the city to obtain money and stop the sale of Violetta's property.

Violetta comes in and begins to read her mail. She has received an invitation to a party at the home of her friend Flora. In the gay and frivolous type of entertainment which is associated with her old life, she has no interest.

An unexpected visitor is announced. It is Giorgio Germont, the father of Alfredo. He has come to threaten Violetta and frighten her into giving up his son, but, when he sees her, he realizes he must attain his ends by other means. He is surprised to find that Violetta has been paying the expenses of the home. Telling her that he has a daughter whose approaching marriage will be impossible as long as Alfredo is living with a woman of Violetta's reputation, he finally prevails upon her to promise to leave Alfredo and let him believe that she has gone back to her former lover, the Baron Douphol. In return, she asks the father to tell the truth to his son after she is dead.

His father is gone, and Violetta is composing a letter, when Alfredo returns. He has received a letter from his father demanding an interview, and Alfredo expects to see him at any moment. Alfredo talks of how his father will love Violetta when he sees her, and she is silent about her recent visitor. Under pretense that she wishes to let Alfredo talk with his father alone first, she leaves the room after a pathetic scene in which Alfredo speaks of their happy future, which she knows is not to be.

After Alfredo has been alone for a while, he receives a message from Violetta telling him that she is returning to her old life. Just at this point, his father enters and urges Alfredo to come home with him. Now, however, Alfredo has become insanely jealous, and when he sees Flora's invitation to a party, he concludes that Violetta will be there. Filled with a desire for revenge, he hurries to Paris.

The scene changes. Alfredo arrives at Flora's masquerade, where gambling is the chief entertainment. When Violetta enters with the Baron Douphol, the two men begin to play together. Alfredo wins so much from the Baron that a quarrel ensues. A duel seems inevitable, until the announcement of dinner postpones it, but Alfredo promises to give the Baron satisfaction at a later date. Violetta manages to see Alfredo alone and begs him to leave. He tells her he will go if she will depart with him and not otherwise. Finally she tells him she loves the Baron. Angered beyond all control, Alfredo calls the guests from the other room. When they have come in, he tells them that he has allowed Violetta to support him and now he is paying his debt in full. He throws all of his winnings at her feet. Everyone is indignant at this insult to Violetta. Even the elder Germont is ashamed of his son, and Violetta is heart-broken.

ACT III

It is early morning. Violetta is lying in bed in her Paris apartment. She is near death. Her manner is calm and resigned and she has turned to religion for comfort. When her maid, Annina, comes in, Violetta gives her money to distribute among the poor. The doctor enters and speaks cheeringly to his patient, but to Annina he says that her mistress will live only a few hours.

In her morning mail Violetta receives a letter from Alfredo's father, in which he tells her that the Baron and Alfredo have fought their duel, and that the Baron was wounded and Alfredo obliged to leave the country. The father tells her also that because she has kept her promise, he has told Alfredo of her sacrifice. They are both coming to see her.

Soon they arrive. So excited does Violetta become that Alfredo at first thinks there is hope for her recovery. He and Violetta sing a touching duet of reconciliation. As she joins her lover in joyous plans for their future, she suddenly falls lifeless in his arms.

TRISTAN UND ISOLDE

Words and music by Richard Wagner (1813-1883)
First produced: Munich, June 10, 1865

The Characters

Tristan, King Mark's nephew	Tenor
Mark, King of Cornwall	Bass
Isolde (Ee-sohl'dah), Irish princess	Soprano
Kürvenal (Koor'vee-nahl), Tristan's servant	Baritone
Melot, a courtier	Tenor
Brangäne (Brahn-gay'na), Isolde's friend	Soprano

A shepherd, a steersman, a sailor; chorus of sailors, knights, squires, and men-at-arms

The story of the two lovers, Tristan and Isolde, is one of the famous romances of literature. It so happens that at the time Wagner was writing the text for his version, he was deeply involved with Mathilde Wesendonck in a love affair which was to become both his inspiration and his despair. It filled him with hope, anticipation, and expectation; but the final emotion was despair, because of his failure to achieve fulfilment of his love. *Tristan* is not an opera of love's attainment; it is an expression of love's desire. For some, *Tristan* is a symbol of that larger human love which seeks the union of the individual with humanity, of the one with the many.

ACT I

The scene is a ship at sea. One end of the deck is divided from the rest by a temporary partition. In this way a gorgeous compartment has been made for Isolde, an Irish princess, and her companion. The ship is bearing Isolde to Cornwall, to become the bride of King Mark. Tristan, nephew of the king, has been sent by his uncle to escort the princess to his domain.

Isolde is lying upon a couch. She hears a sailor singing about an Irish maid and, believing he is referring to her, she becomes very angry. Brangäne tries to calm her. As Isolde is going to be the bride of a man she does not love, her companion tells her that she has a love potion which will make Isolde and the King love each other. Isolde bids her prepare a draught of poison instead.

Courtesy Chicago Civic Opera Co.

MARIA OLSZEWSKA AS "BRANGÄNE" IN "TRISTAN UND ISOLDE"

Courtesy Chicago Civic Opera Co

ALEXANDER KIPNIS AS "KING MARK" IN "TRISTAN UND ISOLDE"

She has sent for Tristan to come to her, but he has refused. The reasons for this refusal go back to events which occurred before the beginning of the opera. Not long since, an Irish knight, Morold, was sent to collect a tax from King Mark, and Tristan slew him and sent his head back to Ireland in lieu of the tax. Gravely wounded, Tristan went to Ireland in disguise because he had heard that Isolde was skilful in ways of healing. She discovered his true identity, but, partly from pity, and partly from love, allowed him to live. Now that he has come as the envoy of King Mark to take her to a loveless marriage, her anger returns, and in desperation she intends to give him the poison and to take it herself, thus revenging herself on both the king and his emissary. Therefore, when the sailors begin to call that land is in sight, she again summons Tristan, saying that she will not land unless he comes to her and makes amends for treating her so coldly. Meanwhile she instructs Brangäne to bring the poison draught.

When Tristan comes, Isolde tells him that she must seek vengeance for the death of the Irish knight. He offers her his sword but she refuses it and says they will together drink a cup in expiation. Tristan understands the implications, but since he secretly loves Isolde, death is welcome.

They both drink deeply, and are awaiting death, when a strange thing takes place. They find themselves rapturously in love; for Brangäne has substituted the love potion for the phial of poison. The two lovers are clasped in each other's arms when the ship arrives at Cornwall, and the approach of King Mark is announced.

ACT II

The scene is the garden outside Isolde's room in the castle. It is midnight. King Mark has gone out with a hunting party, and Isolde has arranged a meeting with Tristan. Although Brangäne urges caution, Isolde sets out a torch and waves her scarf as a prearranged signal to Tristan. Soon he appears, and the two lovers join in a long and beautiful duet "O sink' hernieder, Nacht der Liebe!" (Descend on us, O night of love!). While they are in each other's arms, Kurvenal, Tristan's faithful servant, hastens in and tells his master that the King is coming. The hunt has been merely a plot of Melot, a courtier, to prove to King Mark that his queen is unfaithful. He is grief stricken to find his trusted Tristan also untrue to him. Realizing that there is only one way of escape, Tristan asks Isolde if she will follow him. When she assents, he draws his sword against Melot. Tristan is wounded, and Kurvenal catches him as he falls.

ACT III

The scene is Tristan's castle in Brittany, where Kurvenal has taken the wounded Tristan. The knight is lying unconscious, cared for by his faithful servant. When Tristan regains consciousness, Kurvenal recalls to him the duel with Melot and also tells him that he has sent to Cornwall for Isolde, who may again be able to cure him. Tristan becomes excited when he hears the name of Isolde and begins to curse as he thinks of the past, and of the fatal drink. Finally he drops back again into a coma. Kurvenal finds that Tristan's heart is still beating, however, and takes courage again.

When the wounded man awakes once more, he is in a more serene mood. Soon the signal is given that the ship is in sight, and Tristan sends Kurvenal to escort his beloved Isolde. When she enters, he rises excitedly from his couch and, swaying toward her, clasps her in his arms. Then he sinks, dying, to the ground. He opens his eyes, and says one word, "Isolde," before he dies.

Now a shepherd enters and tells them that another ship is nearing. Kurvenal recognizes the ship of King Mark. When Melot appears, Kurvenal rushes upon him and kills him. Then he attacks some of the king's other men, and is himself mortally wounded.

King Mark, however, has come with peace in his heart. He has been told the entire story, and knows now that Tristan and Isolde were victims of their destiny. He is filled with grief when he finds he is too late to give the lovers to each other.

Meanwhile, Isolde has been oblivious to all about her. Now as she gazes at Tristan, her voice swells into the ecstasy of the beautiful "Liebestod" (Death of Love). Then she falls dead upon the body of her lover.

IL TROVATORE (THE TROUBADOUR)

Music by Giuseppe Verdi (1813-1901)
Words by Salvatore Cammanaro, based on a Spanish drama by Antonio Catteerea
First produced: Rome, January 19, 1853.

The Characters

Leonora (Lay-oh-noh'-rah)	Soprano
Azucena (Ahz-you-chay'nah)	Mezzo-Soprano
Inez (Ee-nez)	Soprano
Manrico (Man-ree'-koh)	Tenor
Count di Luna (Dee Loo'nah)	Baritone
Ferrando, a soldier	Bass
Ruiz, a soldier	Tenor
An Old Gypsy	Baritone

It is necessary to give a short account of the events which have taken place before the drama opens.

Many years before, the mother of Azucena was burned at the stake. She had been accused of bewitching one of Count di Luna's two infant sons. Azucena, who witnessed the burning of her mother, stole the other child and intended to consign him to the same flames in which her mother had perished. However, beside herself in her fury, she made the dreadful mistake of throwing her own child into the fire. She then took the Count's child up into the mountains and reared him as her own. Although she grew to love him, she planned to use him some day

Courtesy Chicago Civic Opera Co.

ACT II, SCENE II, OF "IL TROVATORE"

to revenge her mother upon the Count's family. When the opera opens, the old Count has been dead for many years, and his son believes himself the last of the family. The old Count never gave up the hope that his younger son still lived. On his deathbed, he had his elder son, the present Count, promise to continue the search for his lost brother.

Act I

We first hear Ferrando, who is on guard at Aliaferia Palace, as he relates to other soldiers how Azucena stole one of the old Count's sons, threw him into the flames, and escaped. So realistic is his account that the soldiers become alarmed when the clock strikes twelve, and rush out.

In the garden of the palace Leonora and her companion Inez are walking. She is telling Inez of a troubadour who has serenaded her and with whom she has fallen in love. After a while they reenter the palace.

Now Count di Luna comes to gaze at the window of his beloved Leonora. He hears a harp in the distance and soon Manrico enters singing "Deserto sulla terra" (I am deserted on the earth). Leonora, hearing her serenader, rushes out and, by mistake, goes into the arms of the Count. At this Manrico is indignant, but

Courtesy Chicago Civic Opera Co.

ACT III, SCENE I, OF "IL TROVATORE"

soon he realizes that she has made an error, and the two lovers sing of their mutual love. The Count, in turn, becomes angry and makes threats to Manrico. This brings about a very exciting trio. The Count insists upon knowing the identity of the masked troubadour. The latter removes his mask, and the Count recognizes Manrico, who is in the employ of the Count's enemy, the Prince of Biscay. The two men are immediately ready to fight a duel, and rush out as Leonora faints.

Act II

When the curtain rises, we see a gypsy camp. The men are at their forges working and we hear them sing the well-known "Anvil Chorus." Azucena, now an old woman, sits by the fire, brooding. She sings "Stride la vampa" (Fierce Flames Are Soaring), describing her mother's death by fire and her dying cry "Avenge me!" Azucena tells Manrico that to avenge her mother's death is her sole object in life. She also tells him of the child she burned, but when he says "Then I am not your son," she hurriedly says that she had more than one child. She tells him that she is depending upon him to wreak vengeance upon the Count through his son, the young Count, and reproaches Manrico for not having killed the Count when the latter was lying prone at his feet during the duel. Manrico replies that he heard a voice from heaven saying, "Forbear to strike." Azucena urges him to be more merciless in the future.

Suddenly a messenger arrives to inform Manrico that the Prince of Biscay has appointed him commander of the Fort of Castellor. The messenger also tells him that Leonora, believing that Manrico is dead, is about to enter a convent. Manrico is in haste to depart, but Azucena detains him and they join in a long affectionate farewell.

The scene changes and we see the grounds of a convent. The Count di Luna, who also has heard of Leonora's purpose to become a nun, has come with his men to take her away. He sings a passionate aria in which he tells how her smile and her beauty move him to ardor. Now, with the nuns and her maid Inez, Leonora comes from the chapel. As the Count is about to stop her, Manrico arrives with his men and intervenes. With joy, Leonora departs with her lover.

Act III

In the first scene, the Count is besieging the castle in which Manrico and Leonora are about to be married. The Count's men are singing the familiar "Soldiers' Chorus." When the Count comes in, he vows that the castle shall fall on the morrow and he will have Leonora.

Just then Azucena, caught prowling about the camp, is dragged in for questioning. Ferrando sees that she is the gypsy who stole the old Count's infant son. When the gypsy calls upon the name of Manrico, her son, and the Count realizes that she is the mother of his bitter enemy, he determines that he will have her burned to death.

Now we see a room in the castle. It is just before Leonora and Manrico are to be married, and he is singing to her to calm her fears. Suddenly a messenger enters and tells Manrico that Azucena is about to be burned to death by the Count. As he leaves his tearful bride, Manrico expresses his rage in the aria "Di quella pira" (Tremble Ye Tyrants).

Act IV

As the curtain rises, we see the outside of Aliaferia Castle. In the tower Manrico and Azucena are both prisoners awaiting death.

To save her lover, Leonora has resolved to promise herself to the Count, but as she comes upon the scene she is wearing a ring in which poison is concealed. In front of her loved one's prison, she sings "D'amor sull' ali rosee" (Love, Fly on Rosy Pinions). She has scarcely finished when from the chapel come the strains of "Miserere" in which the choir begs for mercy for departing souls. So somber and prophetic is the music that Leonora is terrified. From the tower, Manrico sings a beautiful song of farewell.

Now the Count enters and says he will spare the life of Manrico and allow Leonora to take the pardon to her lover's cell if she will give up Manrico and marry him. As he sings of his ecstasy, unnoticed she sips the poison from the ring.

The next scene is the interior of the cell in the tower. Azucena is lying sleepless, thinking of her mother's death. We hear again the "fire motive" as heard in her song of vengeance in the second act. Manrico, to calm her, reminds her of their old home as he sings "Ai nostri monti" (Home to Our Mountains), and she joins in. Finally she sleeps.

Now Leonora comes in with the pardon. Manrico guesses how she has gained it and chides her for infidelity, but the poison has begun to work and she sinks lifeless into Manrico's arms.

When the Count discovers how he has been tricked, he sentences Manrico to be burned. Azucena awakens, and the Count shows her the flames, telling her, "Yonder is thy son!" She replies, "Nay! thy own brother!" Then with the cry, "Mother! Thou art avenged!" Azucena dies.

ARTURO TOSCANINI, CONDUCTOR

Courtesy National Broadcasting Co., Inc.

HART HOUSE STRING QUARTET
James Levy, first violin; Harry Adaskin, second violin; Milton Blackstone, viola; Boris Hambourg, 'cello.

WHILE it is rather difficult to define as broad a term as "chamber music," it is much easier to classify some of the compositions which are and which are not included in it. In its widest sense, chamber music includes all music suitable for performance in private rooms, small halls, and similar places. It is played by a small group which needs no conductor, and therefore does not refer to compositions requiring large numbers of singers or players. The term customarily excludes vocal and piano pieces, although they are especially suitable for domestic purposes. In its usual sense, chamber music includes instrumental duos, trios, quartets, quintets, and works for even larger combinations which ordinarily do not require a conductor.

It is also difficult to determine with great precision the origin of this medium. As was the case with singing, however, we believe that it was spontaneous—one musician commenced playing and others joined him.

In the sixteenth century the term "chamber music" applied to compositions written for one voice or more, with an accompanying instrument. Later, more instruments were added, and before the beginning of the seventeenth century we find such music played not only in the theater, but in the church as well.

As the instruments were given greater freedom, special compositions were written for them, known as "suites," or combinations of dance tunes. From its primitive form the genius of Haydn, Mozart, Beethoven, and Brahms developed the instrumental salon combination into the string quartet ensemble of today—the perfect means of expressing the great depth of musical thought.

Such terms as "string quartet," "string trio," "piano quintet," (or simply "quartet," "trio," "quintet"), may refer either to specific ensembles or to compositions written for these groups.

As early as 1685 we find the publication of "12 sonatas da camera a tre" (12 chamber sonatas for three [performers]) by the Italian composer A. Correlli (1653-1713), who is considered the originator of the classical school of violin playing and writing. Henry Purcell was the pioneer of chamber music in England, his first publication appearing in 1683, even earlier than Correlli's sonatas.

The most usual combination at that time consisted of two violins and a 'cello, often assisted by a harpsichord or an organ. With the exception of a few compositions which included a larger number of instruments, the above-mentioned type of chamber music remained fundamentally unchanged from the sixteenth to the first half of the eighteenth century.

THE SIGNIFICANCE OF HAYDN

The generation after Correlli witnessed a new chapter in the evolution of chamber music. Haydn and W. F. Bach, both endowed with a rare gift for instrumental color, wrote compositions which required flutes, oboes, bassoons, the harpsichord, and a little later even trumpets. The stringed instruments were improved.

The viola, until Haydn's time limited in compass and in other possibilities, was admitted as a member of equal importance with the violin and the 'cello. The range of the instrument was increased; its tone acquired beauty, expression, and flexibility unknown before. Similar improvements came about for the violin and 'cello, so that the string combination, as it is known to us to-day, began to take a definite shape. This medium was greatly developed by Franz Josef Haydn, the father of the string quartet. The fact that he wrote most of his music for Prince Esterhazy plays an important rôle in his life as a composer. Haydn had at his disposal one of the best trained groups of musicians of the day, who had all the time necessary to perfect performances of his works. For some forty years he limited himself to writing not for the church or the theater, but for the salon. His earliest symphonies were written for a small group of players, and were thus more in the nature of chamber music than symphonies.

THE ROMANTIC PERIOD

Schubert, Beethoven, Mozart, and even Schumann all show, at one time or another, the influence of Haydn, whose eighty-three quartets they studied carefully. This influence continued until the beginning of the so-called "romantic period," in which such composers as Chopin, Berlioz, Schumann, and Mendelssohn showed very little sympathetic understanding of the classical Haydn, merely because they had an altogether different approach to music.

With the writing of his quintet for piano and strings, Schumann set a new standard of technique for composers of chamber music. The combination of piano and strings was virtually a new medium of expression. It was the dawning of a new era in the writing and playing of chamber music, not only for private, but for public performances as well. The improved piano added new life to the four strings, new color and a technical perfection for which Beethoven would have given anything, since his piano was much too limited.

In the nineteenth century Schumann's example was followed by Dvorak, Brahms and César Franck, whose piano quintets and other compositions with piano accompaniment constitute a very important part of the chamber music literature. Then followed the Slavic composers, Tschaikowsky, Borodin, and Smetana, whose trios and quartets show the influence of romanticism and even of programme music.

Near the close of the nineteenth century Claude Debussy appeared upon the horizon of chamber music. His music is in a class of its own, and is discussed elsewhere. Not long after Debussy, Ravel added flute, clarinet, and harp to his strings, thus aiming for new freshness in color effects. F. Schmitt, Bartok, Vaughan Williams, and many others have made valuable contributions.

THE TWENTIETH CENTURY

In the early part of this century, Arnold Schönberg's harmony, Max Reger's counterpoint, and Hindemith's emphasis on rhythm have opened the page known as modern music in the "salon" group.

Chamber music, as an established art-work, is the only perfected and at the same time the most profound department of all musical creation. And the string quartet of today, possessing independent existence and dignity, has a power, brilliance, and expressive clearness of thought which no other instrumental combination has ever surpassed. For this reason the present discussion will be limited principally to music written for this type of ensemble. Particular mention will be made of those masterpieces which the average music-lover is apt to find on the chamber music programmes of today. Certain compositions, because of their charm, brilliance, intellectual value, and unquestionable superiority, have won the favor of critics and art-loving audiences alike, and have endured through the ages—a definite proof of their greatness. It is on a few such compositions that attention will be focused.

The possibilities and qualities of orchestral and instrumental color in relation to the string section are discussed in other parts of this volume. However, it is essential here to mention a few facts characteristic of the string quartet alone. It should be borne in mind that the elasticity and brightness of each instrument are different; the individual strings of any one instrument are dissimilar. Nevertheless, there is an underlying similarity and uniformity of tone-color throughout the four instruments which may turn against the combination if not handled with the deep understanding, sympathy, and expertness which are elementary prerequisites for the composer. Masters like Beethoven or Franck were able to spread a passage throughout the entire compass with the greatest of ease, and by doing so they could produce the effect of a single instrument. The perfect blending of tone color makes it possible to achieve the most lyrical, harmonic, or unison effects with ideal balance, yet without the sacrifice of that charm which is characteristic of the effect produced by the solo use of the individual instrument.

Like the sonata and the symphony, the string quartet usually consists of three or four movements which are so arranged that, like chapters in a novel, they form a consistent whole, developing an uninterrupted musical idea in which the law of contrast is carefully observed. The classical conception of the different movements was as follows:

The first movement was usually an "Allegro" (fast), lively and impressive, which usually possessed a high degree of importance, even dignity.

The second was an "Andante," or slow movement, of a lyrical or an expressive nature.

The "Finale" or concluding portion was another fast movement.

Sometimes compositions had a fourth and even a fifth movement, which was either of the "Scherzo" or of the "Minuet and Trio" type. The speed of these additional movements gave balance to the entire unit. The compositions frequently had "introductions" and "codas" (or closing sections) which were sometimes made up of material used elsewhere in the quartet. The following examples of such structures will serve to illustrate these points.

BEETHOVEN

The *Quartet in F Major, Opus 59, No. 1,* is universally recognized as a masterpiece. It is one of the three quartets dedicated to the Russian prince Andreas Rasoumowsky, and supplies an excellent example of Beethoven's so-called "second period."

The principal theme (Ex. 1) of the first movement (Allegro,

F major, 4/4 time) is stated simply and without preparation. The theme gradually ascends, and it is later found some three octaves higher. After a somewhat livelier passage, the second theme (in three sections) appears. It is of a less interesting nature than the first subject, and leads into a development section, which turns to the first theme for melodic and rhythmic material.

The second movement (Allegro vivace e sempre scherzando, B flat major, 3/8 time) is an interesting example of the liberties Beethoven took with the conventional scherzo form. It is in a first movement form, contrary to general practice in writing a scherzo. Moreover, there is considerable duplication of material, for there are two principal subjects, two transitory passages, and two development sections. In experimenting with form in this fashion, Beethoven was the forerunner of a greater freedom in the writing of the larger forms, and also suggested the possibility of a new form—the cyclic idea, adopted by César Franck, Rimsky-Korsakov, and many other composers of the nineteenth century. The whole movement abounds in expressive passages as well as very interesting modifications of the original theme. There are also curious transformations of rhythmic patterns into perfectly logical melodies. Here we see the foreshadowing of the "Variation" form, which was highly developed by Beethoven and succeeding composers.

The third movement (Adagio molto e mesto, 2/4 time) is in F minor, a key which is particularly well adapted to mournful, pensive, and sublime melodies. And that is just what this movement is—profound and gentle, reflecting subdued suffering and grief.

The last movement (Allegro, F major, 2/4 time) pays homage to Russian music. An expressive, almost transparent Russian folk song, which is simultaneously idyllic, sad, and hopeful, with the aid of a slow episode, brings this great quartet to a restful conclusion.

The *Quartet in B Flat Major, Op. 130, No. 3,* was Beethoven's thirteenth work in this form. It was begun in 1825, finished the following year, and published on May 7, 1827. The composition was dedicated to Prince Galitzin, and was performed for the first time in 1826. It is considered to be Beethoven's last completed work, for shortly after its completion he left on a journey which indirectly caused his death.

The first movement (Adagio, B flat major, 3/4 time) opens with an introduction, a more or less favorite device of Beethoven. But this is not a mere prelude like the slow introduction of his first symphony; as in the A minor quartet, the introductory

material (Ex. 2) has an important part in the making of the first movement. Beethoven's technique had reached its zenith by then, and every new idea that he used was a source for further development. The introductory theme not only appears in the second subject, but is rhythmically the foundation of the development section. This movement is typical of the later Beethoven, of the artist and his emotional struggle, of the man and his everlasting clash with his desires—a constant struggle between two opposing forces in one individual.

The second movement (Presto) is charming, but due to its shortness leaves very little opportunity for comment.

The third movement (Andante con moto, ma non troppo) is in the sonata form. Although this movement is a picture of rare beauty and tenderness, it is seldom appreciated, because of the fact that it is rarely given authentic interpretation. On account of its intentional lack of contrast, the movement is difficult to understand, despite its richness of melody.

The movement which follows is marked "Alla danza tedesca" (in the style of a German dance). It is in G major, and in the scherzo form with a trio. This is a slow German waltz which, although frequently misinterpreted, still remains one of the most pleasing movements in the string quartet literature.

The beautiful fifth movement is perhaps one of the most remarkable melodies to be found in Beethoven's quartets. Slow and expressive, this melody is full of subdued emotion, suggestive of a life hereafter. We can probably better comprehend its meaning when we realize that this quartet was written in a period of physical crisis. Although Beethoven's illness did not altogether interrupt his writing, the numerous hours of pain and anguish undoubtedly had their effect on his music. Small wonder, then, that the movement under discussion seems in many ways to be a distant echo of an earlier work which was inspired by the death of a dear friend.

The original concluding movement was a great fugue, which was emphatically condemned at the first reading, and, because of its length, was published separately as Opus 133. Beethoven wrote another Finale for the B flat quartet.

This fugue, the *"Great" Fugue, Op. 133,* was originally meant to close the B flat quartet, Opus 130, No. 3. It is a very interesting and great composition, a perfect example of string writing as well as fugue technique, and is well worth the time and energy of those interested enough to analyze and study it in detail. The fugue is rarely performed, due to the fact that it is as difficult to understand as it is to interpret well.

Quartets 1-6, Op. 18, dedicated to Prince Lobkowitz and known under that name, are the works of a Beethoven who had not as yet found himself. These six works belong to his first, imitative period, in which Beethoven was borrowing form and technique from C. P. E. Bach and Haydn. The Lobkowitz quartets, however deficient they may seem to us in comparison to his later chamber music compositions, nevertheless reveal the possibilities of a great genius, the soul of an artist, and the personality of the man who was to become Beethoven the metaphysician, the philosopher, and the supreme master of the string quartet.

HAYDN

A complete list of Haydn's chamber music is not available, as not all of his works have been published. However, of the eighty-three quartets which are known, the six included in Op. 76 are among his last and in all probability his best. They are of such beauty and show such versatility that, had he written no other quartets, his name would occupy just as prominent a place among composers of chamber music.

The *"Emperor" Quartet in C Major, Op. 76, No. 3,* is so-called because one of the movements consists of a set of variations on a well-known Austrian hymn (Ex. 3). Each instrument is given the

solo part and an opportunity to display its brilliance and warmth. Some of the harmonic effects, especially in the higher register of the strings, are very tender and of rare beauty. Like most of

Haydn's later quartets, Op. 76, No. 3, possesses imaginative quality, spiritual force, and deeply touching moments resulting from the perfect blending of the four instruments.

Other frequently played quartets are the following:

Op. 33, composed in 1781. The works which comprise this group are known as the "Russian" quartets, because they were dedicated to Prince Paul of Russia.

Op. 20 also consists of six works, which are known as the "Sun" quartets, for the simple reason that a sun was printed on the title page of the first edition.

Op. 17, No. 5, in G Major, has become a standard number on the concert program. It is a brilliant work, is strong in dramatic possibilities, and well deserves the popularity it enjoys.

Op. 55, No. 2, is known as the "Razor" quartet, because Haydn was overheard to remark that he would give his best quartet for a new razor. (He got one.) The quartet is very well made.

The *"Lark" Quartet (Op. 64, No. 5)* is famous for the delightful "perpetual motion" character of the finale.

ERNEST BLOCH

The *Quartet in G Major,* written partly in Europe but finished in this country, is one of Bloch's best works for the chamber music medium. (Among his other compositions of this type may be mentioned *Three Landscapes,* a Suite for chamber music orchestra, four pieces for string quartet, entitled *Night,* etc.).

The main theme for the first movement (Andante Moderato, written in the sonata form) is a charming and flowing beginning of a clear composition.

The second movement (Allegro frenetico), although harmonically simple, never ceases to be interesting, with its complicated and constantly changing rhythms.

The viola passage which opens the slow movement is a most exquisite melody, endowed with charm and simplicity, conveying melancholy and sorrow. Of this "Pastorale" the composer himself has said that it contains something of his own soul, known to plants and flowers only.

The finale is the most suggestive of all the movements. It recalls the composer's first impressions of America, to him the land of cold steel and machines.

In very true colors it speaks of realism, of the strong desire of an oppressed soul to escape. The clash of tonality and rhythm is at times grotesque and noisy. A European critic once wrote that "it is impossible to listen to this work of formidable intensity without a shudder."

BELA BARTOK

The *String Quartet No. 2, Op. 17,* was composed in 1915. In this work Bartók has resorted to the unlimited richness of Hungarian peasant music. Modal scales, frequently exaggerated dissonances, and adaptation of the folk idiom make the quartet sound strange and weird (see Ex. 4). More than one hearing is advisable

before one can form an intelligent opinion of the composition. Bartók's thorough familiarity with native Hungarian rhythms gives the work energy, vividness, and originality, which almost make up for the harmonies.

PAUL HINDEMITH

The *Third Quartet (Op. 22)* of this composer differs markedly from the preceding two, for it is written in what is known as "atonal" style. This means that the establishment of key centers and relationships is avoided. The work was first performed on November 4, 1922. Here, perhaps for the first time, the composer is himself—the possessor of rich musical background, keen thought, clarity and precision, with no conventional rules to hinder his technique. Throughout this quartet, Hindemith's harmonies sound daring to the unaccustomed ear, at times even harsh. However, the general effect is both unified and convincing.

The fugue-like section which opens the first movement (marked "Very slow quarter-notes") is a satisfying example of good counterpoint which doesn't necessarily have to be built around a certain tonality. Announced very softly by the violin,

the subject (Ex. 5) is then taken up by the viola, and later by the 'cello and there is little difficulty in recognizing the source of its identity.

The Scherzo (marked "Very energetic"), which follows without a break, is based on the alternating rhythms of 5/8 and 3/4 and 3/8; these metrical changes are not indicated either in the parts or in the score. This movement possesses much rhythmic interest and requires a great display of virtuosity on the part of the performers.

The third movement is rather melodious, and is in marked contrast to the preceding portions. Long, melodic lines and well-conceived pizzicato effects lead smoothly to the fading away of the last chord, which is preceded by delicate harmonics in the first violin.

The main theme of the fourth movement is announced in the cello, which difficult part is the most prominent throughout, continuing without a pause to the close of the movement. The last movement is a rondo and opens with a graceful fifteen-measure dialogue between the viola and the cello. This is followed by a rhythmic and melodic development of the theme, reaching a loud, almost wild climax. The soft, weird dialogue between viola and cello returns again on the original tones; after nine measures of thematic reproduction, the quartet closes with a fortissimo unison statement of a rhythmic fragment of the principal theme.

MOZART

Mozart occupies a prominent place among writers of chamber music, for the development of which he shares almost even honors with Haydn and Beethoven. Mozart wrote chamber music all his life, but a complete list of his works is not as yet available. Besides the twenty-seven quartets published between 1853 and 1870, he wrote a great number of trios, quintets, septets, octets, nonets, serenades, and violin sonatas.

Among the quartets most popular today, especially with amateur players, are the so-called "ten celebrated quartets"—

the ones in G, D minor, E flat, B flat, A and C (dedicated to Haydn and known under that name); and those in D, B flat (the fifth and last in that key), and F, dedicated to Frederick William II of Prussia. (This last quartet has a prominent part for the 'cello, the favorite instrument of the king.) The three quartets mentioned last are known as the "Berlin" quartets, and were written in 1789 and 1790.

The *Quartet in C Major* (last of the "Haydn" series) is known for its famous introduction (Ex. 6). Although the composition is

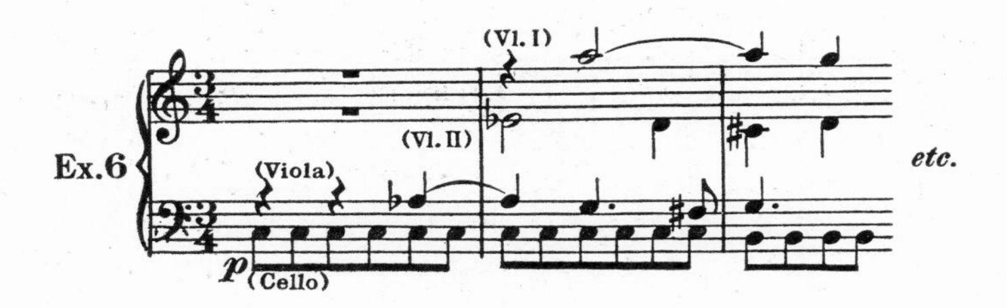

in C major, the viola enters with an A flat on the third beat of the initial measure; this is followed by an E flat in the second violin, on the first beat of the succeeding measure. The next two measures further increase the indefiniteness of the key, thereby creating an oppressing and pessimistic mood. In this quartet, as well as in the one in D minor, Mozart resorts to free modulation and inharmonic changes. Here another outstanding fact arises regarding Mozart's historic significance in the maturity of chamber music. He wrote his first quartet in 1770, at a time when even Haydn himself was in the developmental stage. It was an epoch in which the quartet was struggling to attain independence as a form. In this early, critical period may be found the mature Mozart, composer of the "celebrated ten quartets" previously mentioned, among which is the one in C major, a composition in which the composer freely uses his capacity to express deep emotion through the singing tone of the strings, into which he put his whole soul. This quartet is a characteristic example of Mozart's song-like, colorful style, which distinguishes him from his contemporaries. His free usage of inharmonious changes and almost strenuous modulations point to him as the predecessor of Romanticism and a forerunner of Schubert.

The *Quartets in B Flat* and in F are both tuneful and charming, and are written with extreme care and ingenuity.

The *Quartet in D Major* has a lovely melodious opening. It was written during the last three years of Mozart's life when his writing technique was at its zenith. The last movement is considered to be one of the best things Mozart ever wrote, and is one of the most masterful movements in all chamber music.

There are a few quartets with varied combinations of instruments. Among these, the most frequently heard are the quartets in D and A major for flute, violins and 'cello, and the one in F major for oboe and strings. All three are graceful and gay, and, as may be expected, all favor the solo wind instrument.

The *Quintet in G Minor* is probably the best-loved of the many works which Mozart wrote for this type of ensemble. Many regard this medium as the one in which Mozart excelled. And of all his quintets, the one in his favorite key, G minor, is the greatest. A celebrated Russian scholar and critic calls it "a drama without event, having for its theater and for action a series of psychological studies . . . ."

The quintet is, indeed, passionate and imaginative, full of melancholy and despair. At times dreamy and eloquent (Mozart had an incomparable gift for making the strings sing), at times agitated and even wild, it is nevertheless always subjective and moving in its sincerity.

CESAR FRANCK

In 1886 Franck decided to write a composition which would do justice to the talent of two of the greatest artists of the day—the violinist, Ysaye, and the pianiste, Madame Bordes-Pene. The *A Major Sonata* was composed and was performed by them the same winter. Since then, the violin sonata has been classed with the very few compositions of its kind which have established themselves as masterpieces in the literature.

Franck employs the cyclical type of construction in this sonata—a device introduced by Beethoven. This type of treatment is characterized by the constant use of one or more "motto" or "germ" motives throughout the work. These motives are generally the bases of all the themes, as well as of much of the subsidiary material.

The first movement (Allegretto) is in the sonata form, and opens with a lyrical theme in 9/8 time (Ex. 7) which is the

foundation of the other first subjects of the remaining movements. The changes which the original theme, full of dramatic potentiality, undergoes, and the skill with which it is handled to make it appear fresh, are more intriguing with each appearance and can hardly be described adequately.

The second movement (Allegro) is in D minor, a favorite key of the composer. It is also in sonata form and contains extensive usage of the rhythmic and melodic aspects of the principal germinating motive.

The third movement is in F sharp minor and is marked "Fantasia" (fancifully written), although the structure is more than clear to follow throughout. The cyclical melody, which was calm and carefree at the opening, intensely animated and even full of exultation in the second movement, now subsides to bewail distress and awaken tender and sympathetic feelings. The harmonies, in most instances derived by chromatic progressions, express bitterness and discouragement, hope and consolation, courage and fear—all intermingled in one.

The last movement (Allegretto) is in Rondo form, and may be played more slowly than the indicated tempo without losing its charm and grandeur, which are desirable qualities in any closing movement.

Besides the principal "motto" motive, at least three others can be found in this work. The first of these appears in the second, third, and fourth movements, and the remaining two are confined to the third and fourth movements. This cumulative process accounts for the fact that the concluding section of this sonata consists largely of material from the preceding three movements.

The *D Major Quartet* was probably the last of Franck's chamber works to be composed, and it is one of his greatest. Here again

he uses the cyclic idea; the main theme (Ex. 8) dominates the entire work, giving it distinct power, unity, and balance. Franck wrote the quartet at the age of 68, and for the first time experienced the joy of having a work received with great enthusiasm.

The *F Minor Piano Quintet* was written earlier than the works previously mentioned. It is in three movements: "Allegro" in F minor, "Lento" (in three sections), and "Allegro con fuoco" in F major, with a closing section in the original key. The quintet was first performed on January 17, 1880, with Saint-Saëns at the piano.

As a complete entity, the quintet is melodious, coherent, and clear. The themes are of undisputed beauty and originality. Their working out is next to perfection, and the design of the whole is precise and logical. These are the attributes which elevate César Franck, the modest father of French chamber music, to a height where only the supreme masters of musical expression reign.

Even in a work as early as this, Franck's technique is far superior to that shown in his four trios (1840-1842). By this time he had discovered the style which best suited his temperament, imagination, and intellect.

Franck's compositions do not number in the hundreds; he believed in quality rather than quantity. They do not appeal to the imagination only, but to the intellect and emotions as well. This explains why his Violin Sonata, String Quartet, Piano Quintet, Symphony, and Organ Chorales will remain great music as long, perhaps, as music itself exists as a living art.

Courtesy Italian Tourist Bureau

THE CONTEMPORARY ITALIAN COMPOSER PIZZETTI AT THE PIANO

Courtesy Italian Tourist Bureau

AN EXHIBITION DANCE BY PUPILS OF THE BALLET SCHOOL OF THE SCALA, MILAN, ITALY

THE BALLET

ITS DEVELOPMENT AND INFLUENCE

DANCING AND SINGING are the primary arts of the human race. Recorded history does not tell us which came first. It is not important here that we should know, for both arts have developed as man himself has developed and wished to give outward expression with his body to the inward emotions which he felt. His earliest dances were those which gave expression to his religious emotion, ecstasy, and desire, or those which intensified community of thought and feeling, such as the war dance. One dance symbolized petition, another thanksgiving, and so on through the gamut of his religious life. Later these

Courtesy Italian Tourist Bureau

"DANCING AND SINGING ARE THE PRIMARY ARTS OF THE HUMAN RACE"

Courtesy Italian Tourist Bureau

A BALLET SCENE AT THE SCALA, MILAN, ITALY

grew into dances used whenever he was deeply moved by either joy or sorrow. He created the dance to symbolize happenings and things which he could not rationalize, and for which he had no language to express his deep feelings of mystery or supernaturalism. By bodily movements he was able to communicate his state of consciousness or ecstasy to his fellows. As man has grown spiritually, he has developed an ever increasing power for spiritual expression through the medium of the dance.

THE RUSSIAN BALLET

Our momentary concern is with the late nineties and the pre-war days of our century, more specifically with the Golden Age of the Russian Ballet, both in Russia and in France. In those days the genius of Diaghilev was combined with that of some of the world's most famous painters, designers, composers, and writers for the dance. He produced spectacles that are still cherished memories for all those privileged to see and hear them. For twenty years this great Russian artist was a leader in the contemporary art movements at home and abroad. The Russian Ballet became famous for its music, its feast of color, its combination of gorgeous trappings, decoration, and bodily expressiveness. It was an orgy of the primitive emotions mixed with an element of symbolism.

Courtesy Col. W. de Basil's Ballet Russe, Monte Carlo, France

TAMARA GRIGORIEVA AND DAVID LICHINE IN DEBUSSY'S "L'APRÈS MIDI D'UN FAUNE" (THE AFTERNOON OF A FAUN)

The early Diaghilev ballets dealt with themes of very limited emotions. Their concerns were chiefly with the triangles of human desire and human jealousy. The earlier Russian composer, Tschaikowsky, with his simple and childlike ballet, the *Nutcracker,* could hardly have conceived of his work as the forebear of such realistic descendants as the *Petrouschka* ballet or the pagan *Rite of Spring*, both by the Russian composer, Stravinsky.

Diaghilev and the Russian Ballet fostered the realistic and revolutionary art of Stravinsky. In this same group was the painter, Picasso. All of them combined bodily motion, bewildering sound, and bizarre color in an effort to give us poetic expression, to make us feel without the aid of words. This group even influenced others to try to make us accept words in literature which had no expressive intention, no meaning as words.

But the impress of Diaghilev and his collaborators was not limited to the theater or the concert hall. Our neckties, our cigarette cases, ladies' dresses, children's toys, the pictures on our walls, the draperies of our rooms—all these items of everyday living suddenly took on amazing designs, exotic colors, all bearing the imprint of these extraordinary minds and personalities. Prettiness was changed to splendor, and languid rhythms suddenly became imbued with new power, or fled a universe possessed by the demons of machinery and speed. In any case, none of the arts will ever be the same again.

THE AMERICAN BALLET

The first part of this century found the American ballet beginning to make itself felt in the theatrical and musical world. Though the forms were still largely dependent on standardized European manners and styles, being more imitative than creative or progressive, yet they were decided steps forward in our American art and were the cause of some rejoicing. Particularly notable were the ballets *Krazy Kat,* the *Birthday of the Infanta,* and *Skyscrapers,* by the Chicago composer, John Alden Carpenter. Other ballet composers in America are Borowski, Still, Copland, Bennett, Chavez, Cowell, Eicheim, Elwell, Josten, Maganini, Saminsky, and Whithorne.

RABANA HASBURGH

ANNABELLE LYON

Courtesy The American Ballet Co.

DAPHNE VANE IN "ORFEO" (AMERICAN BALLET)

Photos by George Platt Lynes

RABANA HASBURGH IN ANOTHER DANCE POSTURE

Photo by Maurice Seymour, Chicago

RUTH PAGE BALLET FROM SCHUBERT'S "LOVE SONG"

Photo by Maurice Seymour, Chicago

RUTH PAGE AND HAROLD KREUTZBERG IN RAVEL'S "BOLERO"

Ruth St. Denis was one of the first American dancers to clothe her conceptions of religion and spiritual thought in Eastern, Egyptian, and Indian art forms of the dance. So responsive was she to this thought that she built her whole career upon the expression of the God-consciousness through the dance, as a symbol of a state of being, or of a cosmic awareness which should permeate every act and activity in our lives.

The future of serious American ballet music does not lie in jazz. The new American ballet music will diverge from traditional and accepted classical forms and lines. It will become an unfolding of new forms, not repetitions of old, and will perhaps be symbolical of the unfolding process of life itself. There are many who hope that our dances will not be imitative, not mere displays of virtuosity, but will instead be essentially creative.

All this has much to do with contemporary music. If it were not evident that the true artist of the dance uses the entire body and mind, it might be feared that the dance influence would cause

Photo by Maurice Seymour, Chicago

RUTH PAGE BALLET IN "HEAR YE! HEAR YE!"

most present-day music to be written for the feet. But, like the creative musician, the creative dancer must use both head and heart. Therein lies the hope for the future of American music as well as the dance. Is dance rhythm? Nothing less. Is it color? Exotically and splendidly so. Yet, like its sister art, music, it is more than these. It is symbolical. Of what? Of all the smoke and flame, of all those winnowing winds, of all those dreams, of all that which makes our seeming, real. Through these sister arts, life is not only transcribed—it can also be transmuted.

Centuries ago, the dance was even more important than the music which accompanied it. As music slowly diverged into a more independent art, dance suites were evolved for the orchestra. These comprised a series of dance forms and movements for instruments alone. Out of these suites of folk dances, composed by such masters as Bach, Haydn, and Handel, grew an extended musical development of form known as the symphony. Wagner felt that the Seventh Symphony of Beethoven was the apotheosis of

Photo by Maurice Seymour, Chicago

RUTH PAGE BALLET IN "LOVE SONG" (SCHUBERT)

the dance. By 1900 the symphony had reached its highest expression. Then came the supremacy of the ballet, and innumerable composers turned to that art form as their medium. This influence laid its finger on all the arts. Soon there was a flood of artists dabbling in ill-considered experiments, in a morbid fear lest they seem commonplace, or their art simply natural expression. But this is, in reality, a mere evasion of that problem; it is no solution. Pantomime, culminating in the dance, can hardly be expected to replace the emotional expression found in the difficult medium of the opera. Whether to express happiness or sorrow, the world still loves a song. Intoxicated with the rhythm of our feet, we almost lost the power of the voice to sing.

Rhythmic strength, used with absolute freedom, is Stravinsky's key to the problem of form. Today we are seriously doubting if rhythm, as geometrical or mathematical patterns divorced from melody, can be used as the sole generator of music. If melody without rhythmic vitality degenerates into mere tunes, or if harmonic oddities and curiosities become the end and aim of music, then we find music becoming an artificial pleasantry without organic unity, vitality, or power. In great music no one element predominates at the expense of another. Each component exists at its highest in equilibrium with the others. Certainly that is true in the music of Palestrina, Bach, and the mature works of Beethoven and Wagner. In much of our contemporary music there has been a preponderance of interest in either rhythm, color, or pantomime, one element being sacrificed for another. A technical limitation or deficiency in one aspect has forced the composer to compromise, to evade the problem at issue. Great power or artistic expression through music must presuppose an extensive and comprehensive technique in the composition of music, no matter whether the medium be ballet, opera, or symphony. Such a complete command of material is usually acquired by work, not by dispensation or gift.

In recent years, the artists of the dance have had a command of the problem of form and design which some of their collaborators in music have not possessed. For the dancer, a change in outward symbol or design did not indicate a change in idea. But to the majority of composers, change in pattern meant change in idea, and so they have given us episodic, fragmentary music which could not stand apart from its pantomime, music which was almost meaningless if transferred from the theater to the concert hall.

For centuries we have had cycles of recurring stress on either the dance or music, sometimes dependent on each other, sometimes not. Today we are witnessing the reunion phase in one of these cycles. This is not a reunion of separate arts, but rather a coming together of two great arts out of which we hope will emerge a unified art greater than either might achieve alone.

In America are movements seeking to create new art forms, new thought expressions, which capitalize upon their inheritance from the shores of the past. Ours is the heritage of the nations and the ages. What we shall mold with it, what we shall become, is still part of our destiny.

Courtesy The American Ballet Co.

LEW CHRISTENSEN IN "ORFEO"

RARE EARLY TYPE OF SPINET

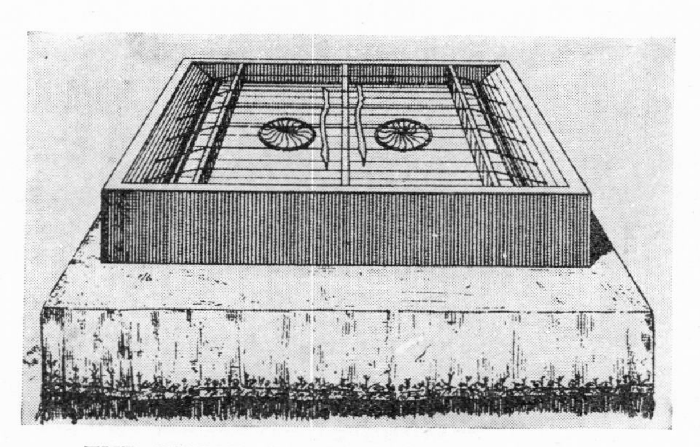

THE CITOLE (THIRTEENTH CENTURY)

THE PIANO—THE INSTRUMENT OF THE MILLIONS

THOUSANDS OF AMERICAN CHILDREN think of the piano only as an instrument of youthful torture. Most adults realize, though, that it is probably the most generally important musical instrument. In the United States, in 1929 alone, more than one hundred thirty thousand pianos were produced. It is an unusual home that does not have a piano of some sort, from the battered old upright for which no one will pay the cost of moving, to the gleaming walnut and ivory of the concert-grand.

The piano, itself, is a relatively recent invention. Although the first one was made in the eighteenth century, it stems from several similar instruments of a much earlier time. In some respects the piano is the descendant of the clavichord, an instrument popular during the later Renaissance. The clavichord had a keyboard of from two and a half to five octaves. Parallel to it were the strings, which were sounded by the striking action of a brass wedge attached to each key. The pitch was fixed according to the part of the string struck by the wedge. The tone of the clavichord was small and metallic.

Somewhat resembling the clavichord were the virginal and the spinet. These instruments differed but little. Virginal, an English term, was bestowed on a form of the spinet, because it was considered especially appropriate for girls, as contrasted with the lute, which the gay, singing cavaliers of Shakespeare's England thought more manly. The spinet and the virginal had but one string to each key, hence the tone was soft; and they were used primarily for homes instead of for concert purposes.

In the seventeenth century, occupying the position of the concert piano today, was the harpsichord, which differed from the spinet in that it had two, three, or even four strings to each note. Its tone was louder and much more brilliant than that of the clavichord, but it lacked the expressive qualities of the smaller instrument. It was used little for solo playing, but occupied an important position in concert and orchestral work, the harpsichord player usually being the conductor. With the coming of the piano the harpsichord passed into disfavor and became virtually obsolete. Recently, however, it has been resurrected by various enterprising contemporary musicians, and its merry tinkle is now heard regularly, even over the air lanes.

The piano had its inception around 1715. It was the invention of Bartolomeo Cristofori, an Italian musical-instrument-maker and expert, who designed the first one for his patron, Prince Ferdinand dei Medici. It was very imperfect, and the famous composer, Johann Sebastian Bach, to whom it was shown, expressed only a mild interest. Cristofori continued experimenting with his new brain-child, which at first was called *pianoforte*, a combination of the Italian words for "soft" and "loud," since, unlike previous keyboard instruments, it could be played either softly or loudly. His later models were much better, and Bach praised one of them highly.

Despite Bach's approval of the pianoforte, it was long in winning favor from the musicians of Europe. Bach, himself, did not compose for it, preferring the clavichord. So different were the two that all of Bach's works for the earlier instrument have had to be transcribed in order to be made suitable for the piano. Mozart had a piano in his rooms for his personal use, but what composing he did for a keyboard instrument was for the clavichord or harpsichord. Other musicians also were slow in adopting the piano.

Gradually German and English craftsmen began to perfect the piano. Broadwood devised an improved key action, and the new instrument began to attain popularity with musicians and their audiences. Not till the advent of Ludwig van Beethoven, however, did the piano attain the eminent position in music that it holds today. Trained well on the instrument, Beethoven made triumphant tours throughout Europe, playing, in concert, works for the piano. He was also the first significant composer to write works of a caliber that recognized the possibilities of the instrument. Beethoven wrote more than one hundred works of various kinds for the piano, but standing head and shoulders above the rest are his five concertos for piano and orchestra, and his thirty-eight sonatas for piano. Even today these sonatas form the very basis of the tremendous piano repertoire, and most famous pianists make a specialty of interpreting them.

SERGEI VASSILYEVICH RACHMANINOV

CHARLES CAMILLE SAINT SAËNS

Courtesy Chicago Musical College

RUDOLPH GANZ, PIANIST-CONDUCTOR, WHO HAS MADE IMPORTANT CONTRIBUTIONS IN THE PRESENTATION OF NEW MUSIC

Paul's Photos, Chicago

IGNACE JAN PADEREWSKI

Firmly established by this time in Europe, as a result of technical improvements and Beethoven's compositions, the piano began to undergo significant developments in the new world. Steinway and Chickering are the great names in the history of early American pianos, and to them were added during the last century, Baldwin, Mason and Hamlin, and many others. One of the most significant changes brought about in piano-making in America was the forging of the frame in one piece of iron by Steinway. Later, the player piano became very prevalent, and in thousands of homes one could hear Beethoven and Chopin as well as the latest popular tunes.

The coming of the phonograph and the radio has caused a serious decline in the manufacture of pianos. The attractions of "canned" music and the opportunity to hear the best of music over the air have led many Americans to drop the piano as a necessary adjunct of the home. It is not likely, however, that the number of pianos will diminish markedly in the near future. Their value in the musical education of the child and as a medium of popular music will undoubtedly continue. The perfection of the pianos of the present day seems to lend support to this view. Mechanically and musically they are a far cry from the frail, clumsy instrument of 1800.

Pianos will, of course, remain significant in formal music, also. The importance given to the instrument by Beethoven was enhanced by the compositions of Schubert and Schumann, and to their work was added soon after, the delicate music of Chopin. In Chopin's hands the piano became a thing of gossamer-like grace, and the beauty of his writings has established them as an integral part of present-day piano repertoire.

With the coming of Franz Liszt there began the age of excessive demands on the piano. He utilized almost every technical possibility in the keyboard, and great skill became a requisite for playing his works. His innovations were carried to excess by succeeding artists and composers, until the "slam-bang" style of piano playing became the characteristic one. To meet the heavy poundings of the virtuosos affecting this technique, the piano manufacturers of the 1870's were forced to increase the strength of their product measurably. Gradually the age of excessive demands on the piano began to pass, however, and today the prevailing style is one that emphasizes precision and clarity in the execution of any work.

Almost every major composer since Beethoven's time has written for the piano, and the maintenance of its important position in music seems assured. Bach, Beethoven, Schubert, Schumann, Chopin, Scriabine, Liszt, Rachmaninov, Tschaikowsky, Saint-Saëns, Debussy,—these are some of the men who have spoken through the piano, and today countless thousands at concerts all over the civilized world sit entranced as some performer weaves a magic spell with this single potent voice of music.

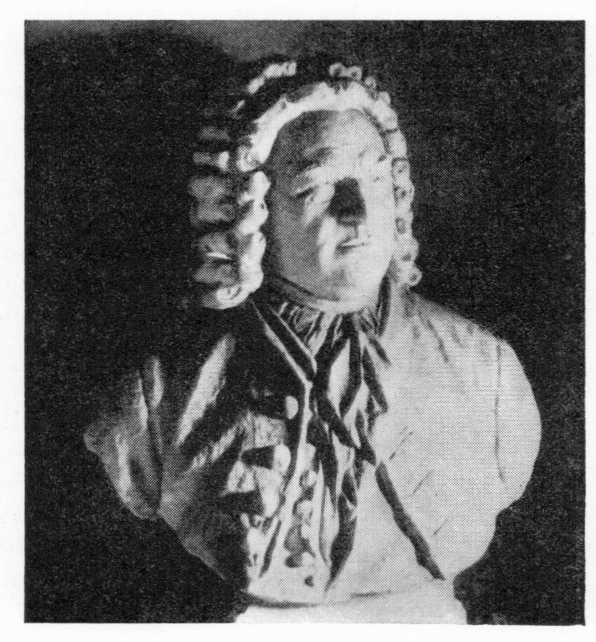

JOHANN SEBASTIAN BACH

Courtesy German Railroads Information Office, N. Y.

Courtesy The Art Institute of Chicago

THE SCALA THEATER, MILAN, ITALY

Courtesy The Art Institute of Chicago

THE ROYAL OPERA HOUSE, VIENNA, AUSTRIA

THE MEN OF MUSIC

MEN WHO HAVE MADE MUSIC

BACH (1685-1750)

JOHANN SEBASTIAN BACH, the "Master of Eisenach," was born in 1685, the same year as Handel. He comes of a long line of Bachs who were musicians. From his father he learned the violin at an early age. When he was a boy his parents died, and he went to live with his brother who was an organist at Ohrdruf. From him he learned harpsichord and organ. He was a boy soprano, and in 1700 acquired a place in the choir and school of St. Michael's at Lüneburg. Here he received a classical education. He secured a place in a court-band at Weimar, but soon became an organist at Arnstadt. He had a fine opportunity for composition and study while holding this post. When he went to hear the music of Buxtehude, who was organist at the cathedral at Lübeck, he outstayed his leave and difficult circumstances arose which caused him to move to Mühlhausen. In 1707 he was married to his cousin Maria. In 1708 he was called to the post of court-organist and violinist to the Duke of Weimar. While holding this position he not only mastered the technique of the organ, but wrote some of his best compositions. He accepted a position as court choirmaster at Cöthen in 1717.

The Prince of Anhalt-Cöthen preferred the Reformed Church in which music was not important, so Bach turned his interests to chamber music. His efforts in this field brought forth the *Brandenburg Concertos* which represented Bach's first attempt at instrumental music along symphonic lines. It was while at Cöthen that he composed the first volume of his *Well Tempered Clavichord* (preludes and fugues). His wife died in 1720, and in 1721 he married Anna Wülken. Being an accomplished musician herself, she became his copyist. In 1723 he became cantor at the Thomasschule in Leipzig, and stayed there until his death. During his stay at Leipzig he wrote choral works including many cantatas: the great *Passions of St. John* and *St. Matthew*, the *Christmas*

Paul's Photos, Chicago

BACH'S BIRTHPLACE AT EISENACH, GERMANY, NOW A MUSEUM

Oratorio, and the monumental *Mass in B Minor*. In 1749 he became blind as the result of an operation, and the following year died of apoplexy. Today he is recognized as the greatest musician of all time. There is a vast literature already extant on his work.

BEETHOVEN (1770-1827)

Ludwig van Beethoven was born in 1770. His father, a singer, was stern and intemperate, and was inclined to exploit the boy, who was a prodigy. He gave him little education except in music. At his meeting with Mozart in Vienna in 1787 the latter prophesied that the youth would make his mark in the world. After holding numerous orchestral positions, Beethoven went to Vienna, where for a time he had a small salary, and when this was stopped after two years, he became dependent upon the patronage of wealthy amateurs. Those who realized his true worth remained his friends in spite of his uncouth appearance and moody temperament. He became one of the greatest pianists of his day. His public playing appearances began in 1795, in which year he also composed some of his first great works. From then on composition became his chief interest.

In 1814 his career as a concert pianist closed due to his deafness which caused him also to withdraw from his friends.

Although he had many love affairs, he never married. He was a very poor business man even in the most simple matters of everyday living.

Courtesy Steinway & Sons

BEETHOVEN AND NATURE
From the painting in the Steinway Collection by N. C. Wyeth.

His affections became disastrously entangled when his nine-year-old nephew was left in his guardianship. He lavished everything possible upon the boy, who, when he became a man, proved worthless. When his nephew was banished from Vienna in 1826, Beethoven went with him to a farm, returning to Vienna late in the same year. On the return journey he took cold. This condition brought about dropsy and he died in 1827.

Chief among the works of Beethoven are the nine symphonies, piano sonatas, string quartets, sonatas for violin and piano, the opera *Fidelio,* the *Mass in C Major,* the violin concerto, and a long list of other works. Analysis of some of his compositions is given elsewhere in this volume.

BERLIOZ (1803-1869)

Hector Berlioz was born in 1803 at Côte-St.-André, where his father was a doctor. When old enough he was sent to Paris to study medicine, but he was interested in music and decided to study it instead. His father was very much displeased, and Hector was left to his own resources, supporting himself by singing in a chorus. In 1833 he married Henrietta Smithson, an actress, with whom he lived until 1840.

Berlioz was an exponent of program music. His lack of respect for musical tradition stamped him as a revolutionary. He was disliked by his French contemporaries, and only with the greatest difficulty did his works gain hearings.

He toured Germany in 1842 and 1843 where he received much recognition, especially from Liszt and the Weimar circle. This caused his status in Paris to be changed.

Due to extensive study of the hitherto unknown technical possibilities of the instruments of the orchestra, and to the inclusion of new instruments, he was able to give valuable advice as to effects which they were capable of producing, thus starting symphonic music on a new era of orchestral color. Though he left cantatas, symphonies, including the *Fantastique,* and songs, he is best known by his work on instrumentation.

After his death in 1869 many honors were bestowed upon him by his countrymen.

BIZET (1838-1875)

Georges Bizet was a member of a group of French composers who gave vitality to a new type of opera known as lyric opera. He was born in Bougival, France, in 1838, the son of a pianist.

Georges entered the Conservatory when he was but nine years old. Among other teachers he studied with Halévy, whose daughter he later married. He won many prizes before he won the Prix de Rome, which enabled him to study for three years in Italy.

His style, although highly individual, showed Wagnerian influence.

He wrote orchestral music, songs, and instrumental music as well as operas. His best known operas are *The Pearl Fishers* and *Carmen*. The latter opera was not a success at first, and the composer died in Paris, France, in 1875, before this opera, which is now one of the world's favorites, gained its popularity.

BRAHMS (1833-1897)

Adhering to the traditions of a magnificent past, Johannes Brahms takes his place as one of the immortal composers in musical history. Brahms achieved the fame that established him as one of the popularly known "Three B's" (Bach, Beethoven, and Brahms). He wished to transcend his wretched living quarters

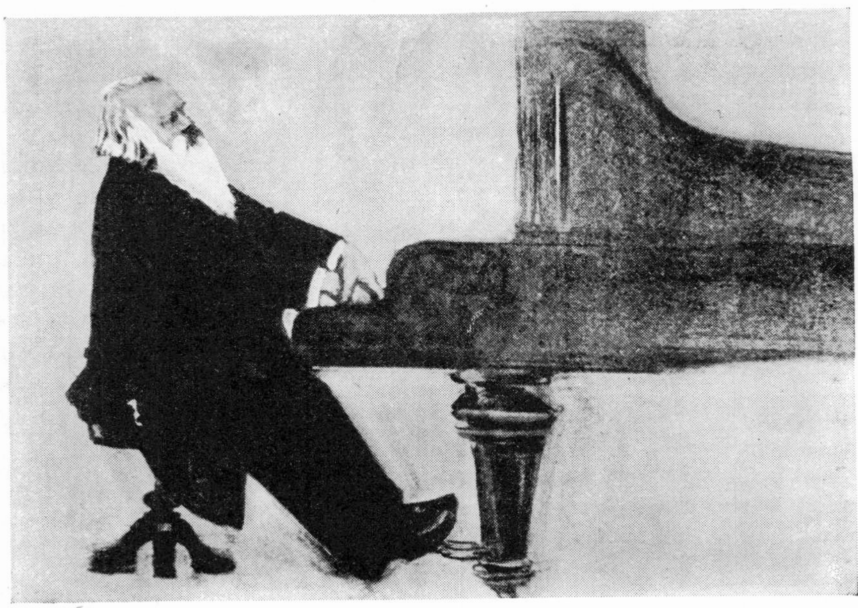

Paul's Photos, Chicago

JOHANNES BRAHMS

and their ugly effect not only on his physical being, but more particularly on his imaginative life. Friedrich Cossel and Eduard Marxsen, two splendid teachers, were messengers of Fate. Through the influence of their teachings Brahms carried on to fame and atonement for the poverty-stricken and disease-ridden surroundings of his earlier life. Indeed the creative genius of the man rose to sublime heights when he produced the *German Requiem* and the *B Flat Major Piano Concerto.*

Brahms was born in Hamburg, Germany, in May, 1833, and fourteen years later made his debut as a pianist. In 1858 Schumann, to whom Brahms had introduced himself, heard some of the rising young composer's work and prophesied in his journal *Die Neue Zeitschrift für Musik* (The New Journal of Music) a brilliant future for him. In reviewing the compositions of a musical creator, whose forms rise from the "lied" (song form) to his four great symphonies, we find that Brahms was unconcerned with the demands or preferences of the superficial music lover. Consequently his music, on the surface, is more intellectual than emotional. However, there is a disclosure of new beauties on each separate audition of his works that eventually rewards the sincere individual. Surely no one can be immune to the somber hues, the tonal beauty, and the passionate nature of the *Intermezzi, Capriccios* and *Ballades.* And who can deny that his numerous songs give him eminence as a composer endowed with the highest conception of lyric values? When Brahms was twenty-one years old he had written three piano sonatas, the *B Minor Trio,* and a number of other works including piano pieces and songs. The originality of these works is remarkable. With the finish and singularly striking beauty that they possessed it is no wonder that his first symphonic attempt, which was completed when he was forty-three years old, was acclaimed as "The Tenth Symphony," implying that it was a worthy successor to Beethoven's Ninth.

Brahms's life was a comparatively contented one, garlanded with honors. He was a genial and affectionate man who made a host of friends. Those events that spelled grief in his existence were comparatively few, and when they did occur there was at least spiritual compensation to be derived. After his mother's death he completed the *German Requiem,* which was an appeasement of the grief that had possessed him after that regrettable experience. The death of his dear friend and benefactor Robert Schumann brought to a climax the development of one of the most romantic episodes in musical history, the friendship that existed between Brahms and his friend's widow, Clara Schumann. If we look to outside influences that inspired some of his greatest creations, it is clear that she was responsible for many of them.

Brahms died on April 3, 1897, in Vienna, from a cancerous condition of the liver that clouded the last years of his life. He was not mourned by a wife, children, or near relatives. His escort consisted of his many loyal and affectionate friends. The words of Agathe Von Siebold, Brahms's childhood sweetheart, had come to pass. He could belong to no one. He went through life wifeless and childless that he might endow the world with the riches of his art and soul.

CHOPIN (1810-1849)

Frédéric Chopin, "poet of the piano," was a contemporary of many great musical personalities who were active in the first half of the nineteenth century. He was born near Warsaw, Poland, where he received his musical education. He was playing in public at the age of nine, and soon began to compose. When he was fifteen he published his first work. He won fame as a pianist, his virtuosity winning him much approbation. He was an intimate of such musicians as Cherubini, Rossini, Berlioz, and Meyerbeer. He had a career as concert pianist and composer, until his health began to fail in 1835. In 1836 began his friendship with George Sand. During the years spent with her at Majorca he became a victim of consumption. Later they went to Paris

Paul's Photos, Chicago

TOMB OF CHOPIN, IN PARIS

and some of his best works were inspired by their friendship. He also gave some private concerts. He died in Paris in 1849, two years after George Sand left him.

In personality, Chopin was very sensitive and refined. He was generous, enthusiastic, and had a fine intellect. Although he left a few songs, most of his important works were for the piano. His nationalistic tendencies, derived from his French and Polish parentage, are clearly reflected in his compositions. The polonaises and mazurkas exhibit strong Polish traits. The influence of the Parisian salon may be seen in his waltzes and some of his nocturnes.

FRANCK (1822-1890)

Founder of the modern French school of music, César Franck exerted a profound influence on many later and contemporary composers. He was born in Liége, Belgium, of German descent. For a time he studied in his native city, but at the age of fifteen he removed to Paris, where he entered the Conservatory of Music. There he began his composing career, at the same time studying the organ under Benoist.

Franck's first significant work was a cantata, *Ruth,* which achieved some success when produced in 1846. Throughout this period, however, he received relatively little recognition, and continued to lead a very quiet and retired life. He was organist at Saint-Jean, Saint-François and then at St. Clotilde, but continued to teach and also composed a mass, several motets, and much other religious music. In 1872 Franck became professor of organ at the Conservatory, and in the following year he received French citizenship.

Greatest among Franck's works, with the possible exception of the oratorio, *Les Béatitudes,* is his major orchestral work, the *Symphony in D Minor.* It has a depth of power and feeling rarely heard in modern French music.

Though he lived amid the garish splendor of Paris, Franck's entire life exhibited a remarkable devotion to his labors as organist, composer, and teacher. D'Indy, Chausson, and Bordes were among the immediate circle of his pupils, but there were many others who felt the breadth of his influence. Franck died in 1890, beloved by his pupils and admired by the public.

HAYDN (1732-1809)

Joseph Haydn, "father of the symphony," was born at Rohrau, in lower Austria, in 1732. His parents were humble people and very devout Catholics. His father was fond of rustic music, and young Haydn acquired his taste.

When Joseph was six he was sent to study music in a nearby town. The Viennese organist Reutter discovered him there in 1740, and took him into St. Stephen's Choir. In the nine years following, he received his support and free training in the choir school. He also did much studying by himself. The period after his voice had broken was filled with many struggles for existence, and only through the kindness of his friends was he spared from starving. By himself he worked upon the clavichord and violin and also upon composition. With the proceeds of some teaching and playing he was able to buy some textbooks. Meanwhile he kept on composing. At one time he served Porpora (singing teacher and composer) as valet in return for lessons. Later he had several royal patrons.

Of these, one of the most important was Prince Esterhazy, at whose country home at Eisenstadt Haydn became assistant choir master in 1761 and director in 1766. When the Prince built a magnificent palace at Esterhazy, Haydn went there to live and work. He remained until the prince died in 1790; and even after leaving did not break his connection with the family. Most of his orchestral and chamber works were written there during the life of the prince.

After leaving Esterhazy, Haydn went to England to give concerts. Besides performances, his stay in England was marked by his activity in instrumental composition. Twelve symphonies were composed in this period. They are known as the "London group" and include such popular ones as the *Drum Roll*, *London*, *Surprise*, and the *Military*. He was received in royal circles and made Doctor of Music by Oxford University.

Leaving London, he returned to Vienna, where he devoted the rest of his life to the writing of the *Seasons* and the *Creation*, the two most important of his oratorios. It was during these years that he received Beethoven as a pupil. He was paid much attention by musicians and others until his death (resulting from old age) in Vienna in 1809.

Haydn wrote 125 symphonies, many sonatas for clavier, numerous church pieces, among which is *The Seven Words,* and oratorios. There were also many cantatas and other vocal works, operas, operettas, and songs.

LEONCAVALLO (1858-1919)

Ruggiero Leoncavallo, like Mascagni, was chiefly an opera composer whose fame is based on one successful work. His father was President of the High Court of Justice in Naples, Italy, where Ruggiero was born.

Leoncavallo was graduated from the Naples Conservatory when he was sixteen. He also studied at the University of Bologna.

An uncle was in the Foreign Office in Egypt, and arranged for his nephew to give some piano recitals in that country. His playing pleased the Egyptian Court and he was invited to be the head of the Egyptian Military Bands. However, at this time, war broke out with England, and Leoncavallo was forced to escape in the guise of an Arab. Finally, with his money gone, he reached Paris, and was obliged to become a café pianist to earn his living. Soon he began to do some teaching and in the meantime was working on some operas. He wrote the words and music of *I Pagliacci,* his most successful work, in five months.

Although educated a conservative in music, Leoncavallo admired the work of Wagner, and brought some Wagnerian influence into Italian opera. He also wrote ballets, songs, and other works.

His death was at Montecatini, Italy, in 1919.

MASSENET (1842-1912)

Jules Massenet was born in Montaud, France, in 1842. His early years were troubled by poverty, and during the time he was getting his education he supported himself with difficulty. His original compositions won some prizes at the Paris Conservatoire, where he was studying, and in 1863 he won the Prix de Rome for his cantata *David Rizzio.* He went to Rome to study. Massenet served in the Franco-Prussian war (1871).

He taught composition at the Paris Conservatoire from 1878 to 1896, and this period was one of his greatest productivity.

Massenet wrote music which was characteristically French, and during much of his lifetime he was one of the most popular living French opera composers. The stories he chose for his libretti were typically French. He succeeded so well in pleasing his countrymen that he received all the honors they could give. He was admitted to France's honorary society of distinguished men, the Academy, in 1878, and enjoyed the distinction of being the youngest man ever admitted.

He died in Paris, France, in 1912.

Among his compositions are operas, oratorios, orchestral suites, and songs. The best known of his operas are *Manon* and *Thaïs*.

MENDELSSOHN (1809-1847)

Felix Mendelssohn-Bartholdy was born in 1809, in Hamburg, Germany, where his father was a banker. His parents were intellectual Jews who provided their children with a well-rounded education. Felix first played in public in a trio when he was less than ten. By the time he was twelve, he had composed many pieces for piano and other instruments and also for the voice. He had rather an unusual opportunity, for his father engaged expert musicians to perform his son's works. It was not, however, until Felix was sixteen that his father became willing for him to make music his life work.

After a period of composition and study in Berlin, Mendelssohn toured England, Scotland, Germany, Italy, Switzerland, and France.

His life was filled with commissions, conducting of festivals, teaching, orchestra conducting, and composing. Despite much opposition he succeeded in conducting, in 1829, a performance of Bach's *St. Matthew's Passion.* This was its first performance after the death of that great master of polyphonic music.

Mendelssohn wrote many orchestral works, among which were four symphonies, a number of concert overtures (one of which was the *Midsummer Night's Dream*), chamber music, organ music, choral music, songs, oratorios (the most important being the *Elijah*) many *Songs without Words,* and other works for piano.

He died in Leipzig in 1847.

MOUSSORGSKY (1839-1881)

Modest Petrovich Moussorgsky was born in Karevo, Pskov, in 1839. He was very much interested in music when he was a

A SCENE FROM "KHOVANTCHINA" BY MOUSSORGSKY

child, and a nurse made him familiar with the old Russian tales. His first piano lessons were given him by his mother.

His early training was received in the Military School for Ensigns. After graduation he began a professional career as an army officer. About three years after his entry into the service he met Borodin and Balakirev, members of "the Five," and became so interested in their efforts to create a new school of Russian music that he left the army in 1858 to devote his time to their cause.

Moussorgsky occupied himself with music until he had to resume his work because of family reverses. He took a government post, and while he remained in the service, he was sent from one post to another because of his careless work. He lived in the country for a time and came into intimate association with Russian peasants and their folk music. He was a member of the "Russian Five" (Borodin, Balakirev, Dargomyzhsky, Cui, and Moussorgsky).

He died in 1881.

Although Moussorgsky wrote many orchestral numbers, among which is *A Night on Bald Mountain,* his greatest achievement is the opera *Boris Godounov.*

Paul's Photos, Chicago

THE LITTLE MOZART HOUSE NEAR SALZBURG, GERMANY

MOZART (1756-1791)

Wolfgang Amadeus Mozart received his early musical training from his father. The elder Mozart was a violinist and court composer to the Archbishop of Salzburg. Here his son was born in 1756. When only seven years of age, Mozart played violin on a concert tour. So precocious was the young Mozart that, before he was ten, he could read at sight any music for violin, clavier, or organ. His first sonatas were published when he was seven, and he wrote his first symphony when he was eight.

His father arranged that the boy should travel to the various music centers in other countries so that in addition to making money and becoming acquainted with many musicians, who would learn of the boy's genius, the young Mozart would become familiar with all of the different national styles of music. He made ten trips away from Salzburg before he was twenty-five.

He married Constanze Weber. The young couple were frivolous and loved gaiety, and were given to extravagance. His income

Courtesy The Art Institute of Chicago

WOLFGANG AMADEUS MOZART

was small and he soon was deeply in debt and had to take on many duties which soon broke down his health.

In 1787 Mozart was appointed private musician to the emperor, but the salary was insufficient. In 1791 he began to compose a funeral service which was ordered by a mysterious stranger, whom Mozart believed supernatural. Mozart feared that this was prophetic of his death. Strange to say he did die before the *Requiem* was completed.

His death took place at Vienna, Austria, in 1791. He was so poor that he was buried in a pauper's grave.

Mozart wrote voluminously for piano, chamber ensembles, and orchestra. Among the many symphonies he composed, the last three, in E flat major, G minor and C major (the *Jupiter)* are the most outstanding. Mozart realized his ambition to be an opera composer when he wrote such successful operas as *The Magic Flute, Don Giovanni,* and *Figaro.*

RIMSKY-KORSAKOV (1844-1908)

Nicolai Rimsky-Korsakov, the son of a well-to-do landowner, was born in Tikhvin, Novgorod, Russia, in 1844. As a boy he had opportunities to learn at first hand the folk songs of the Russian peasants which were later a strong influence in establishing him as a Russian nationalistic composer.

Acquiescing in his parents' wishes, he attended and graduated from the St. Petersburg Naval Academy. While there he studied music as a recreation. After graduation he served three years as a naval officer, during which time he composed a symphony which was produced by Balakirev. He retired from the navy in 1873 to accept a position as professor in the St. Petersburg Conservatory, an institution that had opposed the ideas of Rimsky-Korsakov and

A SCENE FROM "THE INVISIBLE CITY" BY RIMSKY-KORSAKOV

the other members of the "Five." During the same year, he married and also had his first opera produced. Later he succeeded Balakirev as conductor of the symphony orchestra.

He wrote many operas and songs but is best known for his orchestral music, which includes the popular *Scheherazade.* His most popular opera, *Le Coq d'or* (The Golden Cockerel), was produced in 1908, the year he died in St. Petersburg. He was one of the "Russian Five" (Moussorgsky, Cui, Balakirev, Borodin, and Rimsky-Korsakov) who were so influential in the development of Russian music.

SCHUBERT (1797-1828)

In 1797 Franz Schubert was born in very humble circumstances in Vienna. His family was very much interested in music, and Franz received his early instruction from his father and elder brothers. His beautiful voice enabled him to enter the choir school of the Imperial Chapel. Here he also had his early orchestral experience, becoming first violinist and assistant conductor in the school band. After his voice broke he began to give music lessons in his father's school. In 1816 von Schober induced Schubert to give his entire time to composition. The composer left his teaching post and went to share lodgings with his friend. For a while during the summer of 1818 he taught at the country place of

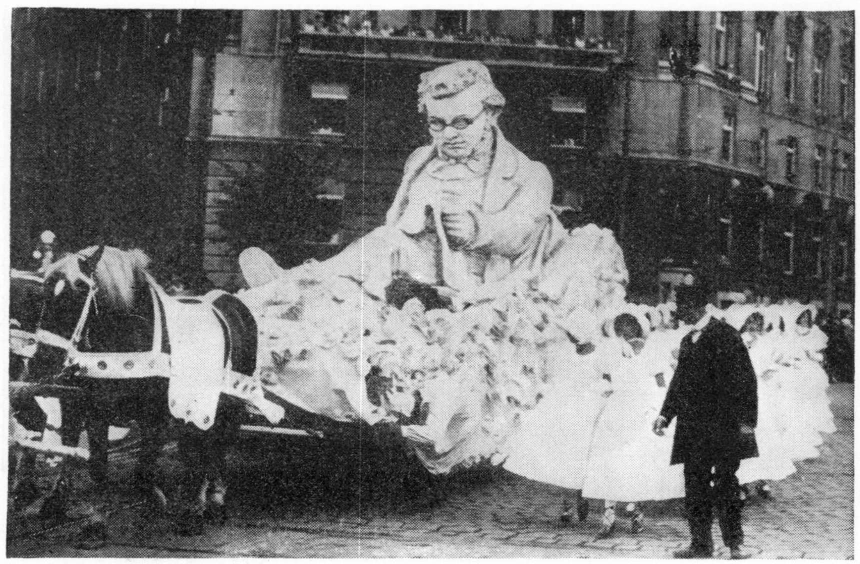

Paul's Photos, Chicago

SCHUBERT'S MEMORY HONORED IN VIENNA
Heroic figure of the composer on a float in a procession of Song Festival Week in Vienna.

Count Esterhazy, and in contrast lived in very poor lodgings the two following years. He was so bashful that when he met Weber and Beethoven in 1822 nothing came of it. In the summer of 1824 he again taught at the home of Count Esterhazy and fell hopelessly in love with his daughter. During the winters he composed constantly. This, together with a rather reckless way of living, impaired his health, causing him to become melancholy and to have frequent mental delusions. He died in 1828, at the age of thirty-one.

Schubert left an almost unbelievable amount of music. Among his works are over six hundred songs and eight symphonies, including the ones in B minor ("Unfinished") and C major. In all, he left more than eleven hundred works. He will be remembered as one of the greatest song writers in musical history.

SCHUMANN (1810-1856)

Robert Schumann was an important member of the group of composers who were exponents of Romanticism. He was born at Zwickau, in Saxony, in 1810. His father was a book-seller and author, and taught his son much of his trade and interested him in literature. As a boy he was a leader among his playmates and organized a boys' orchestra. As he grew into his teens, he became more retiring. His father fostered his interest in music, but the father died when Robert was sixteen, and his mother insisted that the boy study to become a lawyer. After many years his mother consented to his making music his career. In 1830 he went to Leipzig and studied with Wieck and others to make up for the deficiencies in his early musical training. He crippled his right hand by use of a device to make the fourth finger more free. This caused him to make composition his principal occupation. He was the chief motivator in a group organized to oppose the commonplace in music. Pursuant with this policy, he, with the assistance of others, started the *Neue Zeitschrift für Musik* (New Journal of Music), which stood for the most advanced ideas in music. He held the editorship of this until 1844. In 1840 he married Clara Wieck, a very fine pianist. He became a member of the faculty of Leipzig Conservatory when it was started by Mendelssohn in 1843. A year later he had a nervous breakdown and moved to Dresden. He gradually recovered, and finally took up his composition again.

An unusual feature of Schumann's activities in composition is that he devoted his attention to certain musical forms in a given period. Up to 1840 all his compositions were for piano. Then for a year he did nothing but write songs, in which field he ranks with Schubert. There followed successively periods of symphonic writing and chamber music composition. Of Schumann's symphonies the *Spring* and the *Cologne* are best known.

He held a position as conductor and later one as director, but from 1852 on he suffered from melancholy and delusions. Once he was rescued from the Rhine, where he had attempted to drown himself. He was then placed in a private asylum where he died in 1856.

VERDI (1813-1901)

Giuseppe Verdi, successor to Rossini, Bellini, and Donizetti, was born near Busseto in 1813. His father was an innkeeper. Giuseppe's musical talents were evidenced at an early age. At the age of ten he was appointed organist of the village church, and ten years later became leader of the local music society.

Courtesy Chicago City Opera Co.

SCENE FROM ACT III OF VERDI'S "RIGOLETTO"
Rigoletto pleads with the Duke to return his daughter, Gilda.

Awarded a scholarship by his townspeople, he went to Milan to study but was refused entrance to the conservatory. He started to study with the accompanist of La Scala Theater, and in 1839 his first opera, *Oberto,* was performed. He was under contract to write three more when his wife and two children died suddenly. The opera on which he was working at the time was a failure, but Merelli persuaded him to write the other two and they were successes. These were written in the Italian style.

The tremendous popularity of *Rigoletto,* produced in 1851, and *Il Trovatore* and *La Traviata,* in 1853, established Verdi as Italy's outstanding musical representative of the nineteenth century.

When he was almost sixty, Verdi began to write operas which are often said to reflect the influence of Wagner. In this period, 1871-1893, some of his best works were written, *Aïda, Othello,* and *Falstaff.* The last was written when he was eighty years old.

Verdi left little music outside of operas, of which he wrote more than thirty. He led a simple life. In character he was sincere, generous, and brilliant intellectually.

His death occurred in 1901.

VON WEBER (1786-1826)

Carl Maria von Weber was born in 1786 near Lübeck. His father had been a choirmaster and band leader, and his mother was a soprano. As all the family had musical talent and the father was a rover by disposition, they went from one place to another giving concerts. So until he was twenty-five years old Carl was traveling most of the time. He did his first serious studying in 1796.

In 1804 he became conductor at the theater of Breslau. While here he lost his voice by accidentally swallowing acid.

He became secretary to Duke Ludwig of Württemberg at Stuttgart. The court here was corrupt and von Weber became dissipated and got into financial difficulties. At this time he became interested in philosophy. He finally got into difficulties and the King banished him.

He was very much interested in musical criticism. After teaching in Darmstadt for a short time, he began to travel and concertize. He held the position of director of the Opera House at Prague for three years. In 1816 he was appointed chapel master of the German Opera at Dresden, and later in the same year the tenure was made for life. In that year he married Caroline Brandt, a famous singer. Now his interest naturally turned to opera and in 1820 he completed *Der Freischütz*. He was commissioned in 1824 to write an opera for Covent Garden, England.

At this time he was suffering from lung trouble. Ignoring his doctor's advice against assuming the task in his state of health, he set to work on *Oberon,* which he completed in 1826. He made his condition worse by going to England to supervise the rehearsals and performances of his new work. The strain was too great, and he died in his sleep two months after he had scored a complete triumph with his last work.

Weber established German romantic opera and with it the romantic movement. His methods became an influence in both the operatic and symphonic fields.

WAGNER (1813-1883)

Richard Wagner was born at Leipzig in 1813. His father, who was a civil officer, was very much interested in the theater. Shortly after the death of his father, his mother remarried and Richard was brought up by a stepfather. In his early educational period he was more interested in Greek, drama, and poetry than in music. Later, at Leipzig, he became interested in music. In his early period his interest was in instrumental music, although

Paul's Photos, Chicago

RICHARD WAGNER IN CHARACTERISTIC POSE

Courtesy German Railroads Information Office, N. Y.

NEUSCHWANSTEIN CASTLE, SETTING FOR WAGNER'S OPERA, "LOHENGRIN"

his first dramatic libretto was commenced when he was nineteen.

While he was director of the theater at Riga between 1837 and 1839, he began his opera *Rienzi,* which, when completed in Paris in 1842, scored a definite success. The next year *The Flying Dutchman* was produced and also was acclaimed.

After the Parisian performances of his successful works, they were produced in Dresden. The cordial reception of the operas brought Wagner the appointment of musical director of the court at Dresden in 1843. His dogmatic attitudes brought about troubles with conservatives. Due to political difficulties he had to flee to Weimar in 1849, and thence to Paris.

In the sixteen years following, Wagner composed other operas that added to his fame, notably *Tannhäuser, Lohengrin* and *Tristan and Isolde.* The last work was conceived in Switzerland and completed in Italy. In addition to his operas he spent much time in writing articles and books on music, musical criticism, and esthetics.

He was separated from his wife in 1861. In 1864 he was called to Munich by Ludwig II, of Bavaria, there to carry out his dramatic ideas. From now on his music became increasingly more favored by the people. The king had hoped to found a Wagnerian theater at Munich, but local opposition was too great. At the close of the year 1865 Wagner went to Triebschen, where he met Cosima Liszt, who later became his wife.

The famous theater at Bayreuth, built according to his ideas, was completed in 1875. Here complete performances were given of the Nibelungen cycle which includes *Das Rheingold, Siegfried, Die Walküre* and *Götterdämmerung.* So elaborate was the scale upon which these were given that heavy debts were incurred which were later paid off by proceeds of concerts and operas at other cities.

He died in 1883 and was buried at Bayreuth.

Courtesy National Broadcasting Co.

A SESSION IN BRASS AND WOOD

Into each of the concerts of the series broadcast by the NBC Symphony go many hours of the hard rehearsal that makes easy lis·ening. In some rehearsals, strings and wind instruments separate and drill over each measure of the scores. Here the candid camera has caught some of the woods and brasses as they smooth out difficult passages. Upper left: a quartet of clarinets—B flat, E flat and bass—practice a rippling arpeggio. Upper right: The French horns join in wi:h a call reminiscent of the hunting horn. Lower left: A quartet in brass—trumpets lend their brilliant tones to the coloration of the score. Lower right: Reed instruments of assorted sizes—clarinets, bassoons, and oboes. The English horn, another reed, is not shown.

MEN WHO ARE MAKING MUSIC TODAY

ANTHEIL (1900-   )

GEORGE ANTHEIL was born in Trenton, New Jersey, in 1900. His father was a political exile from Poland. When he was four his parents took him back. Later he returned to America and studied at the Curtis School in Philadelphia. He took up residence in Europe in 1921, returning to America in 1927. A Guggenheim fellowship was awarded to him in 1932 and he went to Europe, where he composed his opera, *Helen Retires,* of which John Erskine was the librettist. He is also the composer of some symphonic music, chamber music and some piano pieces.

At present he is living in New York City with his wife, Böske Markus.

BARLOW (1893-   )

Samuel L. M. Barlow was born in New York City in 1893. He still resides there. Much of his musical study was abroad under Respighi and Phillip. He has written a number of orchestral works, chamber works, and operas. His principal interest is in orchestral composition.

BARTÓK (1881-   )

Béla Bartók is one of the most nationalistic of contemporary composers. He was born in Hungary in 1881, the son of an amateur musician. When Béla was eight his father died and his mother had to take up teaching to support her family. In pursuit of her profession she traveled throughout Hungary. During this period Béla came to know folk song, learning it in the different parts of his country where it was indigenous.

Before he was ten Bartók had started to compose and had also appeared publicly as a pianist. During his early training at Pressburgh he met Dohnanyi, who advised him to go to Budapest for further study. He was appointed a professor of piano in the Conservatory there in 1907. With the co-operation of Kodály he unearthed folk songs that were unknown to the present-day public.

After five years as piano teacher in the Royal Hungarian Musical Academy at Budapest, Bartók resigned to devote his entire time to composition and research in folk songs. His style has been greatly influenced by his studies in folk song. He makes advanced use of dissonance.

He has written for the orchestra, chamber music ensemble, piano, and voice.

BAUER (1887-)

Marion Bauer was born in Walla Walla, Washington, on August 15, 1887. Her musical training was acquired in this country and in France. She has written a large number of songs which have been sung with much success by many leading artists. They bear the mark of excellent musicianship and sensitive beauty. She has also written works for orchestra and chamber ensembles. Her contributions to the field of musical essay and criticism, as well as history, have been stamped with lucidity of style and authority.

BECKER (1886-)

John J. Becker, born in Henderson, Kentucky, received his musical training in America. His compositions, in which he displays much of the contemporary dissonant counterpoint, are largely for orchestra and the stage. He has been identified with the New Music group in the United States and abroad.

BENNETT (1894-)

Early sickness did not deter Robert Russell Bennett, who was born in Kansas City in 1894. At the age of six he contracted infantile paralysis, was taken to the country, and for the following nine years studied piano with his mother; violin, trumpet, and other instruments with his father, who had a band and an orchestra. When he was fifteen he went to Kansas City and began his study of harmony under Carl Busch. In 1916 he went to New York, where he was engaged as copyist and arranger by G. Schirmer. After a year's service in the war, he was married in

1919. A while later he went to Paris and studied with Boulanger. He won a Guggenheim fellowship in 1927, which was renewed at the end of the year. Bennett's orchestral work *Sights and Sounds,* and his symphony *Abraham Lincoln* won for him the R. C. A. Symphony award. However, the major portion of his works shows much use of the jazz idiom. He has written two operas, music for orchestra, chamber music, and songs, also one ballet. His orchestrations display much skill.

BEREZOWSKY (1900-)

A great portion of the musical activity of Nicolai Berezowsky, born in Russia, has been connected with the United States. His life as a professional musician began in 1918 when he became concertmaster in the Saratov National Opera. A couple of years later, he became first violinist in the opera at Moscow. He came to America in 1922, and, after studying privately, finally went to the Juillard School of Music, where he studied violin with Kochanski and composition with Goldmark. In 1926 his sextet for strings, piano, and clarinet was presented at the Coolidge Chamber Music Festival in Washington. In 1929 he went abroad for two years and devoted his time entirely to composition. He has also conducted some of the leading symphony orchestras. He is at present living in New York, where he is on the staff of the Columbia Broadcasting System, and also an assistant orchestra conductor. He has written one opera, several orchestra numbers, including two symphonies, a choral number, and several works for chamber ensemble.

BERG (1885-1935)

Alban Berg was born in Vienna in 1885. He became an Austrian government official in 1905, and two years later decided to devote his life to a career in music, which heretofore had been his avocation. After becoming a pupil of Schönberg in Berlin, he began to write atonal music, making use of his teacher's "twelve tone system." He became one of Schönberg's most distinguished pupils.

Berg taught theory and composition in Vienna after 1910. During the war, he served in the Austrian army for three years. Upon his return he began composing his opera *Wozzeck* which took him four years. It was completed in 1922. In it he makes

NBC photo by Sydney Desfor

NBC SYMPHONY ORCHESTRA

effective and dramatic use of atonality and uses the speaking voice instead of singing. *Wozzeck* has had one of the most spectacular successes of any opera since Debussy's *Pelléas.*

His compositions were slowly and painstakingly written. He revised them many times. Berg's last opera was *Lulu.*

BLOCH (1880-)

Ernest Bloch was born in 1880, in Geneva, of Swiss-Jewish parents. When only a child, he was determined to become a composer and in his native city he studied with Dalcroze. At the age of sixteen he began the study of the violin with Ysaye at Brussels. One of the teachers whose influence made its mark upon Bloch's life, was Knorr, at Frankfort-on-the-Main, who taught him to learn by himself. His first symphony was composed while he was in Munich. He went to Paris after that. It was so long before his works began to be performed that he had to enter business for a

NBC photo by Sydney Desfor

NBC SYMPHONY ORCHESTRA

living. When, in 1910, his opera *Macbeth* was produced at the Opéra Comique in Paris, and met with great success, he gave up business to devote himself to music. In 1927 he entered his symphony *America* in a contest conducted by *Musical America*, and won a prize of five thousand dollars. Four years after this he received an endowment, gave up all his teaching, and went to Switzerland, where he composed his greatest work. It was a musical service to the Sabbath morning prayers of the Jewish synagogue. Because of the depression the endowment was stopped in 1934, and Bloch returned to the United States.

CADMAN (1881-)

Charles Wakefield Cadman was born in Johnstown, Pennsylvania, in 1881. He became interested in music when he was a child, although the family did not have a piano until he was thirteen. He was, however, far more interested in composition than in piano playing. He had great difficulty in getting his works published. When some of his songs were finally accepted by Ditson Company, they lay dormant until John McCormack began to use *At Dawning* on concert tours. Through Nellie Richmond Eberhart he became interested in the music of the American Indian, in which he has specialized since 1909. He is now living in La Mesa, California. He has written three operas, of which *Shanewis* and *Witch of Salem* are the best known. He has also written for the orchestra, songs, piano pieces, and chamber music.

CARPENTER (1876-)

John Alden Carpenter was born in Park Ridge, Illinois, in 1876. On his paternal side he is descended from the John Aldens of Plymouth. His early musical education was under Amy Fay in Chicago. He entered business, but was more interested in music. After once being refused, he persuaded Elgar to take him as a pupil. After studying with him for a short time, Carpenter returned to Chicago and began his studies with Bernhard Ziehn. In 1914 his songs, settings of poems by Tagore, under the title of *Gitanjali* were favorably received. In 1924 Diaghilev commissioned Carpenter to write a ballet, whereupon he wrote *Skyscrapers,* which he dedicated to the modern city. He has produced other works for orchestra, chamber music, songs, and piano selections. He is a resident of Chicago.

CHARPENTIER (1860-)

Gustave Charpentier was born in Dieuze, Lorraine, in 1860. He began his study of music in Turcoing, where his family was forced to move as a result of the Franco-Prussian War. He secured work as an accountant when he was fifteen. His employer, being interested in music and recognizing the talent of the boy, founded an orchestra and musical society as an outlet for Gustave's musical gifts. Charpentier matured musically so rapidly that his employer sent him to the Conservatory of Lille. Later he went to the Paris Conservatory. After having been in military service for a year, he began to study composition under Massenet.

While holding the Prix de Rome, Charpentier familiarized himself with Italian life. It was while in Rome that he composed an orchestral suite, *Impressions of Italy,* one of his most popular works. Later he lived the life of a Bohemian in Paris.

During the time that he was writing his opera *Louise* he was so poor that he would have starved had he not been given credit by a kind-hearted baker. The opera, produced in 1900, was a great success. Although he wrote another opera, *Julien,* and works for orchestra, chorus, and some songs, *Louise* is his greatest work.

CHAVEZ (1899-)

The most important contemporary Mexican composer is Carlos Chavez, who was born in Mexico City in 1899. For the most part he has been his own music teacher, although he did receive a few lessons from his sister when he was ten years old. He learned much from books about the different instruments of the orchestra and from the same source acquired his knowledge of musical theory.

When he was eighteen he began composing, modeling his works on classical compositions which he analyzed. After touring Europe, he returned to Mexico and began to express the music

ROY HARRIS
American composer.

SERGE KOUSSEVITZKY
Conductor, Boston Symphony Orchestra.

of Mexico in modern form. He is now living in Mexico City and is director of the symphony orchestra there.

He has written for orchestra, ballet and chamber ensembles. Among his ballets *New Fire, H.P.,* and *Four Suns,* are outstanding.

COPLAND (1900-)

Aaron Copland was born in Brooklyn, New York, in 1900. He began his musical education when he was about thirteen. In 1921, he went to Paris where he studied three years under Boulanger. After he returned to America he was awarded a Guggenheim Fellowship that enabled him to go to Europe for two more years of study. When he was twenty-two, he composed an orchestral number *Cortège Macabre* which first brought his music into prominence. He has a very facile technique, and makes much use of jazz rhythms and dissonant harmonies.

As well as being a composer, Copland is a magazine writer and lecturer. He is also a sponsor for concerts of modern music. In his intense desire to further the cause of modern music, he became one of the organizers of the Yaddo Music Festival, which takes place at Saratoga Springs, New York, each fall. He has written aggressive music for chamber ensemble, orchestra, and piano.

DEBUSSY (1862-1918)

Claude Achille Debussy was born in 1862, at Saint-Germain-en-Laye. His early schooling was meager, due to the fact that his father, a poor shop-keeper, could not afford more. As a boy, Debussy had opportunity to hear music only in open-air concerts. His father wanted him to become a sailor, but Claude showed a marked liking for all things beautiful and artistic. When he was nine he began to study the piano. Later he entered the Conservatory in Paris, where he won numerous medals. Through the conservatory he secured a position in a trio which toured Florence, Vienna, Venice, and Moscow. He won the Prix de Rome in 1885 with his cantata *L'Enfant prodigue.* After his time in Rome had expired he returned to Paris. During his early creative period, he composed songs and choral works which showed his sensitiveness, but showed too that his musical aim was not as yet definitely delineated. He became interested in the poetry of the French Symbolists and wished to express the ethereal in his music. For this effect he began to use the whole-tone scale. In about 1890 he began to compose a series of compositions that defined his new style of musical Impressionism. One of these was the well-known *L'Après-midi d'un Faune* (The Afternoon of a Faun). The high point of his musical career was reached when he composed the opera *Pelléas et Mélisande* which was first presented at the Opéra Comique in 1902. Debussy died in Paris in 1918. He had very great influence in the development of modern music, and will always be considered one of the foremost composers of France.

D'INDY (1851-1931)

Paul Marie Théodore Vincent D'Indy was born in Paris in 1851. To please his father he took up the study of law, studying harmony and counterpoint in his free time. He served in the army during the Franco-Prussian War, after which he gave up any pretense of studying law and made music his profession in spite of parental opposition. In 1872 he submitted to César Franck for criticism a quartet that he had written. Franck liked it so well that he advised D'Indy to enter the Conservatory. After a short stay at the Conservatory he persuaded Franck to take him as a private pupil. In 1873 D'Indy went to Liszt at Weimar.

With César Franck he founded the Société Nationale de Musique for the promoting of contemporary chamber and orchestral music. He became president of the society upon Franck's death. When, in 1893, the French government placed him upon a committee to reform the Paris Conservatory, his suggestions were so revolutionary that the committee disbanded and the reformation was postponed for several years. When at last it took place, D'Indy was put on the faculty. While D'Indy is generally thought of as a composer, he was equally important as a teacher. He has wielded great influence in modern music, many of the contemporary composers having benefited from his teaching either directly or indirectly. Although the subject which he taught at the Conservatory was conducting, he also criticized the compositions of his pupils. He wrote operas, symphonies, and other orchestral and choral music, chamber music, songs, and piano pieces.

DE FALLA (1876-)

A significant representative of the Spanish people in the writing of modern music is Manuel De Falla, who was born at Cadiz in 1876. He began the study of music at an early age, and when he was twenty-nine years old won the award of the Academy of Fine Arts for his opera *La Vida breve* ("The Brief Life"). Later he moved to Paris, where French composers encouraged him to continue in his pursuit of a musical career.

Although De Falla's music is fundamentally national, Spain was slow to recognize the ability of her composer son. He remained in France until 1914, but with the beginning of the war returned to his native country. There he made a thorough study of Spanish folk music and then settled in Granada amid the crumbling ruins of the romantic Alhambra. His studies in the ancient music of Spain served De Falla in good stead, and in his music can be observed the influences of early church music and the oriental style of the music of the Moors, who ruled Spain for many centuries.

The painstaking revision to which De Falla has subjected all of his work has served to limit it in quantity, but what there is has a spontaneous freedom as well as well-rounded finish. Best known of his music is that he composed for the ballet, *El Sombrero de tres picos* ("The Three-cornered Hat"). Other important works written by De Falla are *Noches en los jardines de Espana* ("Nights in the Gardens of Spain"), for piano and orchestra, *Pièces Espagnoles,* for piano, and a group of Spanish folk songs.

ENESCO (1881-)

Georges Enesco, born in Dorohoiû, Rumania, on August 19, 1881, is the outstanding composer today in that country. His principal studies were in Vienna and Paris. His *Symphonie Concertante, Rumanian Rhapsodies,* symphonies, and other large orchestral works, have brought his fame to audiences all over the world. His native penchant for tonal color, and an inherent gift for melody writing, have given him a high place in the field of contemporary music. In addition to his contributions as a composer Enesco has made an important place for himself as a concert violinist and a conductor.

Photo by Rembrandt Studios, Philadelphia

EUGENE ORMANDY
Philadelphia Orchestra Conductor

WALTER DAMROSCH
Conductor.

GERSHWIN (1898-1937)

George Gershwin was born in Brooklyn, New York, in 1898. His early piano training was forced upon him by his mother, his interests being in playing on the street at punch ball and other kindred sports. His first position in the musical field was as pianist for Remick and Sons. While he was engaged as a jazz player he met Paul Whiteman. They found that they had a common interest, that of using jazz in a serious composition. It was decided that they would co-operate, Gershwin doing the composing and Paul Whiteman and his orchestra producing it. The result was the *Rhapsody in Blue.* Although he began to write things of more serious interest, Gershwin did not abandon the writing of musical comedies. With *Of Thee I Sing,* a political satire, he won the Pulitzer Prize in 1931. His last important work, *Porgy and Bess,* was a successful effort to incorporate native folk material into opera. He died in 1937 after a brief illness.

GRUENBERG (1883-

Louis Gruenberg was born in Russia in 1883. He was brought to America at the age of two and received his early education in the schools of New York. When he became older, he determined to become a professional musician. He returned to Europe, where he toured as concert pianist, being soloist with the leading orchestras. When he turned his talents to composition he won a ten-thousand-dollar prize for a symphonic poem, *Hill of Dreams*. Among four operas which he wrote in his earlier period, was *The Man Who Married a Dumb Wife,* based upon a play by Anatole France. He neglected to ask permission of the author to use the play, and encountered the refusal of France's executors. As yet he has not received permission to produce the opera. It was, however, *The Emperor Jones,* an opera, which placed him in the foremost rank of American composers. Gruenberg has written five operas, including *Jack and the Beanstalk,* several works for orchestra, and a few for chamber ensemble. After teaching in Chicago for several years, he went to live in California in 1937.

HADLEY (1871-1937)

Henry Kimball Hadley, born in Massachusetts, was one of the most prominent of American composers. His mother was very much opposed to his following a musical career in spite of the fact that he was vitally interested in music at an early age. However, when one day his parents saw some waltzes that the boy had composed, they realized his talent, and gave him the best musical training that could be had in Boston. Under this excellent training he matured musically with great rapidity. In 1893 he toured as violinist with the Mapleson Operatic Company. The next year he went to Vienna. His orchestral debut was made in New York as conductor at the Waldorf Astoria. Later, after touring about six years in Europe, he returned and was made conductor of the Seattle Symphony Orchestra. Afterwards he conducted many leading orchestras. In 1918 he married Inez Barbour, a concert singer.

He was a very prolific composer, his symphonic works being his best. He has written a number of suites, symphonies, and other compositions in the larger forms. A most unusual aspect of his work was the fact that he could compose while friends were talking to him, and often had his wife read to him while he was writing a score. He died in 1937.

Courtesy Eastman School of Music, Rochester, N. Y.

HOWARD HANSON

HANSON (1896-)

Another middle western composer is Howard Hanson, who was born in 1896 in Wahoo, Nebraska, of Swedish parents. His parentage and early environment later bore fruit in his *Nordic Symphony*. His musical education and first attempts at composition began when he was seven. After graduating from the local high school, he graduated from Luther College. Then he left Wahoo and went to New York City where he studied with Friskin and Goetschius. He was graduated from Northwestern University at the age of nineteen. The following year he became professor of theory and composition in the College of the Pacific in San Jose, California. This post he held for three years and then became Dean of the Conservatory of Fine Arts. In 1921 he was awarded the Prix de Rome which he held for the next three years. Returning from Rome in 1924, he became Director of the Eastman School of Music in the University of Rochester, a post he still holds. Among his works are the *Lament of Beowulf* for chorus and orchestra, *Pan and the Priest,* and the *Romantic Symphony.* His opera, *Merry Mount,* was produced at the Metropolitan in 1934.

In his capacity as Director of the Eastman School, Hanson has done much to encourage American music and its composers.

HARRIS (1898-)

A log cabin was the first home of Roy Harris, who was born in Oklahoma in 1898 on Lincoln's birthday. His parents were pioneers. Due to his mother's ill health they moved to California, when Harris was five years old, and he was reared on a farm. In his early years he had a meager training in music and also in general subjects, though he had two years at the University of California.

After serving in the army as a private during the war, he returned to California and made his living by driving a truck. Studying at night, he made such rapid progress that within three years his first symphonic work was performed in New York. In 1927 he won a Guggenheim fellowship, as the result of which he lived in Europe, where he studied with Boulanger. In 1929 he had the misfortune to injure his spine and was in the hospital for six months. When he was recovering he had to compose while lying flat on his back. This circumstance freed him from what he had formerly considered the necessity of composing at the piano. As a result his music gained in clarity and became more contrapuntal. He is the only American whose most important works have been recorded in their entirety. These are his concerto for piano, clarinet, and string quartet, and his symphony. At present, he is in Princeton, New Jersey, and is teaching there at the Westminster Choir School.

VICTOR HERBERT

HERBERT (1859-1924)

Of Irish birth, but with great influence on light music in America, was Victor Herbert, born in Dublin in 1859. His mother was the daughter of a novelist and playwright who was also a composer of Irish songs.

He was educated at the Stuttgart Conservatorium in Germany. After holding the conductorship of the Pittsburgh Symphony for a number of years, he went to New York to devote his time to composition.

Victor Herbert was a prolific writer of operettas, writing thirty-five between 1894 and 1917. Among these are the popular *Mademoiselle Modiste* and *Naughty Marietta.* He also wrote the grand operas *Natoma* and *Madeleine.* There were also compositions for violincello, voice, and symphony orchestra. He died in New York in 1924.

HILL (1872-)

Born in Cambridge, Massachusetts, in 1872, Edward Burlingame Hill comes of a distinguished family. His father was a professor of organic chemistry at Harvard, and director of the Boylston Chemical Laboratory. He attended Harvard University where, in 1908, he went to teach in the Division of Music, during Professor Spalding's leave of absence, and has remained there. While most of his time has been taken up with teaching musical history, orchestration, and French and Russian music at Harvard, Hill has found time to compose three symphonies and other works for orchestra, and works for chorus and for chamber ensemble.

HINDEMITH (1895-)

Paul Hindemith was born in Germany in 1895. His earliest musical study was at the age of eleven, when he began to study the viola and violin. He studied composition at the Hoch Conservatory in Frankfort, and became more engrossed in this branch of music. From 1915 to 1923 he was with the Frankfort Opera, first as concert master of the orchestra, and later as conductor. Beginning in 1921, his works were produced at the Festival at Donaueschingen, and his chamber works were produced at the Salzburg Festival in the three succeeding years. It was 1925 when his first atonal work (without an established key center) was presented at the Venice festival of the International Society for Contemporary Music. This was his *Kammermusik.*

Hindemith's ambition is to popularize modern music among the masses. While he has written all types of music, his chamber music is best known, particularly his string quartettes and a sonata for viola which he played first in 1937. In that year Hindemith's works were featured at the great Elizabeth Sprague Coolidge Festival of Chamber Music, held in Washington. While his compositions are all ultra-modern, the freshness of their design and soundness of musical ideas have led many conservative critics to praise them highly.

HONEGGER (1892-)

Arthur Honegger was born in Havre, in 1892, of Swiss parentage. His early musical training was in violin. He studied at the Conservatory of Zürich, returned to France in 1912, and studied at the Paris Conservatory with Widor and Vincent D'Indy, among others. Then he applied himself to the mastering of the technique of composition. He studied carefully scores by modern composers before he himself began to compose. Consequently his works show very skilful craftsmanship. Outstanding among his works are *Le Roi David* ("King David"), *Judith,* and *Pacific 231* for orchestra. His works are episodic, and not extended in form. He makes use of harmony as a color medium.

JACOBI (1891-)

Though Frederick Jacobi was born in San Francisco in 1891, he won his reputation as a composer in the east where he studied at the Ethical Culture School of New York. After studying composition with Goldmark, he went to Berlin and studied with Juon in the Hochschule für Musik. When he returned to America he became an assistant conductor at the Metropolitan Opera House in New York. His interest in primitive music caused him to spend much time studying Indian music in Arizona and New Mexico. He was a saxophone player in the United States army during the war. He is very active in the cause of modern music, having served on the jury at the Coolidge festival in 1926, and has been a delegate to the festivals of the International Society for Contemporary Music a number of times. His ideal in his own composition is to make it as personal and free from outside influences as possible. His compositions include works for choruses, chamber ensemble, and orchestra.

LOEFFLER (1861-1935)

Charles Martin Tornov Loeffler was born in Alsace in 1861. His father was a scientist, with music for an avocation, and his mother a devotee of poetry. Charles received his early music training in Kiev where he studied violin with a German who became interested in him, though when the family moved to Hungary he had to discontinue his studies. In 1875 he determined to make music his life work and went to Berlin and Paris. He secured a position in the orchestra of Baron von Derwies.

In 1881 he came to America. First he held a position as violinist in Damrosch's orchestra, and later in the Boston Symphony, where he had first chair. In 1891 the Boston Symphony played his *Les Veillées de l'Ukraine* and during the next ten years produced three of his other compositions. His *Pagan Poem,* which he wrote in 1901, was the work which first established his prestige. Since that work his others sustained the same level of importance. He was an Impressionist. His compositions are for orchestra, chamber ensemble and chorus.

KELLEY (1857-)

Edgar Stillman Kelley was born in Sparta, Wisconsin, in 1857. His orchestral and chamber works have been frequently performed in the United States and Europe. His symphonies, choral works, and chamber music were important contributions to musical composition in America in the first quarter of the twentieth century. Among his best known works are the *New England Symphony,* and the oratorio *Pilgrim's Progress.*

MacDOWELL (1861-1908)

Edward MacDowell, regarded as one of the foremost American composers, was born in New York City in 1861. His early education was in America under various teachers, among whom was Teresa Carreño. Later he studied in the Paris Conservatory and Stuttgart, Germany, and also Wiesbaden, to which, after teaching in other places, he returned remaining until 1887. Later he accepted the chair of music (newly established) in Columbia University, from which he resigned in 1904. The University of Pennsylvania and Princeton University conferred upon him the honorary degree of Doctor of Music. He died in 1908 as a result of a cerebral collapse due to worry and overwork.

As a composer MacDowell was a Romanticist and favored poetical suggestion and programmatic titles. The influence of his

PIETRO MASCAGNI

German training in the romantic school is reflected in most of his works. He wrote songs, as well as orchestral, choral, and piano music. His *Indian Suite* is a well-known orchestral work, as are the two piano concertos.

MASCAGNI (1863-)

Pietro Mascagni's father was determined that his son should be a lawyer, so Mascagni at first kept his musical study secret. When his father discovered that he was studying at the Instituto Luigi Cherubini, it was only by the intervention of his uncle that he was permitted to continue. His symphony for small orchestra and a chorus were both performed at the Instituto in 1879. When his uncle died in 1881, his father, who had been pleased by the success of his son, relented and allowed him to follow the career of a musician. Count Florestano heard a performance of Mascagni's *Ode to Joy* and sponsored the boy's education at the Conservatory of Milan. After a short time Mascagni, who did not enjoy the formulas set down by the Conservatory, left, and became conductor of a traveling opera company. Finally he settled down in Cerignola, as manager of a municipal school of music and teacher of piano. His obscurity was broken when he wrote *Cavalleria Rusticana* and won the first prize offered for a one-act opera. It was produced at the Costanzi Theater and its success was phenomenal. He became famous overnight. The King of Italy made him a Chevalier of the Order of the Crown. After touring America as a conductor in 1903, he returned to Europe and now resides in Rome. He has written orchestral music and a number of operas.

MASON (1873-)

Daniel Gregory Mason is a grandson of Dr. Lowell Mason, composer of "Nearer My God to Thee," and a son of the founder of the Mason and Hamlin Piano Company. He was born in Massachusetts in 1873. He received a thorough academic training before he specialized in music, graduating from Harvard in 1895. In the summer of 1913 he studied composition under D'Indy. In the following year he became a professor of music at Columbia University.

Mason has acquired a reputation as a composer and a writer of numerous books on music. He is also a critic and lecturer. He is the head of the Music Department at Columbia University at present. His numerous works include symphonies and other large orchestral works, many for chamber ensembles, songs, and piano pieces.

MIASKOVSKY (1881-)

Among the modern Russian symphonic composers, Nikolai Yakovlevich Miaskovsky is probably the most prolific. He was born in Russia in 1881. He was trained as an engineer in the army; music was his hobby. Finally he entered the Petrograd Conservatory in 1906 and gave up his engineering profession entirely. He spent five years there and early in his training began to concentrate on composition. His musical life was interrupted by the war when he served in the Russian army on the Austrian front in 1914. After the war, he returned to composing and in 1921 took a professorship in composition in the Moscow Conservatory of Music. Since that time his fifteen symphonies have been performed by the leading orchestras throughout the world. Among other works, he has written three string quartets. He follows in the tradition of Tschaikowsky.

ORNSTEIN (1895-)

Another American composer of European lineage is Leo Ornstein, who was born in Russia in 1895. His father was a cantor and began to teach the boy the rudiments of music at an early age. He wanted him to devote his life to being a cantor instead of following a more active musical life. However, due to the intervention of his uncle, he was allowed to study the piano. He played for Josef Hofmann, who was so astonished at the boy's technique that he wrote a letter of recommendation to the Petrograd Conservatory. Ornstein did not take advantage of this until 1904. When he had been in Petrograd a short time he went to play for Glazunov. Ornstein was annoyed because the piano was a half-tone lower than it should have been and, as he played it, transposed an entire Bach fugue a half-tone higher than written.

After studying several years in Petrograd, he came to America, where he finally entered the New York Conservatory of Music. His compositions include works for orchestra, chamber ensemble, and chorus, as well as songs and piano numbers. His early works were considered radical.

PARKER (1863-1919)

Horatio William Parker was born in Auburndale, Massachusetts, in 1863. His mother, both a musician and literary woman, taught her son in early years and later collaborated with him. In 1881 he went to Munich to study in the Hochschule für Musik, where he perfected his organ technique and laid the foundations of his contrapuntal facility in later years.

Parker's cantata *The Dream King and His Love* won for him a series of prizes offered by the National Conservatory of Music in New York to stimulate the creation of music in America. At the "Three Choirs Festival" held at Worcester, England, Parker's oratorio, *Hora Novissima,* was given. This was the first time that an American composition was admitted to the Festival.

Cambridge granted Parker the degree of Doctor of Music in 1902. From 1894 until his death in 1919 he was a professor of music at Yale University. He was the winner of many prizes and composer of music for orchestra, voice, and various other types of music. His opera *Mona* won a ten-thousand-dollar prize from the Metropolitan Opera Company, and was produced in 1912.

PISTON (1894-)

Among distinguished New England composers is Walter Piston, who was born in Maine. His early training was in art, which he studied in Boston. It was only because of his interest in kindred arts that he took up the study of violin and piano in leisure time. He began to be very much interested in music and studied harmony, counterpoint and theory at Harvard. Then he went to Paris, where he studied under Boulanger and made his debut as a composer. He is now a member of the faculty in the Division of Music in Harvard University. Among his works are orchestral compositions and chamber music, which have been played much in the east and abroad.

POWELL (1882-)

Outstanding among southern composers has been John Powell, who was born in Virginia in 1882. His musical studies began when he received instruction in piano playing from his sister. Later he studied with Hahr of Richmond. In 1902 he went to Vienna and became a pupil of Leschetizky. After a debut as soloist with the Vienna Tonkünstler Orchestra he began a concert tour of Europe and the United States. His greater interest, however, was in composition. In 1918 his *Negro Rhapsody* for piano and orchestra was performed by Walter Damrosch. Powell resides in Richmond. Composition and concert playing receive about equal attention; he has written extensively for the orchestra, chamber ensemble, chorus, and piano.

PUCCINI (1858-1924)

Giacomo Puccini was born in Lucca, Italy, in 1858. He came from a family of musicians; his father was a composer, who taught Giacomo when the boy was small. When Giacomo was six, his father died and the boy's musical education for a while was carried on by one of his father's pupils. Then Giacomo was sent to Pacini Institute. As a boy, he played the organ very well and traveled about playing in different churches.

GIACOMO PUCCINI

His early years were filled with struggles. His first great

success came with *Manon Lescaut* in 1893. Then *La Bohème* was produced in 1896. After this his operas all met with success. When he died in Brussels, Belgium, in 1924, his last opera, *Turandot,* was unfinished. It was completed by his friend Alfano and produced in 1926.

Other famous operas by this composer are *La Tosca, Madame Butterfly,* and *The Girl of the Golden West.*

RAVEL (1875-1937)

Maurice Ravel, the most significant figure in modern French music, was born in 1875, in the little village of Ciboure, near St. Jean de Luz. He studied music at the Paris Conservatory, and in 1901 was awarded the second Prix de Rome. For refusing to give him the much sought-after Grand Prix de Rome, the judges were criticized severely. Fauré, Chabrier, and Satie all influenced Ravel during his early years, but from the first he was known as a master of orchestration and was famed for the daring effect of his harmonies.

Characteristic of Ravel's compositions is a curiously cynical, detached attitude. A certain refinement and reserve nearly always present has served to remove them from the purely experimental classification. Of his earlier works, *Rapsodie espagnole, Gaspara de la nuit,* and the superb ballet music of *Daphnis et Chloé* are the best known. This ballet suite in particular evidences the extreme impressionism of much of Ravel's work.

Ravel's later music includes much chamber music, and *La Valse* for full orchestra. Probably the most popular of his works is the famous *Bolero.* Its fascinating rhythm, resounding use of the brass instruments, and the color of the woodwind parts, are enough to stir into dancing warmth the most sluggish blood.

Critics quarreled for a time over Ravel's music, but his position is now assured, and many rank him as second only to Debussy in his influence on modern French music. In his later years Ravel did little composing. He died December 28, 1937.

READ (1913-)

Gardner Read was born in Evanston, Illinois, on January 2, 1913. He became a pupil in composition of Bernard Rogers at the Eastman School of Music, Rochester, New York, in 1933,

Courtesy The Art Institute of Chicago

STAGE SETTING FOR RAVEL'S "BOLERO," PRODUCED BY LEONIDOFF AT RADIO CITY, NEW YORK

Photo by

THE CLEVELAND ORCHESTRA . . .

where he has been since. He has written a number of orchestral works which have been played by some of the major symphony orchestras in America. His principal work so far has been a symphony with which he won the thousand-dollar prize offered by the New York Philharmonic Society (1936). He has also written works for chamber ensemble.

SAMINSKY (1882-)

The influence of the East is reflected in the work of Lazare Saminsky, who was born in a village near Odessa, Russia, in 1882.

Geoffrey Landesman

. . . ARTUR RODZINSKI, CONDUCTOR

He inherited his love of music from his mother and began composing songs when he was a boy. His father was interested in literature and politics. At St. Petersburg University, Saminsky specialized in mathematics and philosophy. When he was graduated from the University, however, he decided to take up seriously the study of music. With this idea, he became a pupil of Rimsky-Korsakov in 1906, and later of Liadov. His public debut as composer came in 1909 when an overture of his was performed by the St. Petersburg Conservatory Orchestra. Finally with several of his faith he started the Society of Hebrew Folk Song. In 1913 he was commissioned by the ethnological expedition of Baron

Photo by Renato Toppo, N. Y.

ARTHUR RODZINSKI
Conductor, The Cleveland Orchestra.

Guinzbourg to study the religious folk music of Caucasia. The result of this research was that he became more and more interested in folk music, and he began to use Hebrew folklore in his own creations. *The Lament of Rachel* was his first work to evidence this.

After a period of travel, Saminsky settled in Paris. In 1920 he came to America, becoming an American citizen in 1926, and has since lived in New York. He married Lillian Morgan, an American writer. He takes an active part in the promotion of the music of today as both essayist and composer. His compositions include many works in all forms.

SCHÖNBERG (1874-)

Arnold Schönberg was born in Vienna in 1874, of Jewish parents. Due to the death of his father he was forced to earn his own living at an early age, so music was merely an avocation to him. Upon the advice of an American, who saw some of the things that the boy was writing, he went to Zemlinsky, a Viennese composer, who immediately recognized his talent. Zemlinsky supervised his training carefully, and succeeded in bringing Schönberg's music before the public. In 1901 Schönberg married Zemlinsky's sister. Two years later, Schönberg met Mahler, who encouraged and inspired him.

When Schönberg's *First String Quartet* had its première in 1907, it was hissed. Always his work has been revolutionary and experimental in character. In order to free himself from the influence of Wagner and romanticism, Schönberg struck out on new paths of his own devising. He broke down the domination of one tone as key center (the old diatonic system) and replaced it with a free use of every chromatic tone without relationship to any center. At first it appeared as a tonal anarchy, rather than an evolution. Then he welded it into what has become known as the "twelve-tone" (duodecuple) system, which demands an intricate technique. Out of the composer's seeking and experimenting he has wrought works of enormous musical influence, in spite of their being a welter of dissonance to many auditors.

His latest string quartet, the *Fourth*, is far less nebulous, more direct, is more sustained in its lyrical aspects, and may be indicative of a new tendency which will make his music more readily understood, at least by the initiate.

SCRIABIN (1872-1915)

Alexander Nicolaevich Scriabin was born in Moscow in 1872. His mother was a pianist, who died when Scriabin was only two, leaving him to be reared by his grandmother and an aunt. He taught himself to read and write, and play simple melodies on the piano. He became more and more interested in the piano, and his aunt, observing his evident talent, took him to play for Anton Rubinstein, who was greatly impressed. Rubinstein advised the aunt to allow the boy to follow his own impulses, which probably would be better for him than systematic study. However, Scriabin was still destined to have a military career and pursuant of that was sent to the Moscow Military School. He was not at all interested in the military life, and devoted much time to his musical studies in addition. When he finished military school he decided to make music his career. He worked so hard at his piano that he finally paralyzed his hand. In spite of the fact that doctors did not think he could use it again, he persisted and worked with it until he regained its use. In 1891 he was awarded the gold medal for piano playing at the Conservatory of Moscow. Because his ideas in composition were opposed to those taught by his teachers, and he would not be bound by the rules and laws of harmony and composition, he left the Conservatory without a diploma.

The publisher and critic, Beliayev, became interested in Scriabin's work and decided to sponsor his career and publish all of his music. It was he who later organized for Scriabin a concert tour in Russia, and abroad, and accompanied him. Scriabin taught at the Conservatory from 1898 to 1904 and then decided to devote his entire time to composition. After numerous concert tours, he died in London in 1915.

THE OPERA, IN PARIS

Courtesy Chicago City Opera Co.

OPERA HOUSE, BERLIN

Courtesy E. W. Forkert

ALBERT MEMORIAL HALL, LONDON

In his later works Scriabin displays extreme modern tendencies. Besides his many piano works, he has composed such prominent orchestral works as *The Poem of Ecstasy*, *The Divine Poem*, and *Prometheus*.

SESSIONS (1896-)

Descended from a long line of New England clergymen, Roger Sessions was born in Brooklyn, New York, in 1896. He graduated from the Kent School, in Connecticut, and then from Harvard University. He studied two years with Horatio Parker, at the Yale School of Music. From 1917 to 1921 he taught music in Smith College. In 1923, while he was Assistant Director to Bloch in the Cleveland Institute of Music, his first important work, the *Black Maskers*, was produced. He resigned from the Institute when Bloch was forced to leave. He was awarded a Guggenheim Fellowship and made a sojourn in Europe. His musical development has been marked by a slow but steady growth.

In 1934 he was commissioned by Stokowski and the Philadelphia Symphony to compose a symphony, which was later produced. He has written for the orchestra, organ and piano.

SHEPHERD (1880-)

Arthur Shepherd, born in Idaho, is an American-trained musician. Among the orchestral works he has written is *Horizons,* depicting four western musical impressions, which has been frequently performed at home and abroad. He has won a number of prizes for orchestra, chamber, and choral works. At present he is head of the music division, Western Reserve University, at Cleveland, Ohio.

SIBELIUS (1865-)

Jean Sibelius, one of the greatest living composers, was born in Finland in 1865. The improvisations he made as a young boy gave early evidence of his musical talent, and he began to study the violin when he was fifteen. For a time he studied law, but finally he gave up all idea of following it as a profession, and in 1889 went to Berlin to study music. He went to Vienna to complete his studies and returned to Finland in 1892. The tone poem, *En Saga,* had already established his reputation, and for a time he taught composition and violin at the Helsingfors Institute of Music. The Finnish government then granted him an annual stipend, and ever since Sibelius has devoted himself solely to composition.

The world was quick to recognize Sibelius' genius, and his major works have been played by leading orchestras all over the world. Although he is modern in technique, the general public has taken a great liking to the works of Sibelius, particularly to his tone poems. *Finlandia* is the most popular, and to many, its ponderous chords, flaring trumpet phrases, and somber harmonies represent the essence of Finland's national spirit and people. *En Saga* has also long held a place in the affections of music lovers. Its misty, flickering surges of the strings, and the heavy coldness of the themes create in the listener's mind an impression of a dark night on the bleak wastes of the Arctic.

Although until recently little known, Sibelius' symphonies are the culminating achievements of his superb musical ability. His

Courtesy The Art Institute of Chicago

OPERA HOUSE, DRESDEN

Courtesy The Art Institute of Chicago

MUSIC HALL, PRINGSHEIM HOUSE, MUNICH

earliest symphonic works are heroic sagas in music, and depart but little in fundamental style from the romantic tradition. True, they are definitely racial and national in character, but they are easily understandable, permeated as they are with a definite melodic structure. It is in his later work, however, that Sibelius has risen to lofty heights. The *Fourth Symphony,* in A minor, is one of the best examples. A "series of great musical ideas," it is at times almost darkly motionless, but its scope of design and tremendous thematic development stamp it as one of the greatest modern musical works. Truly, as Olin Downes has said, "It is pure music, of the most transparent and unadorned kind."

In recent years Sibelius has lived in seclusion at his woodland home near Helsingfors. There he is still writing music, having received all the honors that man can heap upon a member of his profession. Eight great symphonies, numerous tone poems, pieces for chamber orchestra, compositions for the piano, and songs—these are Sibelius' gifts to the present age. That the world is cognizant of his genius is shown by the tremendous ovation given him on his seventieth birthday, and by the esteem with which he is regarded today.

SMITH (1877-)

David Stanley Smith was born in Ohio in 1877. His father was a church organist, who composed anthems and songs, and his mother was a singer. They had a small pipe organ in their home. He received his B.A. degree from Yale in 1900, and continued his study of music under Horatio Parker, having been in his classes while at college. Subsequently he took a position as church organist. In 1901 he spent a year and a half abroad. Since 1903 he has been on the faculty at Yale, where he is at present Dean of the School of Music and Conductor of the New Haven Symphony Orchestra. He has written choruses, one opera, much chamber music, and among his orchestral compositions are three symphonies.

SOWERBY (1895-)

Leo Sowerby was born in Grand Rapids, Michigan, in 1895. His mother died when he was three years old and his father married again. It was the influence of his stepmother that caused him to take up music. He began his study of piano when seven and learned elementary harmony and theory by himself when he was eleven. After studying piano, he took up the study of theory with Arthur Olaf Anderson. Later Sowerby began the study of organ and now holds an important position as organist. During the war he went into the army, served six months abroad, and received his honorable discharge in 1919. In 1921 he was awarded the Prix de Rome, which gave him three years in Rome. He has written many works for orchestra, chamber ensemble, organ, and chorus. These have been performed extensively in America and in Europe.

RICHARD STRAUSS (1864-)

Richard Strauss, modern German composer, was born in Munich in 1864, the son of Franz Strauss, a famed horn player. Like many earlier composers, he showed his musical ability at an early age. At the age of four he could play the piano, he began to compose when he was but six years old, and at ten he was studying music intensively. In 1885, when he was but twenty-one years old, Strauss became conductor of the Meiningen orchestra, and later in the year he was appointed third conductor of the Munich Opera orchestra. Later he became first conductor at Munich and then at Berlin.

Strauss's earlier works were not recognized as very significant, but in 1888 the appearance of his tone poem, *Don Juan,* won him an immediate place in modern music. Based on the interpretation of the Austrian poet Lenau, it portrays in music the gay and dashing career of the legendary Spanish cavalier. To Strauss as well as to Lenau, Don Juan was not the mere seeker after sensuous pleasure; he was also the dreamer who longed to find the ideal woman. In music filled with warmth and passion Strauss follows his hero's endless quest, and among the motives expressing various episodes in Don Juan's life are several magnificent themes. But the Don's search is futile; in the end he is stabbed in a duel, and the music ends with a picture of drab and dark despair.

Following *Don Juan* in close succession came other tone poems that were to make every music lover familiar with his name. *Tod und Verklärung* (Death and Transfiguration) appeared in 1888. It portrays a dying man who in fitful dreams recalls the events of his past life. At last death comes, but the magnificence of Strauss' closing chords gives evidence of the triumph of faith over terror and death and darkness.

Strauss' next tone poem was the delightfully gay *Till Eulenspiegel,* which pictures the merry pranks of this fantastical figure out of the tradition of nearly every nation in Europe. In the following year he composed another, *Also sprach Zarathustra,* after reading the book of the same title by the famous German philosopher, Nietzsche. In this tone poem Strauss tells the story of the career of Nietzsche's "Superman." *Don Quixote,* written in 1897, is based on Cervantes' well-known tale. In some of the most realistic music ever written, the composer takes up episode after episode in the life of the wistful knight and his squire, Sancho Panza.

Photo by Maurice Schubert, Chicago

RUTH PAGE AND BALLET IN SCHUBERT'S "LOVE SONG"

Strauss' last tone poem, *Ein Heldenleben* (A Hero's life), portrays his own life. Though he wrote this tone poem to pillory his critics, the greatness of the music more than compensates for the egotistical spirit he displays in it.

In his later career Strauss left the medium of the tone poem. In 1905 appeared the *Symphonia Domestica*; but best known in this period are his operas, especially *Salome, Elektra,* and *Der Rosenkavalier,* which is tremendously popular at the present time. Both *Salome* and *Elektra* are excellent examples of realism in modern opera.

Romantic and yet realistic, the music of Strauss is the expression of a fiery genius. From tone poems to operas, he displays a magnificent power of portraiture in music. His orchestrations are marvels of color and tonal beauty. Extremely difficult to play, his music is at times filled with strange harmonic combinations, but its qualities so far outweigh any possible faults that it will undoubtedly remain significant.

STRAVINSKY (1882-)

Igor Feodorovich Stravinsky was born near St. Petersburg in 1882. His father, an actor and singer, fostered his musical talent, besides providing him with an education in law. In 1902 Stravinsky met Rimsky-Korsakov who was amazed at his knowledge of music since he was only an amateur. He urged Stravinsky to give up law in favor of music, and became his teacher.

Diaghilev, whom Stravinsky met later, was so interested in the score of *Fireworks* that he commissioned him to write a ballet. He therefore composed *L'Oiseau du Feu* (The Fire Bird) in 1910. This was the beginning of a relationship from which came some of Stravinsky's greatest works, like *Petroushka* and *Le Sacre du Printemps* (Rite of Spring). After this Russian period, came a period when Stravinsky veered to a more classical idiom.

At present Stravinsky lives in the St. Cloud district of France. Among his most outstanding orchestral works are a number of ballets, symphonies, choral works, and music for chamber ensemble. He has also written in the smaller forms.

Steeped in folk-song and folk-lore though he was, Stravinsky has, from the beginning of his career as a composer, transcended all possible conventional bounds. Opposed to the long, extended forms of the earlier, romantic composers, Stravinsky writes in short, incisive forms that are like splintered mirrors. His meter and rhythm embody complete freedom, and his harmonies and chord combinations are clamorously different from the staid writing of the past. Sensational and dazzling as it is, Stravinsky's work has rhythmic power, orchestral color, and such an original approach to the whole concept of music that it must command attention. His music is the product of our own time, and must be judged on that basis. The relentless pounding of the machines of the factory, man's irresistible search for truth, the ennui and monotony of life in a machine civilization, all these are readily heard in Stravinsky's music.

SZYMANOWSKI (1883-1937)

Following in the tradition of Chopin, one of the most outstanding Polish composers is Karol Szymanowski, who was born in Poland in 1883. He studied in Warsaw from 1901 to 1904 and at seventeen began to compose piano pieces, becoming a member of a society known as "Young Poland in Music." After studying in Berlin he went to live and work on his estate in the Ukraine. In 1917 his property was confiscated by the Bolshevists, leaving him destitute. In 1919 he returned to Warsaw, where he became the leader of the contemporary Polish composers. He died in Switzerland in 1937. The Polish government has erected a monument in his honor. Among his best known works are the masque *Scheherezade* for orchestra, and *Myths* for violin. He wrote many large compositions for orchestra, two operas, choral music, chamber music, piano pieces, and songs. He is the heir to the Chopin-Scriabin tradition of color effects and advanced harmonic trends.

TAYLOR (1885-)

The versatile Deems Taylor was born in New York in 1885. After he graduated from New York University, he took up the study of music. Although he took a course in harmony under Oscar Coon, most of his knowledge of composition and orchestration is self-acquired.

He had a great variety of occupations after he left college, including acting on the vaudeville stage, carpentering, editing technical journals and a music magazine, and translating songs.

In 1921 he became music editor of the *New York World*, in which capacity he distinguished himself. In 1925 he gave up newspaper work to spend his time in composition. In 1926 he went to Switzerland where he collaborated with Edna St. Vincent Millay upon the opera *The King's Henchman*, which had its first performance at the Metropolitan Opera House in New York in 1927. For a while in 1930 he was editor of *Musical America*. In 1934 he became master of ceremonies on a radio program. Among his works are two operas, two choral numbers, various orchestral numbers, and some piano pieces.

WALTON (1902-   )

William Turner Walton was born in Oldham, Lancashire, England, in 1902. After studying at Christ Church, and for a time with Sir Hugh Allen, he was self-taught from the age of sixteen.

A string quartet of his was played at the Salzburg Festival of the International Society for Contemporary Music in 1923, and in 1926 his overture, *Portsmouth Point*, was played at the Zürich Festival of the same society. The latter work was also used in the Diaghilev ballet season at His Majesty's Theatre in 1926, as an interlude.

Among other works of Walton are a symphony, songs, chamber music, and orchestral music.

WHITHORNE (1884-   )

Cleveland, Ohio, and Vienna contributed to the musical education of Emerson Whithorne, who was born in Cleveland, on September 6, 1884. His reputation was first made as a music-critic abroad. Composing at first in the smaller forms, he later turned to chamber music. In 1923 he startled the musical world with an orchestral work, *New York Days and Nights*, a serious symphonic piece in which he made use of the jazz idiom. Its audacious harmonies seem less startling now than when it made its appearance at Salzburg. Since then Whithorne has traveled much in the Orient, and continues to make significant contributions to musical literature in all mediums.

VAUGHAN WILLIAMS (1872-)

To Ralph O. M. Vaughan Williams, English music owes much of its present-day significance. The son of a clergyman, he was born in 1872 in Gloucestershire. From his youth he showed a marked bent toward music, and later he studied at the Royal College of Music, at the same time attending Trinity College, Cambridge. He received the degree of Doctor of Music in 1901. In 1908 he studied in Paris with Ravel. Vaughan Williams served during the entire World War, first in the R.A.M.C., then as a gunner, and finally as a lieutenant. After the war he became a teacher in the Royal College of Music and conductor of the London Bach Choir.

Vaughan Williams' most significant contribution to the music of England has been his emphasis upon the merry old English folk tunes. He revived their popularity by arranging and harmonizing many of them for modern use, and by incorporating many of them in his own compositions. His *Norfolk Rhapsodies* were based on folk songs, and in the symphonic impression, *In the Fen Country,* he used original themes of a folk-song character. Vaughan Williams also found in Tudor Church music, and in that of Purcell, further stimulus to the use of his creative abilities in the development of a truly national music.

Vaughan Williams' musical genius suffered no ill effects from his long service in the World War, and his post-war works are regarded as his greatest, although his important *London Symphony* appeared in 1914. In this later period Vaughan Williams occupied himself with the production of many choral works, some inspired by the poetry of Walt Whitman. In addition he composed other significant works, among them *A Pastoral Symphony for Orchestra, A Mass in G Minor,* and the oratorio, *Sancta Civitas.*

Vaughan Williams' music is characterized especially by the clearness of his melodic outline. He used many new harmonic ideas, but his use of counterpoint was in line with that of the great contrapuntal masters of the eighteenth century. Vaughan Williams will be remembered primarily, however, for his part in beginning the great revival of English folk music. He may be said to be the leader in this trend, which has emphasized much great English music otherwise buried in undeserved obscurity.

Courtesy The Art Institute of Chicago

ST. CECILIA
(After the painting by Dolci)

GLOSSARY OF MUSICAL TERMS

A cappella (ah kahp-pel-lah). Unaccompanied vocal music.

A capriccio (ah kah-preet-sho). In a capricious manner.

Accelerando (aht-chay-lay-rahn-do). Gradually increasing the speed.

Accentuare (aht-tchen-too-ah-reh). To mark in an accented manner.

Acciaccatura (aht-tshahk-kah-too-rah). An extremely short accessory or grace note.

Accidentals. Chromatic signs such as sharps, flats and naturals used in music to temporarily alter a given note.

Adagietto (ah-dah-jiet-toe). Not quite as slow as adagio.

Adagio (ah-dah-jio). Slow; not as slow as largo, but slower than andante.

Adagio assai (ahs-sah-ee). Very slow.

Adagio di molto. Very slow.

Addolorato (ad-doh-lo-rah-toe). Sad, sorrowful.

A deux mains (ah-du-main) Fr. For two hands.

Ad libitum. At the will or discretion of the performer.

Affabile (ahf-fah-bee-leh). In a pleasing manner.

Affettivo (ahf-feht-tee-vo). Tender, pathetic.

Affettuoso (ahf-feht-too-o-zo). With feeling; in a passionate manner.

Agitato. Agitated, restless.

Agnus Dei (Day-ee). A movement of a Mass.

Air. A short song.

Air varié (Fr.) (ayr-vah-ri-ay). An embellished song, or a song with variations.

Al fine (ahl-fee-neh). To the end.

Alla Breve (ahl-lah bray-veh). A term originally applied to 4/2 rhythm, but used today to denote a 4/4 meter played in a rhythm of 2.

Allargando (ah-lahr-gahn-doe). Broadening the musical line, by increasing the tone and slowing up the tempo.

Allegretto (ahl-leh-gret-toe). Lightly and in a cheerful manner. Not as fast as allegro.

Allegro (ahl-lay-grow). Rapidly, lively.

Allegro assai (ahs-sah-ee). Very fast.

Allegro di bravura (brah-voo-rah). Fast and spirited.

Allemande (Fr.) (al-mahnd). A rather slow dance in 4/4 time. Also a spirited German dance in 2/4 or 3/4 time.

Al rigore di tempo (ahl-ri-go-reh di tem-po). In very marked, strict time.

Alto. The lowest type of the female voice.

Amore (ah-mo-reh). Con amore. With affection.

Andante (ahn-dahn-teh). Slowly. The term is also used as a name for a movement in certain compositions, in moderate time.

Anima; con anima. With animation; lively.

Animato (ah-nee-mah-toe). Animated.

A poco a poco (ah po-ko ah po-ko). Little by little; gradually.

Appassionato (ahp-pahs-see-oh-nah-toe). Passionately; emotionally.

Appoggiatura (ahp-pod-jee-ah-too-rah). An embellishing note; a grace note.

Aria (ah′-ree-ah). A song which assumed its form in early opera. It is more elaborate than the ordinary song, being constructed generally in two and three parts.

Arpeggio (ahr-ped′-jee-o). The notes of a chord arranged or played consecutively instead of together.

Assai (ahs-sah-ee). Very; to a great degree.

A tempo. In time. The term indicates a return to the original tempo after some deviation from it.

Atonality. Without key center.

Attacca (aht-tahk′-kah). Continue; go on.

Attacca subito (soo-bee′-toe). Begin immediately. Generally used to indicate that there is to be no pause in going from one movement of a composition to another.

Audace (ah-oo-dah′-tcheh). Bold, spirited.

A una corda (ah-oo-na kor-dah). By one string. The term denotes the use of the soft pedal on the piano.

Avec (Fr.) (ah-vehk). With.

Ave Maria (ah-veh mah-ree′-ah). A prayer to Virgin Mary. The literal translation of the words is Hail, Mary.

Bagatelle (Fr.). The term denotes an easy piece of music. A trifle.

Barcarolle (Fr.) (bahr-kah-role). A Venetian boatman song, usually in 6/8 time.

Baritone. A male voice whose range is between the tenor and bass.

Bass. The male voice with the lowest or deepest pitch.

Basso. Same as above.

Bel Canto. The term is used to describe a pure, legato style of singing as opposed to very spirited or dramatic styles.

Benedictus. A movement of a Mass.

Ben Marcato (mahr-cah-toe). In a strongly marked, accented manner.

Berceuse (Fr.) (bayr-say′s). A lullaby.

Bolero (Sp.) (bo-lay′-ro). A spirited Spanish dance, usually in 3/4 time.

Bourée (Fr.) (boo-ray). A very lively old French dance in duple time.

Bravura; Con Bravura (brah-voo-rah). With spirit. The term is used to indicate a display of skill and audacity in the execution of the music at hand.

Brindisi (breen-dee-zee). A drinking song.

Buffa, Opera (boof-fah oh-peh-rah). Comic opera.

Cadence. The group of chords or notes that close a musical phrase or sentence.
Cadenza (kah-den-zah). This word generally refers to a brilliant, embellished passage for soloist, often near the end of a composition.
Calando (kah-lahn-doe). A gradual diminution of tone and retardation of tempo.
Cantabile (kahn-tah-bi-leh). In an expressive, melodious manner.
Crescendo (kreh-shen-doe). Increasing the tone.

Da Capo (dah cah′-poe). (D.C.) From the beginning.
Da Capo al fine (ahl-fee-neh). From the beginning and end at the word Fine.
Decrescendo (day-kreh-shen-doe). Diminishing intensity of tone gradually.
Destra mano (des-trah mah′-no). The right hand.
Diminuendo (dee-mee-noo-en′-doe). Gradually diminishing the tone.
Di Molto (dee mol-toe). Very much.
Dolce (dol′-tshe). Sweetly.
Doloroso (doe-low-row′-zoe). Sadly.
Dur (dewr). Major mode. As A Dur or A Major.

Energico (ay-nair′-gee-koe). Energetic, in a vigorous manner.
Espressivo (es-pres-see′-voe). Expressive.
Forte (for′-teh). Loud.
Forte piano (fp). Accent note strongly and diminish tone immediately.
Fortissimo (ff). (for-tees′-see-mo). Very loud.
Forzato (for-tzah-toe). }
Forzando (for-tzahn-do). } A strong accent on one note or chord.

Grandioso (grahn-dee-o′-zo). In a grand manner.
Grave (grah′-veh). Serious, solemn. This term is also used to express the slowest tempo.
Grazioso (grah-tsee-o′-zo). Gracefully.

Incalzando (in-cal-tsan′-do). With increasing warmth.

Legato (leh-gah′-to). In a smooth, closely connected manner.
Leggiero (led-jee-ay′-ro). Delicate and light.

Marcato (mahr-cah′-toe). Strongly accented.
Maestoso (mah-es-to′zo). Majestic.
Meno (may-no). Less—Meno mosso—slower.
Mezzo Forte (mf). Medium loud.
Mezza voce (met-tsa vo-tshe). Softly.
Moderato (mo-day-rah′-to). Moderately.
Movendo (mo-ven′-do). Gradual diminution of the time and tone.

Opus. Composition; work.

Piano. Soft.
Poco a poco (poe-coe). Little by little.
Perdendosi (payr-den-do′-zee). Gradually dying away.
Pesante (peh-zahn-teh). Heavy, important, impressive.
Più forte (pee-oo). Louder.
Pianissimo (pee-ahn-is′-see-mo). Very soft.
Presto. Very fast.
Prestissimo (pres-tis′-see-mo). As quickly as possible.

Rallentando (rahl-len-tahn-do). Gradually diminishing the time.
Rinforzando (rin-for-tsahn-do). Emphasized; marked.
Ritardando (ree-tar-dahn′-do). Gradually slower.
Ritenuto (ree-te-noo′-to). Held back; slower.

Scherzando (sker-tsahn′-do). Lively; animated.
Smorzando (smor-tsahn′-do). Diminishing in volume—fading away.
Sostenuto (sos-teh-noo′-toe). Keeping the tone sustained and even, full value to the notes.
Staccato (stah-kah′-toe). Separated, detached.
Stringendo (strin-jen′-doe). Speeding up, increasing the tempo.

Tre Corde (tray kor′-deh) (in piano music only). Soft pedal in natural position—hammer strikes all three strings and the piano produces its normal tone.
Tonality. The key of a piece or section.

Una Corda (unah kor′-deh). Used in piano music—calls for use of soft pedal.

DESIGNER'S NOTE

This volume was set in twelve point Linotype Garamond. The style of typography and the art work, together with the illustrations, received a treatment similar to that of other volumes of the *"University of Knowledge."*

OTTO MAURICE FORKERT
Director of Design and Typography